D1739194

The Design of
Energy-Responsive
Commercial Buildings

THE DESIGN OF ENERGY-RESPONSIVE COMMERCIAL BUILDINGS

Steven Ternoey, AIA
Larry Bickle, P.E.
Claude Robbins, R.A.
Robert Busch, P.E.
Kitt McCord

SOLAR ENERGY RESEARCH INSTITUTE
Operated for the U.S. Department of Energy
by Midwest Research Institute
Golden, Colorado

A WILEY-INTERSCIENCE PUBLICATION
JOHN WILEY & SONS
New York · Chichester · Brisbane · Toronto · Singapore

Library of Congress Cataloging in Publication Data:

Main entry under title:

The Design of energy-responsive commercial buildings.

   "A Wiley-Interscience publication."
   Includes index.
   1. Commercial buildings—Design and construction.
2. Commercial buildings—Energy conservation.   I. Ternoey,
Steven.   II. Solar Energy Research Institute
TH4311.D47 1984   690 ′.52   84-11864
ISBN 0-471-80463-0

Printed in the United States of America

10 9 8 7 6 5 4 3 2 1

In loving memory
of our friends

William W. Caudill and Sital Daryanani

FOREWORD

This work, concerning the design of energy-responsive commercial buildings, represents the confluence of two important streams of activity. The first is the evolution of architectural design of medium- and large-size buildings. The design profession reacted in some degree to the energy problems of the early 1970s. Not only had the energy costs of large buildings become of concern, but the capital cost of mechanical plants had become very high as had demand charges for peak electric use. Thus, there was a well perceived rationale for energy-conscious design, and many architectural and related engineering professionals responded to the need.

The second stream of activity, the conservation and solar programs, sprang forth in direct response to the 1973 energy crisis. These were accelerated by both strong enthusiasm and generous government backing. The buildings sector, accounting for 37% of national source energy use, was an obvious target for major emphasis. The initial thrust focused on small buildings, usually residential, with mixed results. Straightforward envelope-related conservation measures were very successful, but active solar heating and cooling installations proved to be trouble-prone and expensive. Passive approaches to space heating proved to be much more cost effective in most cases and fit better into the design, construction, and operation pattern of dwellings. How these successes could be extended to the much complex situation of commercial buildings became a major topic for discussion.

One place these streams came together was at the Solar Energy Research Institute. Formally charged with solar concerns, the group assigned to this job took a broad view of the energy issues. This book is one of the major results of that effort. I regard it as the most important contribution to the topic yet written.

There are a number of important characteristics that distinguish the work. First, it was not conducted strictly in-house at SERI. Design professionals were brought in both to consult and to carry out specific tasks. A case method approach was adopted rather than a completely generalized analysis. Hypothetical and real architectural programs were addressed in an atelier fashion with competing solutions strongly argued and compared. The book itself adopts this format, choosing to discuss the key issues by reference to specific existing buildings. The diversity of the strategies taken lends credibility to the widely perceived view that there are no unique best solutions. A series of short courses was organized under the purview of the American Institute of Architects, providing valuable feedback from the many participants.

An important feature of the book is the up-front admission that there is no known comprehensive "design process" for energy-efficient commercial buildings, a direct result of the large number of situations that can arise considering different climates, building types, client preferences, site constraints, and utility rate structures. Nonetheless, the authors do propose an approach that has proved to be successful in practice. This approach starts by setting up a base case building that provides a reference point and identifies the key energy issues at an early stage. Specific evaluations of proposed solutions are recommended, including methods of presenting and analyzing the results in a manner that will assist understanding the implications to design.

Key words to note in the book title are "design" and "responsive." Combined, these mean that the design process responds to energy issues, a necessary feature if the resulting design is for a building that will respond properly to internal occupant and equipment influences and also to external climate influences. Because these are both highly variable, this requires a building that is resilient, that is, a building that will function well not only under average or typical conditions, but will also coast comfortably through abnormal situations. The design challenge posed is a large one, significantly adding to the already complex architectural design process. Ultimately, the test will be whether the building provides a visually and thermally comfortable working environment for many years, well beyond our present ability to make energy supply and cost projections.

The *Design of Energy-Responsive Commercial Buildings* is an important initial step toward a full understanding of the complex and interrelated set of issues involved.

J. DOUGLAS BALCOMB

Los Alamos National Laboratory
Los Alamos, New Mexico
July 1984

PREFACE

The Design of Energy-Responsive Commercial Buildings is a guide for building designers who want to reduce the nonrenewable energy needs of commercial and institutional buildings. This book takes a unique approach by addressing energy issues from a whole-building context rather than from a component-specific level.

This work has as its premise that architecture is in a transitional period with energy as a prominent design issue. Substantial research and knowledge are presently available concerning individual components, systems, and design concepts, yet building owners and designers disagree on the impact of energy-related design issues on architecture. The traditional way of dealing with a design challenge is to place it in the context of existing design conventions. Design solutions, therefore, become a logical incremental extension of past designs rather than a leap into new solutions, procedures, or techniques. This book represents a departure from that method by presenting new ideas in commercial building design and encouraging designers to consider new approaches.

The principal effort involved in researching and developing the final manuscript for this work was funded by the U.S. Department of Energy as part of its passive solar research and development technology transfer activities and its Solar Technical Information Program. The U.S. Department of Energy regards this book as a valuable contribution to the literature of architecture. All those who have worked on this volume hope that the architectural community will consider it worthwhile in its treatment of innovative approaches to commercial building design.

STEVEN TERNOEY
LARRY BICKLE
CLAUDE ROBBINS
ROBERT BUSCH
KITT McCORD

Golden, Colorado
August 1984

ACKNOWLEDGMENTS

"Information is like love; the more you share, the more there is!"

Sital Daryanani

We express our sincere thanks and indebtedness to the following colleagues and friends whose support, contributions, and helpful suggestions have made this book possible.

Administrative Team

A very special thank you is extended to Ted Kurkowski of the U.S. Department of Energy. Without his aid, this task would not have been initiated. We are also indebted to Michael Maybaum, Bob Shibley, Mike Davis, and Michael Holtz for their administrative assistance and technical suggestions. The Office of Solar Heat Technologies under Dr. Frederick Morse provided final review and approval of the document. Specifically, this review was conducted by Lawnie Taylor, Director, Passive and Hybrid Solar Energy Division and Mary-Margaret Jenior of the same division. The final development and production was supported by the Solar Technical Information Program under Jay Holmes. Without their help, this work would have died on the vine.

Research Team

For their persistence, long hours of work, and continuous personal support, we extend our love and thanks to the following SERI Design Group Members:

Henry Mueller—building type classifications
Kerri G. Hunter—daylighting energy calculations
Leo Dwyer—daylighting case studies
Dennis Carlberg—original isometrics/case studies
Nancy V. A. Smith—energy calculations/Part II bar graphs
Debra Berger—historical case studies
Mike Doyle—original renderings/case study coordinator
Steve Hogg—production/coordination
Anna Gasbarro—historical case studies
Craig Christensen—chief computer analyst, Part II
Robert Perkins—computer analysis, Part II
Ted Bechtel—computer analysis, Part II
Sally Dulin—preliminary editing
Fran Spencer—manuscript typing

Production Team

A very special thanks to Nancy Reece and Richard Meyer of the SERI Technical Information Branch, and Cathy Hawthorne and Mary Schuyler of the SERI Publication Services Branch. Their efforts saw the book through its final stages of completion and production.

Consultants/Contributors and Reviewers

Few aspects of this publication match our original outline and intent. Numerous brainstorming meetings, information exchanges, case study contributions, and a never-ending series of draft reviews have all slowly molded this work to what it is now. In one way or another, all of the following professionals have made a contribution to this work. To every one of you, we express our thanks. We only hope our final product matches the high standards of your professional contributions.

Doug Balcomb	Bill Fisher	James Hedstrom
Clark Bisel	Richard Fitts	Bruce Hunn
L. Britt Blaser	Robert Floyd	Blair Kamin
Dave Bullen	Harrison Fraker	Ron Kammarud
Peter Calthorpe	Greg Franta	Doug Kelbaugh
William Carrol	Gary Gillett	Ralph Knowles
William Caudill	Harry Gordon	Don Kraft
Jerry Caully	Jan Hansen	John Kurtz
Jeffrey Cook	Sarah Harkness	William Lam
Sital Daryanani	Kimball Hart	Ed Mazria
Sally Draft	S. R. Hastings	Robert McKinley

Marietta Millet

Bob Mizell

William Morgan

Scott Noll

John Peterson

Wayne Place

Randle Pollack

Don Prowler

David Reese

Richard Rittelmann

Kalev Ruberg

Al Sain

Steve Selkowitz

Robert Shannon

Michael Sizemore

Marguerite Villecco

Don Watson

John Weidt

Bill Whidden

Bill Wright

John Yellott

CONTENTS

The Design of
Energy-Responsive
Commercial Buildings

chapter one

INTRODUCTION

There is no finality in Architecture, only continuous change.

WALTER GROPIUS

The Design of Energy-Responsive Commercial Buildings is a guide for the building design professional who wishes to reduce the nonrenewable energy needs of commercial and institutional buildings. By presenting, comparing, and interpreting the best available information on the topic, we hope to inform the design professional of the principles, advantages, and disadvantages of a great many energy-related design alternatives. To this end, the book concludes with a recommended method for appraising the energy-related needs and opportunities of specific buildings.

Numerous approaches have been developed to limit the nonrenewable energy needs of commercial and institutional buildings. As demonstrated by the case studies presented in Part One, there is no consensus by either clients or designers of the specific problem to be solved or of the types of solutions. In light of this situation, the present state of the art of the design of energy-responsive commercial buildings can be described as an unresolved design challenge.

Transition periods often link the introduction of a new invention or design challenge to the ultimate resolution of that challenge. Solutions to new design challenges are seldom obvious. As history has shown, several decades of experimentation often precede the resolution of a new challenge. At the outset of a transitional period, the inclination is to interpret the new design challenge in the same context as an existing solution. As such, the changes implemented may represent incremental steps rather than a bold innovative leap. An example of an incremental step toward a solution is

1

Figure 1.1. Early trolley. From *Auto Motion and Power*. Courtesy of Time-Life, Inc.

the rendering of the earliest horseless carriages to resemble a horse and buggy (Fig. 1.1).

A design challenge is resolved when the process of incremental improvement of an existing concept gives way to the development of a wholly unique solution. This pattern is particularly apparent in the history of architecture. For example, the invention of the elevator and the steel frame led to several decades of experimentation with the proper design and aesthetic expression of the resulting tall building. At the beginning of this period, tall buildings looked like a series of short buildings stacked upon each other. For instance, the Montauk Building (Fig. 1.2) towers above the adjacent pre-elevator structures, yet embodies the same classical aesthetic expression of the horizontal design typical of the earlier buildings. In the words of Paul Goldberger in *The Skyscraper*,* the Montauk Building ". . . makes clear how little, thus far, architects had been able to give new form to what they were doing, for the Montauk is essentially 10 horizontal floors piled on top of each other." In this transitional period, it just did not look right to go more than a story or two without a cornice.

The challenge represented by the design of tall buildings was eventually met by disassociating the new form and technology problem from historical precedent. There is limited agreement on which specific building represents the first skyscraper paradigm, yet the Wainwright Building (Figs. 1.3 and

*Paul Goldberger, 1981. *The Skyscraper*. Alfred A. Knopf: New York.

Figure 1.2. Montauk building, Chicago, John Wellborn Root, 1882. Courtesy of Chicago Historical Society.

Figure 1.3.   Wainwright Building, St. Louis, Louis Sullivan, 1891. From *American Architecture and Building News*. Courtesy of Architectural Record.

1.4) by Louis Sullivan is typically exemplified to distinguish between early attempts at tall buildings and the final resolution. According to Goldberger, "What Sullivan managed to do here was create the facade that could not have existed on a short building. It is not merely a low building made bigger; it is a tall building in its very essence."

Energy as a new design issue is in a transitional period. At present, a great body of research and knowledge exists concerning individual components, systems, and design concepts. The lack of agreement by building owners and designers of the role and impact of energy-related design issues on architecture, however, suggests that the resolution has yet to be achieved.

Figure 1.4. Wainwright Building under construction. From *The Engineering Magazine.* Courtesy of *Factory Management.*

> *He (Sullivan) was the real radical of his day, and his thought gave us the skyscraper. You see, the building was—when buildings first began to be tall, they didn't know how to make them tall. They would . . . one two-story or three-story building on top of another until they had enough. And I remember Liebermeister would come in and did come in and throw something on my table, the Wainwright Building in St. Louis. He said, "Wright, the thing is tall. What's the matter with a tall building?" And there it was, tall.*
>
> FRANK LLOYD WRIGHT[*]

[*]From an interview with Lewis Mumford, 1953.

Based on this belief, this book does not solely present existing information on components or systems. Rather, the major emphasis is on the assessment of current knowledge within the context of a design challenge that is still seeking resolution. The approach presented in *The Design of Energy-Responsive Commercial Buildings* has been formulated to represent one step of many in the transitional phase between the initiation and resolution of energy issues in building design. The following section defines that step.

THE PATTERNS OF INNOVATION AND CHANGE

Understanding how major new design challenges typically proceed from initial ideas and concepts to resolved solutions can provide important insights into the current state of the art in the design of energy-responsive commercial buildings. In addition, this process leads to a clearer picture of the challenge that remains. In this section, a model is presented that traces new ideas or products from their early emergence through resolution.

The model presented here is based on diffusion research, a field of study that explores how social systems are changed through the diffusion of new ideas. Diffusion research traces the flow and change of new ideas from their originator to potential users.†

Innovations (i.e., some new idea, process, or technology) follow an evolutionary sequence of events between the origin of a general concept to the adoption of sets of users or behaviors by the majority. Diffusion research indicates that innovations are seldom directly conveyed to the majority by the original Innovator. Rather, innovations are invented or initiated by one group or type of people, the Innovators, and modified, reinvented, or resolved by another group of people, the Adopters. Innovations follow a process toward wide acceptance and use and are not a single act performed by one person. For instance, Sullivan developed a paradigm for the skyscraper, but did not invent the elevator or the steel frame.

One way to define the start and end of the diffusion process is by assessing the changing identity of the innovation as it migrates through and beyond specific groups of people. At the start of the process, innovations have a distinct, separate identity. An Innovator typically focuses much energy on a single new or unique element that is often an incremental improvement to an existing problem or need. Later, Adopters of innovations are typically concerned with broader issues than is the Innovator. In one form or another, innovations are modified or changed to make them appropriate for a larger and often different set of concerns. Final resolution

†The material presented here has been adopted from personal conversations with Dr. Floyd Shoemaker, and from *Communication of Innovations/A Cross-Cultural Approach* by Rogers and Shoemaker, *Reinvention in the Innovation Process* by Rice and Rogers, and *The Diffusion of Innovations: An Assessment* by Radnor, Feller, and Rogers.

of a new innovation is reached when it loses its separate identity and is absorbed into much larger everyday concerns and procedures.

Reinvention is the term used to define the act of changing an innovation by an Adopter in the process of its use and implementation. Reinvention is necessary to make an innovation more appropriate to a larger set of concerns or objectives. Reinvention is both general acceptance of an innovation and a rejection of some of its elements. Reinvention is associated with implementation, a point in time after the origination of a specific innovation.

Innovators and Adopters can be distinguished by their personal motives and the degree of risk they are willing to take. The changing level of risk associated with an innovation is the cue that signals or invites the participation of people beyond the originator of the idea.

Innovations always begin as high-risk ventures. Without a proven track record, early innovations are developed by people who like or are motivated to take that risk. Innovators are motivated by a need to be first and intentionally seek uncertainty and change. Innovators are the first to adopt new ideas in their communities and professions. However, they tend to be innovative in only one focused facet of their lives. Innovators' focus on change often isolates their interactions to those of national or international peer groups, since the local community may not reflect an equal desire for change.

Since innovations are a speculative venture, many experimental mistakes are made compared to the final number of successes that emerge. Once a limited number of successes are achieved, the level of risk is reduced and a new sequence of activities begins. A new set of people, who desire constructive change but are less venturesome than the high-risk-taking Innovators, begin to adopt and change innovations to make them appropriate for their needs and uses. Diffusion research calls the first set of such people Early Adopters.

Early Adopters are prestigious, respectable leaders of their business and community. To maintain this position of respectability, Early Adopters are willing to take some risk to explore the new and useful; yet, accountability and success are important too, and the degree of risk that is acceptable is much less than that of the Innovators. Early Adopters usually track the activities of Innovators but pick and choose only a limited number of innovations that appear useful to the wider concerns of the Early Adopter and offer an appropriate degree of risk.

The value of the Early Adopters is threefold. First, they filter and approve the work of Innovators for the rest of the community and/or profession. Second, they experiment with the new ideas or products and arrive at generalized principles that increase the probability of success. Third, they integrate the new information with a larger set of concerns that may not be important to Innovators. All three of these activities result in the reinvention of the original idea, product, or concept.

Diffusion theory offers a good model to appraise the present state of the art in the design of energy-responsive commercial buildings. At present, a rapidly expanding information base is being formulated that reflects the abilities and benefits of individual energy-related components, systems, and concepts. This research has produced both successes and failures and has been generated at a very high level of risk. Component-specific patterns of success are emerging, and this large collective effort at the component level is reducing the risk associated with energy-related options. At present, our research base is topical or technology-specific, documented under titles such as energy analysis, active solar, passive solar, daylighting, and improved conventional systems. Results that focus on the pieces rather than on the overall final product are characteristic of the work of Innovators. Yet, to reach resolution we need to know more than how the pieces work. What remains to be done is to define the appropriate role and impact of energy-related design issues in the context of the overall intended result at the whole-building level. In the language of diffusion research, the design of energy-responsive commercial buildings is at the Innovator/Early Adopter transition point. The state of the art is reinvention. What we need now are models of success at the whole-building level, an area of concern better understood by Early Adopters.

This book is specifically written to inform the Early Adopters of the benefits and liabilities of existing energy-related alternatives on a whole-building level. The goal is to translate existing energy-related design information into a format that supports the Early Adopters' role of integrating and reinventing innovations to respond to wider concerns and needs. To achieve this goal, two levels of information are presented. In Part One, Reviewing and Interpreting Our Collective Learning Experience, many case studies and examples are presented to summarize the abilities and impact on design of existing alternative means of environmental control and the methods that are being used to assess this problem. In this part of the book, the intent is to present the principles, advantages, and disadvantages of alternative solution types and design approaches as well as to comparatively assess them. In effect, Part One represents a source book or seeds for reinvention.

Part Two, A Framework for Design, presents a detailed, nontechnology-specific approach to the design of energy-responsive commercial buildings. Based on the lessons learned from the most successful examples of Part One, this framework provides a logical basis for considering energy issues in the design process and is formulated to encourage innovation and reinvention by the reader. A major premise of this book and the framework presented in Part Two is that through reinvention major energy-related innovations beyond our present collective knowledge and experience are not only possible but probable. These new innovations will be the product of the work of Early Adopters.

part one

REVIEWING AND INTERPRETING OUR COLLECTIVE LEARNING EXPERIENCE

Introduction to Part One

The clearest advantage we have today is the experience of yesterday.

R. BUCKMINSTER FULLER

Since uninformed intuition alone is not always accurate when applied to an unfamiliar design challenge, a detailed review of the related work of others offers a better starting point. The purpose of Part One is to demonstrate the energy-related design experiences of many talented professionals. This information gives the reader an understanding of the current level of knowledge in this field of study, and identifies the principles, advantages, and disadvantages of environmental-control alternatives and their impact on other build-ing design considerations.

As the review of these learning experiences shows, there are a great number of legitimate alternatives to treating energy as an additional building design consideration. The design of energy-responsive commercial buildings is indeed a matter of choice. Seldom is finding a legitimate alternative the major problem. Rather, the more common problem is deciphering which of an endless list of possible components and systems provide best value and advantage in a specific building. As one colleague so aptly summarized, "Reviewing energy-related information is like taking a drink from a fire hose. There is more available than can be comfortably swallowed."

Part One organizes this large volume of information under two major topics. First, Chapters Two to Four present case studies to highlight the range of possible choices. These chapters contrast the design principles and comparative advantages and disadvantages of these fundamentally different environmental-control solution types on a whole-building basis. In practice, it is as important to understand the comparative value and design impact of competing choices as it is to know the individual principles and techniques of each. Certainly, the most fundamental choice in the design of energy-responsive commercial buildings is what type of environmental control should be provided.

The second major topic of Part One centers on the design methods that have been used to determine appropriate solutions for a specific design problem. How can design aids help or hinder the search for appropriate solutions? Chapter Five addresses this question. As shown, methods of analysis themselves can easily influence the problem statement and, in so doing, bias the solution that is derived.

Summarizing our collective experience in five short chapters is a difficult task. This review is intended to stimulate and challenge the reader's beliefs concerning the impact of energy-related issues on building design and to suggest which variables beyond energy-related components are central to reinvention. Obviously the interpretation of the material represents only one possible view. Since the design of energy-responsive commercial buildings is an unresolved design challenge, it is ultimately the reader's responsibil-ity to formulate a personal opinion of the key variables and best means to address energy-related issues in commercial buildings. Part One can only aid in the completion of this task.

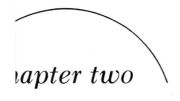

apter two

RANGE OF
E SOLUTIONS

humanely disposed, and more
e the prime human responsibility
. . it would have been apparent
e art and business of creating
divisible into two intellectually
-structures . . . and   mechanical

ᴿEYNOR Bᴀɴʜᴀᴍ

Buildings do not use energy, people do. Heating, cooling, lighting, and ventilation adjustments are made in response to people's needs and desires. The design of a building represents a choice of how these needs and desires are met. These same design choices also dictate how much nonrenewable energy is necessary to provide these services.

For the better part of 30 years, one standard environmental-control solution type has been used in the United States: commercial and institutional buildings have been electrically illuminated, fan ventilated, and thermally tempered with limited equipment and controls. This approach to environmental control has been the norm for so many years that most building owners, users, and designers do not consider alternatives. The purpose of this chapter is to introduce the basic principles of the solutions that are emerging from our collective search for energy-responsive commercial buildings. By contrasting these fundamentally different solution types, we will clarify the range of choices available and their comparative impact on people and architecture.

A difficulty arises in determining the impact of environmental-control alternatives on other design considerations. As mentioned in Chapter One, the diffusion of innovations typically follows a path that progressively absorbs the innovation into broader sets of concerns. In the end, innovations are totally integrated into the whole of a larger product or process. Rather than dealing with individual pieces of energy-related equipment or isolated design concepts on a component-by-component basis, this chapter presents the range of possible solutions in terms of whole-building types.

The whole-building classification system used in this book is based on the use of architectural form and envelope as elements of environmental control in commercial buildings. This system enables a designer to identify the purpose of a particular environmental-control solution type, its individual elements, and the second-order decisions it dictates. Other classification systems could be used, such as energy source or technology-specific equipment. A system that focuses on architectural form and envelope has been selected because such an approach provides a visual picture of the impact of environmental-control alternatives on people and architecture.

As illustrated in Figure 2.1, solutions are categorized along a range of possibilities between two opposite types defined as the climate-rejecting building and the climate-adapted building. Although both extremes use form and envelope as elements of environmental control, these elements are used in opposite fashion: the purpose of form and envelope is distinctly different.

The climate-rejecting building, the standard environmental-control solution type of the past 30 years, uses form and envelope to diminish climate-imposed loads. Environmental-control strategies are handled from within by equipment such as electric lighting and some form of heating, ventilation, and air-conditioning (HVAC) systems. Form and envelope serve solely as barriers between climate and conditioned space for environmental-control purposes.

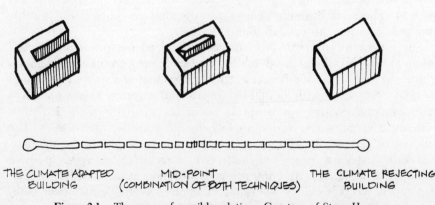

THE CLIMATE ADAPTED   MID-POINT   THE CLIMATE REJECTING
    BUILDING   (COMBINATION OF BOTH TECHNIQUES)   BUILDING

Figure 2.1.   The range of possible solutions. Courtesy of Steve Hogg.

In a climate-adapted building, positive and negative influences of climate are selectively filtered and balanced at the building boundary to provide internal environmental control. External climatic energy sources are filtered and distributed to occupied space, via the envelope, for end uses such as lighting, cooling, heating, and ventilation. These environmental-control techniques are based on age-old architectural and engineering concepts.

These two extreme solution types, as well as solutions that combine elements of both, are best illustrated with three examples. The design principles and conceptual differences of the two extreme solution types are identified in two case studies. A third case study presents an innovative design that combines the two extreme solution types into one building. Examples presented are the Wainwright Building designed by Louis Sullivan, the Larkin Building designed by Frank Lloyd Wright, and the Seagram Building designed by Mies van der Rohe and Philip Johnson.

Historical examples are used in lieu of contemporary case studies in this chapter for two reasons. First, the basic design principles and comparative differences are easier to visualize in familiar buildings. Second, by placing these solution types in their historical context, one can understand the search for environmental-control solution types as an evolutionary process. The chronological sequence illustrates the development of present conventions, and how they affect the use of nonrenewable energy. This discussion establishes the point of departure for Chapters Three and Four, which cover how these basic environmental-control solution types have been optimized in contemporary use.

ONE EXTREME: THE CLIMATE-ADAPTED BUILDING

The Wainwright Building (1890–1891)
St. Louis, Missouri
Louis Sullivan

To secure the highest lighting values in a side-lighted room it is recommended that the room be so designed that no work-space is more distant from the window than twice the height of the top of the window from the floor.

1924 IES Recommended Lighting Practice

Environmental control in buildings is seldom addressed in architectural history texts. For instance, the Wainwright Building by Louis Sullivan (Fig. 2.2) is typically presented in history texts as a broad office block. Without knowledge of the standard design practices of this period, one could assume that it is a solid mass similar to contemporary designs. However, as shown in Figures 2.3 and 2.4, the building is actually notched. What appears to be a large block from the front is actually a very narrow U-shaped building. The

Figure 2.2.   Wainwright Building. From *American Architecture and Building News*. Courtesy of Architectural Record.

requirement of a notch, or a reentrant as it was called, was so typical during this period that it was not even mentioned in most writings by Sullivan and his contemporary architectural critics.

The environmental-control requirements of the building were the major determinants of the Wainwright Building's narrow U-shaped architectural form. At the time it was built, mechanical cooling and humidity control did not exist. Incandescent lighting had just become available, but the high cost of electricity and the large heat release of the bulbs made it useful only as a supplement to daylighting. For these reasons, all work areas required access

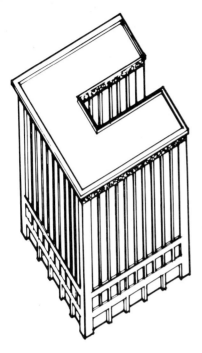

Figure 2.3. Wainwright Building, axonometric. Courtesy of Dennis Carlberg.

to windows for natural ventilation and illumination. The depth of the building was limited by the extent to which light and air could penetrate.

Designers of this period used simple rules of thumb for the provision of natural ventilation and daylighting. The proportions of these rules are evident in nearly all designs of this time. For instance, architectural form in the Wainwright Building reflects the rule that useful daylight on a cloudy day will be available in a building up to a distance of 1.5–2 times the height of the window head. The cloudy day rule was used since it takes into account the time of least daylight availability. Other conditions, such as a clear day with direct sunlight on the windows, were not considered design limitations. An overabundance of light and heat was a problem easily solved with operable windows, awnings, and blinds. As a result of the cloudy day rule of thumb, window size in the Wainwright Building does not vary by orientation. For the design condition of the overcast day, the sky near the horizon is uniformly lit in all directions.

Space planning was also influenced by the external climate in the Wainwright Building. As shown in the floor plan in Figure 2.4, transient spaces such as corridors, stairtowers, and elevators were placed in the central areas where there was limited access to light and ventilation. The double-loaded corridor and the central elevator core originally evolved from these environmental-control concerns. This spatial organization permitted the maximum amount of leasable office space.

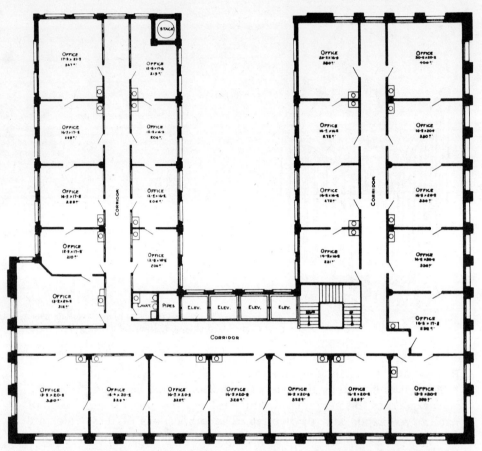

Figure 2.4. Wainwright Building, 5th floor plan. From *Recommendations for Renovation of the Wainwright Building*. Courtesy of the St. Louis Chapter of American Institute of Architects.

Also necessary to provide environmental control in the Wainwright Building were high ceilings that allowed better circulation of air and deeper penetration of natural light. The floor-to-floor height of the Wainwright building is 12 ft 9.5 in., similar to contemporary construction. However, false ceilings were not typically used at this time. The Wainwright Building floor-to-ceiling height is 11 ft. High ceilings allow higher window heads, permitting deeper penetration of light and, therefore, a deeper building.

A classic environmental-control trade-off is represented by the Wainwright Building's heating system. As with most historical climate-adapted buildings, the Wainwright Building used an internal-combustion heating system: a boiler in the basement generated heat which was then distributed to the rest of the building. The climate-adapted building form and envelope, with the narrow U-shape and many operable windows, are not efficient for a heating system that uses a concentrated energy source. Filling

Experience has shown that only under quite unusual conditions is it possible to carry a sufficient volume of daylight for purposes of reading and writing—as found necessary in the transaction of ordinary office business—to a greater distance than twenty-five feet from the source of light. There are many cases where this limit is twenty feet or less. Taking these figures as the basis of our calculation, it would appear that a building having light from front and rear, and two tiers of offices, one to the front and one to the rear, should not be made deeper under any circumstances, after making due allowances for halls, corridors, and partitions, than about sixty-five feet, and that there may be instances where this depth could be very advantageously reduced to even less than forty feet. As the measure of strength of any piece of construction is that of its weakest part, so to a great extent is the character of a building determined by that of its least desirable portions. A number of poorly-lighted rooms occupied by undesirable tenants will do more toward driving good tenants from a building than will be accomplished as a matter of attraction by an equal number of tenants of a high grade. In planning a building, therefore, no matter how much space there may be, the distance from outside wall to outside wall should not be too great for the satisfactory lighting of the interior. Again, there should be an endeavor to have the inside rooms as well lighted as the rooms which obtain light from the street. This can be done only by approximating as nearly as possible in the dimensions of internal light-courts the width of the street on which the building fronts. In many instances it will be found advisable, in the design of light-courts, to face them externally, and make them in a certain sense an enlargement of the street. By this means the efficiency of the source of light is very materially increased, because its horizon is enlarged by a distance equal to the width of the street; and, on the other hand, the efficiency of the street as a general source of light and air is materially enhanced.

DANKMAR ADLER[*]

in the U-shape with additional office space would make a more efficient form that would require less boiler output. However, such a change would render the building useless during warmer weather since hot gas or electric lights would be required. Combined use of external and internal environmental-control sources often produces this dilemma. Climate-adapted systems require narrow buildings that are punctured to allow climatic energy sources to be diffused throughout the building. Internally distributed systems are more efficient when form is collapsed toward a cube and the envelope is sealed, insulated, and opaque. However, one has almost absolute control over forced environmental systems but only relative and dampering control over the natural environment.

The Wainwright Building exemplifies the simple climate-balancing

[*]Dankmar Adler, "Light In Tall Office Buildings," *The Engineering Magazine*, Vol. IV, No. 2, November 1892.

design principles of a climate-adapted building. Bounded by the limits of the penetration of light, heat, or air, architectural form must be narrow and extended, and envelope must be punctured or opened. To connect all internal space to openings in envelope requires a specific relationship between surface, volume, and form. This relationship typically dictates a high surface-to-volume ratio. Likewise, total building volume is typically large, depending on both the use of high ceilings that permit a proportionally deeper building and the treatment of circulation requirements within the relatively narrow building form. If internal environmental-control systems are also used, which is the usual case, an extended, punctured form is typically a liability. This ageless environmental-control trade-off is very often the major concern in the design of a contemporary climate-adapted building. In the Wainwright Building there was little choice. Contemporary climate-adapted buildings generally balance this contradiction in the use of form and envelope according to the relative energy magnitudes of internally and externally distributed environmental-control systems.

As demonstrated by the Wainwright Building, renewable energy sources represent a legitimate alternative choice to nonrenewable energy in commercial building designs. On the simplest level, contemporary climate-adapted buildings are based on the application of age-old architectural principles and techniques. As shown in the contemporary climate-adapted building case studies presented in Chapter Four, however, the availability of new materials and technologies is augmenting the effectiveness of these simple techniques to a point never envisioned by their early users.

THE MID-POINT: MIXING THE CLIMATE-ADAPTED AND CLIMATE-REJECTING BUILDING

The Larkin Building (1904–1906)
Buffalo, New York
Frank Lloyd Wright

More and more, so it seems to me, light is the beautifier of the building.

FRANK LLOYD WRIGHT

Around the turn of the century, new developments in mechanical environmental-control systems provided new design possibilities. The high cost and limited abilities of these early mechanical innovations restricted their usefulness to projects with large budgets or special requirements. The Larkin Building by Frank Lloyd Wright (Figs. 2.5–2.8) is such a special case that used mechanical environmental control to mitigate the effects of the

Figure 2.5.   Larkin Building. Courtesy of the Frank Lloyd Wright Memorial Foundation.

polluted external environment. The resulting building represents a unique approach to environmental control in a commercial building best described as a mix of the two extreme solution types defined at the beginning of this chapter.

The Larkin Building stands alone in the history of environmental control because it was one of the first "hermetically sealed" buildings. All thermal and ventilation needs were handled internally by mechanical equipment. Daylight was the primary light source. Incandescent lights were used but only for night occupancy, decoration, and as a daytime supplement to natural light. As in the Wainwright Building, the limits to daylight penetration required the use of a narrow building form. Rather than having a narrow U-shape, the Larkin Building surrounded and capped a void to make an atrium. As in the Wainwright Building, environmental-control requirements directly influenced architectural form.

The Larkin Building site was adjacent to a railroad yard and surrounded by industrial buildings. The foul air surrounding the site was the primary reason for selecting the sealed building approach. In the Larkin Building, outside air was pulled from above the stairtowers down to the basement where a water wash filtered solid particles from the airstream. In the summer, the same water wash evaporatively cooled the air approximately 2°–3°F and, along with venting hot air from the top of the atrium, provided

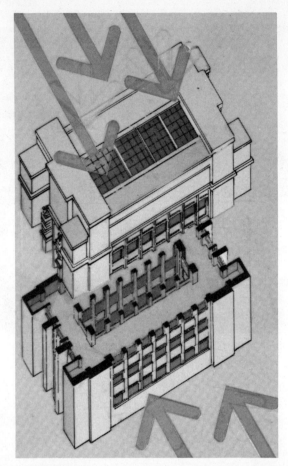

Figure 2.6.   Larkin Building, axonometric. Courtesy of Communication Arts.

the only means to cool the building. In winter, the washed air was heated and distributed by fans to each floor.

A disadvantage of the modest evaporative cooling process was that it increased the relative humidity of the air. In addition, heat generated within the building could quickly overextend the cooling ability of the system. This is a major reason why incandescent lighting was only a supplement to daylighting. Heat is a by-product of all light sources. Natural light, however, is a much cooler source of light than incandescent bulbs (i.e., more light per unit of heat). Incandescent lighting would have been an impractical primary light source for the Larkin Building because of the great amount of heat it would have released to the space.

As with the Wainwright Building, the conflicting envelope and form needs of internally distributed point-source environmental-control strate-

Figure 2.7. Larkin Building, atrium. Courtesy of the Frank Lloyd Wright Memorial Foundation.

Figure 2.8. Larkin Building, workspace. Courtesy of the Frank Lloyd Wright Memorial Foundation.

gies and the use of diffuse external climatic energy sources had to be addressed. A hermetically sealed building with a very modest cooling capacity requires a tight, compact architectural form with limited exposed exterior surface area. However, daylighting requires a narrow building section with a large external surface area exposed to climate. These two contradictory needs are so restrictive that a workable balance cannot be achieved with a conventional building form.

Wright's solution to this problem is best expressed as an architectural form that has two different environmental-control building boundaries. The office floors were placed around an atrium and the top was capped with a large glazed skylight, resulting in a tight building form with limited exterior exposure. Unlike the Wainwright Building with its open notch, the Larkin Building placed the thermal barrier at the top of the atrium. This choice greatly reduced the building area exposed to the exterior environment. In comparison, the Larkin Building's "thermal boundary" is 30% less than the Wainwright Building's thermal boundary.

Since the Larkin Building was capped with a glazed skylight filter, the "daylighting boundary" of the architectural form functioned as a typical narrow building section. The only disadvantage with this lighting approach was a slight reduction in the daylight available in the atrium due to reflection and absorption by the glass. The atrium was treated like an open court. The majority of the Larkin Building was bilaterally illuminated by exterior windows and the atrium. Note in the accompanying interior photographs that the incandescent lights are off, yet the space appears to be well illuminated. Also note the high placement of exterior windows. The industrial blight that surrounded the site led Wright to develop a design which focused inward on the atrium. The exterior windows were for light, not view; their high placement and the use of high ceilings was for better light penetration and quality.

As an element of environmental control, the Larkin Building atrium was essentially a buffer zone, a spatial control device that creates a sequence of environments in series. A buffer zone establishes a unique environmental-control zone between the inside and outside environments. Although the Larkin Building does not represent the first time architectural form was used as buffer, the building used a very inventive extension of the concept that included, for the first time, the ability to cool a building from within.

The greatest advantage to buffer zones is their versatility. They may be exterior to the building, such as a veranda, or centrally located in a building, such as an open court or closed atrium. These elements represent architectural compromises to the ageless trade-off between the need to open a building to diffuse external climate energy sources and the need to close it when internal environmental-control systems are used. Architectural form as buffer may be a spatial filter in a climate-adapted building, a spatial barrier in a climate-rejecting building, or, as in the Larkin Building, it may be used as both for different environmental-control end uses. If the form and envelope characteristics of climate-adapted buildings and climate-rejecting buildings are defined as hypothetical extremes in the range of possible solutions, the Larkin Building can be described as the midpoint. In the Larkin Building, Wright simultaneously extended and collapsed form and punctured and sealed the envelope in a way that mutually meets what at first appear to be contradictory needs. Architectural buffers typically increase overall building volume in an attempt to reduce the skin area of a building exposed to the extremes of climate. This principle may at first appear redundant, but it represents the trade-off in combining objectives of the climate-adapted and climate-rejecting buildings.

As shown in Chapters Three and Four, many contemporary commercial buildings use architectural buffers to reduce the need for nonrenewable energy. With lighting as the typical major energy need in contemporary commercial buildings, the buffer/double-environmental-perimeter approach of the Larkin Building is popular in combination with existing and innovative mechanical systems. However, buffers are being used in many other fundamentally different ways as well in both climate-adapted and climate-rejecting buildings. The use of buffers is illustrated in case studies of both solution types in the next two chapters.

THE OTHER EXTREME: THE CLIMATE-
REJECTING BUILDING

The Seagram Building (1955–1958)
New York, New York
Mies van der Rohe and Philip Johnson

*At night, the entire building will switch to a second lighting circuit which will
give it a "tower of light" appearance.*

ARCHITECTURAL FORUM, FEBRUARY 1957

Practical mechanical air-conditioning systems with both temperature and
humidity control were developed during the 1920s. The fluorescent light, a
more efficient and therefore cooler alternative to incandescent light,
became commercially available in the 1930s. These technological advances
did not immediately lead to commercial and institutional buildings with
total internal environmental control. Narrow buildings using daylight and
natural ventilation were common until the 1950s. At that time increased
equipment reliability, reduced initial equipment cost, and the low price of
electricity allowed the internal environmental-control approach of the
climate-rejecting building to become the standard solution.

The Seagram Building by Mies van der Rohe and Philip Johnson (Figs.
2.9 and 2.10) illustrates the role of architectural form and envelope in
buildings that exclusively use internal environmental-control systems. This
case study also demonstrates two important areas of change in environmental-control conventions that took place during the 1950s: the purpose
of environmental control in commercial and institutional buildings and the
perception of occupants' space-conditioning needs and desires.

The major differences in architectural form between the two preceding
case studies and the Seagram Building are its depth and configuration.
Light, air temperature, humidity, and ventilation were all handled internally
in the Seagram Building. Except to provide a view, no direct connection
was required between occupied space and the external environment. The
need for a notch was eliminated. Whereas the Wainwright and Larkin
Buildings had a limit of about 18 ft between occupied space and window, the
Seagram Building had no such limit to building depth. A deeper simple
rectilinear floor plan could be used.

Because of the increased building depth, the area of exterior building skin
required to encase a unit of gross floor area was sharply reduced. For the
Seagram Building, only 0.3 units of building skin area were required to
encase a unit of gross floor area. This same skin-to-floor-area ratio for the
Wainwright Building is 0.8. By greatly reducing the amount of building skin

Figure 2.9. Seagram Building. Courtesy of Esto Photographics, Inc.

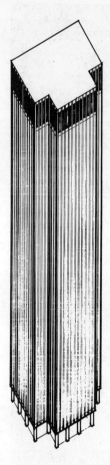

Figure 2.10.   Seagram Building, axonometric. Courtesy of Dennis Carlberg.

area exposed to the external environment, the heating and cooling output required to counteract climatic extremes is correspondingly decreased.

The use of internal environmental-control strategies eliminates the trade-off between the need to open a building to positive climatic resources and the need to close the building to defend against extreme cold and/or heat. Total internal environmental control has the singular form and envelope goal of climatic exclusion. In addition to reducing exposed skin area, the designers of the Seagram Building excluded the climate with fixed, tinted glass. Sealed windows provide a better barrier to climate than do operable windows. Internal thermal-control systems are also better balanced in a sealed environment. Gray-pink polished plate glass rejects daylight and reduces solar-imposed cooling loads, thereby providing visual comfort by balancing the contrast between windows and a luminous ceiling. (The luminous ceiling

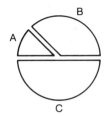

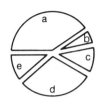

By Energy Cause
A. Envelopes
B. Contents
C. Lighting

By Equipment
a. Interior Lighting
b. Heating
c. Fans and Pumps
d. Cooling
e. Other Uses

Figure 2.11. Energy use by equipment and building energy need by cause. Courtesy of Caudill Rowlett Scott.

was just one of many innovative elements in the Seagram Building.) As is evident in both form and components, the overall goal of this environmental-control method is to exclude the direct influence of climate on space and provide all services internally from controlled point sources.

Although reduced skin area, sealed windows, and tinted glass significantly reduce the relative impact of climate as an environmental-control load, they also hold in the heat from lights, people, and machines and reduce the infiltration of fresh air. In most commercial buildings at this time, the major yearlong task of internal environmental-control systems changed from counteracting climatic extremes to offsetting self-imposed internal loads. Typically, providing light and removing heat are the two major environmental-control needs of the sealed building approach. Climate-rejecting buildings represent a major transformation in the use of environmental-control systems. With this change came a major shift in the proportion of total building energy use for specific tasks or needs.

This shift in the purpose of environmental control has not changed fundamentally from the mid-1950s to the present. A revealing source we have found that expresses this transformation in terms of energy use are the pie charts shown in Figure 2.11. These charts, generated by Caudill Rowlett Scott (CRS) of Houston, Texas, indicate the typical proportions of total building energy use in Btu at the site of various end uses in a mid-1970s climate-rejecting office building. These charts present annual energy requirements in two ways. The chart on the right shows the proportions of total annual energy use by equipment type. Although this chart is informative, the actual causes of these energy needs are unclear. The chart on the left presents the same data in energy-use cause categories. Three causes of energy need are listed:

Lights (which include removing the excess heat of lights from a sealed building).

Contents (which include tempering code-required ventilation air, supplying power to office equipment, and removing the heat of people and machines).

Envelope (which includes the energy required to counteract the extremes of climate through the entire building membrane).

Figure 2.11 clearly shows that the major energy needs of a closed office building are internal and not envelope-related. As shown in Table 2.1, CRS found this pattern reflected in other commercial building types. CRS formulated these data in Table 2.1 from an American Institute of Architects (AIA) Research Corporation data base developed to support the proposed Building Energy Performance Standards (BEPS). This study is based on a 1977 statistical sample of over 1600 buildings designed and built in the mid-1970s. These energy-use patterns reflect the proportions of energy use before substantial efforts were made to limit the use of nonrenewable energy in commercial buildings.

These energy-use patterns are in sharp contrast to those of earlier climate-adapted buildings. For instance, the Wainwright Building used well over half its total annual building energy to counteract winter heat loss through the building envelope.[*] For this reason, past and contemporary climate-adapted buildings are often called envelope or skin load-dominated buildings. In contrast, climate-rejecting commercial buildings are often called internal load-dominated buildings. In contemporary use, both solution types seek similar end results but the technical means to this end are fundamentally different.

With the technical transformations of the time came a similarly profound transformation in the environmental-control needs and desires of people. The shift to internal environmental-control solutions was swift and pronounced. The most obvious reason for the quick change was comfort. New artificial environmental-control systems offered building occupants a

TABLE 2.1. BUILDING TYPES. COURTESY OF CAUDILL ROWLETT SCOTT.

% Allotment	School	Housing	Office	Hospital	Commercial
A. Envelope	15	50	11	10	15
B. Contents	45	30	39	40	45
C. Lighting	40	20	50	50	40
D. Total	100	100	100	100	100

[*]For more information on the energy requirements of the original Wainwright Building, see "Energy Analysis," by Vladimir Bazjanac, Ph.D., *Progressive Architecture*, November 1981.

marked increase in the control of light, air, temperature, and humidity. Thermal comfort on the hottest summer afternoon was achievable and soon expected in commercial buildings. New possibilities, such as the exclusive use of filtered air within buildings, added to the advantages of such systems. In a very few years, no one needed to explain the difference between a new office building and an old one to a prospective tenant. As Figure 2.12 illustrates, to avoid demolition even the best examples of the past had to be upgraded to meet these new expectations.

Building users were not the only people who perceived advantages in the new environmental-control systems. Designers found old limitations were abolished by new design possibilities. A simple example of this is the Seagram Building's use of light. A special circuit illuminates the entire building at night to create a "shimmering tower of light." Building owners also found economic advantages in the use of internal environmental-control systems. This topic is very well summarized by Reyner Banham in *Architecture of the Well-Tempered Environment* (Chicago, Illinois: University of Chicago Press; 1969):

> *(Buildings) . . . had always exhibited a notch or re-entrant in the back . . . and this re-entrant served to bring light (and ventilating air) to the centre of the block . . . But a plan bitten into in this way was more difficult to subdivide and contained more awkward corners that were difficult to let, than would the plain rectangle of what was to be called the "full-floor" type of plan, with its ancillaries islanded in the centre—a possibility that existed, profitably, only with air-conditioning and low-heat lighting. Given these, however, it was calculated by a Chicago real-estate man, George R. Bailey, that full-floor development can be produced, complete with air-conditioning, fluorescent lighting and acoustic ceilings, for only about 8% more than a standard floor (i.e., with notchback) without air-conditioning and with only ordinary lighting. His calculus was timely—not only was the clear, well-serviced rectangular floor plan attractive enough for its rents to absorb the extra eight percent, but architects had by now more or less unanimously decided that their post-war skyscraper dreams were going to be realized in a starkly aesthetic way. Both the United Nations Building and Lever House were in design and construction at the time Bailey's results were published, and though both were prestige buildings which, for differing reasons, could support "uneconomical" standards of servicing, the innumerable rectangular glass slabs which appeared in their imitation soon showed that such a format and its necessary standard of servicing was not at all uneconomic—or, at any rate, not unprofitable.*

The swift transition to the new environmental-control systems of the 1950s was a consequence of the new systems being welcomed by all. Designers, builders, and occupants alike perceived new advantages in comfort, aesthetics, and economics. This is a lesson well remembered in our present search for environmental-control strategies that both meet the needs and desires of people and limit the use of nonrenewable energy. Any

Figure 2.12. Wainwright Building with window air conditioners. Courtesy of John Scarkowski.

substantial modification to commercial buildings for energy-related purposes must address the impact these changes will have on people. The design of energy-responsive commercial buildings is as much a study of people's motives and tastes as it is the application of technology. Modifications must have advantages beyond energy efficiency that will appeal to users. Technological developments that break quickly with existing design conventions involve issues of aesthetics, amenity, profit, health, and human productivity.

A climate-rejecting building represents the other hypothetical extreme in the range of possible environmental-control solution types for commercial buildings. Compared to other design issues such as comfort, amenity, and initial construction cost, the annual fuel cost for a building was a far lesser design concern in the period of plentiful and inexpensive fossil fuel energy supplies. The relative low cost of energy has led to the great number of internal environmental-control solutions with large nonrenewable energy appetites. However, energy waste need not be synonymous with each solutions any more than discomfort need be associated with the direct use of climatic energies. Today, as utility costs rise and the supply of conventional energy sources becomes less reliable, a new balance of design concerns is emerging. As shown in the case studies presented in Chapter Three, ample opportunities are being found for significant energy-related improvements in contemporary climate-rejecting buildings.

In this chapter, the range of possible solutions has been defined as a continuum of possibilities between two extremes. The key difference between the two extreme solution types is the simple choice to accept or reject the direct influence of climate on occupied space. This decision defines a specific nature for a building by establishing the roles of form and envelope and, as the examples in Chapters Three and Four will show, for environmental-control equipment as well. This decision also dictates whether a building is envelope or internal load dominated.

In our review of hundreds of case studies in preparation for this book, we have not found one solution type that decisively outcompetes all others. Be they first cost, comfort, or total energy use, a great many legitimate solutions exist. It is possible to design at either extreme, or somewhere in between, and meet or exceed the needs and desires of people as well as substantially limit the use of nonrenewable energy.

That many appropriate solution types exist does not mean they are always interchangeable and equally applicable for every design challenge. Each alternative has unique abilities, qualities, and limitations. In Chapters Three and Four, the contemporary energy-related choices and possibilities of climate-rejecting and climate-adapted buildings are explored. The principles of these two hypothetical extremes are examined, as well as case studies that mix elements of each, to clarify the purpose of the many existing alternatives, options, and components. Solution types do not represent a comparative list of interchangeable parts; rather, the present range of possible solutions represents a wealth of alternative design opportunities well suited to unique purposes.

chapter three

ENERGY-RESPONSIVE CLIMATE-REJECTING BUILDINGS

How can we accomplish, with minimal expenditure of energy, the things to which we've become accustomed.

JOHN YELLOTT

Designers of contemporary climate-rejecting buildings are faced with the challenge of improving the energy-effectiveness of this solution type. This chapter covers the means currently used to limit the use of nonrenewable energy within a sealed building. As in the preceding chapter, individual alternatives or options are contrasted as competing choices to gain a better understanding of the benefit and design potential of each.

The material in this chapter is based on the assumption that the goal is to improve the energy-effectiveness of a climate-rejecting building. The alternative to this choice would be to use climatic energies in combination with an extended and punctured architectural form. These topics are intentionally divided between Chapters Three and Four to permit the potentials, principles, and limitations of each to be better exemplified.

Once a designer decides to improve the energy efficiency of a climate-rejecting building, other decisions come into play. The first major choice is where to execute such improvements. Because the nature of the climate-rejecting building presumably does not change, the potential to limit the use of nonrenewable energy in this solution type evolves directly from the building's climate-excluding, internally serviced, environmental-control features. Specifically, the energy needs of a climate-rejecting building can be reduced by either making form and envelope a better barrier to climate or by improving the effectiveness of internal systems. These two categories of options serve as a focus of the discussion in this chapter.

The second major choice depicted in this chapter is the degree of change that is permitted to derive energy-related improvements. In order to be successful, any significant change to building design conventions must be perceived as advantageous by owners, designers, and occupants. The degree of change is perhaps the most important choice in the design of energy-responsive commercial buildings. One can choose to make small energy-related improvements within existing design conventions that do not impact overall building design, use, or ownership. Conversely, if one opts to break existing design conventions, new motives and perceived advantages must be central to such solutions. These two levels of change are termed "incremental" and "nonincremental."

Incremental changes are conservation measures that are made within the present design conventions of climate-rejecting buildings. Incremental changes have limited impact on overall building design and, to the untrained eye, may be virtually impossible to detect. Maintaining an appearance of sameness precludes the necessity of creating new perceived advantages. The major advantage of incremental changes is that less effort is required to improve the existing than to formulate a new approach, and the lax attitude of the past toward energy use enables very simple incremental changes to achieve impressive results. The major disadvantage of incremental changes is that the potential for energy-related improvement is bound by existing design conventions.

Nonincremental changes offer possibilities for maximizing energy efficiency beyond those attainable by incremental changes alone. Nonincremental changes achieve energy-related improvements by altering existing design conventions. Although these changes are made within the bounds of the basic nature of the climate-rejecting building solution type, such modification requires that new perceived advantages be found and judged acceptable by building users, owners, and designers. With changes, however, and the subsequent need to develop new perceived advantages, come an increase in complexity of the design challenge.

Distinguishing between incremental change and nonincremental change alternatives signals whether new motives and perceived advantages are integral issues to the successful utilization of the alternative. Quite often, the people-related issues associated with nonincremental change are a much greater design challenge than technological issues.

In the following overview of form and envelope improvements and system-related improvements, incremental changes are discussed first, followed by the presentation of contemporary examples that use the same basic design principles at the nonincremental change level. More emphasis is placed on the nonincremental change alternatives since most designers are relatively familiar with the process of making incremental changes.

FORM AND ENVELOPE OPTIONS

Designers know the opportunities for energy conservation are better for cube-shaped buildings.

ARCHITECTURAL RECORD, NOVEMBER 1981

The purpose of form and envelope in a climate-rejecting building is to reject climate-imposed, environmental-control loads. Form and envelope options isolate occupied space from the influence of climate. Envelope options include such strategies as external solar shades, reflective window films, double or triple glazing, and additional insulation. The energy-effectiveness of form is improved by using cubelike shapes of limited skin-to-floor-area ratios that contain the smallest volume necessary to fulfill the intended building function. These defensive options can be used to nonselectively reject heat gains and minimize heat losses throughout the year or to selectively offset seasonal and peak-demand-period heat gains or losses.

From our review of hundreds of incremental change case studies, we have found that four significant factors should be considered in evaluating the value of form and envelope options compared to system-related alternatives. First, *form and envelope options need not be additive components.* Using existing design elements to best advantage is much better than correcting problems with additive components. Care in the design of form, orientation, and fenestration can limit both annual consumption and peak-period demand. Where possible, reducing surface area by modifying form is generally better than adding insulation or layers of glass. Compact forms also tend to cost less, thereby reducing energy consumption and initial construction cost. Similarly, moving west-facing glazing to a more favorable orientation can reduce both consumption and peak demand by modifying exposure.

The second favorable consideration with form and envelope options is *the opportunity to reduce the size and cost of heating and cooling plants* and associated elements such as ducting or piping. Where load reductions are significant, decreases in equipment cost can offset cost increases of additive defensive options. This result is achieved by designing defensive form and envelope elements that reduce peak loads. Very often, these same options also reduce annual energy use.

These two positive factors are countered by two negative factors, the first of which is *the law of diminishing returns.* As mentioned in the Seagram Building case study, the major need for environmental control in most commercial buildings has shifted from counteracting the extremes of climate to offsetting self-imposed internal loads. Existing design practice emphasizes relatively deep-bayed buildings with sealed envelopes and tinted or reflective glazing. The majority of climate-imposed loads are already neutralized. Any further investments in climate-rejecting form and envelope options represent an attempt to improve this process. If the added expense of a defensive form and envelope option is offset by an HVAC system initial cost reduction, the change is definitely a good one. Otherwise, however, designers incorporating form and envelope changes may find themselves getting proportionally less results for the investment.

The second factor that makes form and envelope options less desirable than system-related alternatives is that many options which reject climate also *trap internally generated heat within the structure*. The total energy use of a building is increased, therefore, since mechanical removal of excess heat is required. During fall, winter, and spring, when outdoor temperatures are mild, it is usually advantageous to lose internal heat through the building envelope. In all climate-rejecting buildings, advantages gained by excluding climate are somewhat offset by the need to mechanically extract the heat of lights, people, and machines. As a minimum, the envelope should always be insulated to provide occupant comfort under the extreme outdoor design conditions. Beyond this point, advantages gained by further excluding climate will be partially offset by increased swing-season cooling loads. This liability is not great enough to suggest that defensive options are always inappropriate, but it indicates that combining system options which reduce self-imposed internal loads with defensive form and envelope options may be the preferable solution.

Where form and envelope options are combined with system-related improvements in a climate-rejecting building, climate-imposed loads may begin to be a more significant proportional cause of total annual building energy use. For instance, when heating needs are increased and cooling needs are decreased by a switch to a high-efficiency lighting system, further investments in defensive form and envelope strategies may be justified. When incremental changes are made to a climate-rejecting building it may not be wise to start with selecting form and envelope options, but such options may be appropriate once substantial system improvements have been made. Knowing when the envelope represents a significant cause of total building energy use is the key to employing appropriate defensive options. The recommended design approach presented in Chapter Six illustrates one way this may be done.

In conclusion, the purpose of defensive incremental changes to form and envelope is to minimize energy exchanges between the inside and outside of a building. The general means used are to seal and insulate the envelope, push form toward a cube, and reduce the volume of space that requires conditioning. Beyond using the existing elements of design to best advantage, these options will often prove disappointing if not coupled with system-related improvements because most climate-rejecting buildings are dominated by internal loads. If most energy use is internal, then the greatest potential to limit energy use is to be found behind the building skin. Form and envelope options assume greater importance only as these internal energy needs are diminished. We feel that many designers miss this connection and overrate the singular use of incremental form and envelope options. This belief is probably a result of the association of these strategies with the advantages derived by similar improvements to residential buildings.

The following two case studies illustrate the value of form and envelope revisions once internal system improvements have been made, and their effectiveness at the nonincremental change level. As these examples show, a simple insulated cube is not always compatible with other important design objectives. At first, the need to balance defensive form and envelope goals with other design concerns may seem limiting. However, if one integrates energy concerns with other major design objectives, the result need not be a compromise. Ideally, a solution can be developed that exceeds the capabilities of a conventional building in meeting major design and energy requirements.

The two buildings presented are the Federal Building–U.S. Courthouse, Ft. Lauderdale, Florida, designed by William Morgan Architects, and 33 West Monroe, Chicago, Illinois, designed by the Chicago office of Skidmore, Owings & Merrill. Both buildings generally fit the definition of a climate-rejecting building because all environmental-control needs of the buildings are serviced by internal systems. However, both buildings deviate from the definition of an incrementally changed climate-rejecting building by expanding either form or volume as a means of simultaneously limiting overall energy need and meeting other important design objectives.

Federal Building–U.S. Courthouse

The Federal Building–U.S. Courthouse is a four-level, 336,014-ft^2 structure located in downtown Ft. Lauderdale, Florida. The building houses four federal courts, a variety of other governmental agencies, and a 230-car below-grade parking garage. The General Services Administration (GSA), the client for the building, originally requested a conventional office block with an attached, above-ground parking garage. As shown in Figures 3.1–3.9, the City of Ft. Lauderdale gained much more than just another conventional office building. Most critics agree that Morgan's building gives a new tone and focus to the loosely organized Ft. Lauderdale urban center.

The architects were presented with two seemingly incompatible qualitative design mandates: the building should be a functional, public facility yet be a stately, monumental structure as well. The solution derived by Morgan is both formal and informal. Formality is achieved with an impressively

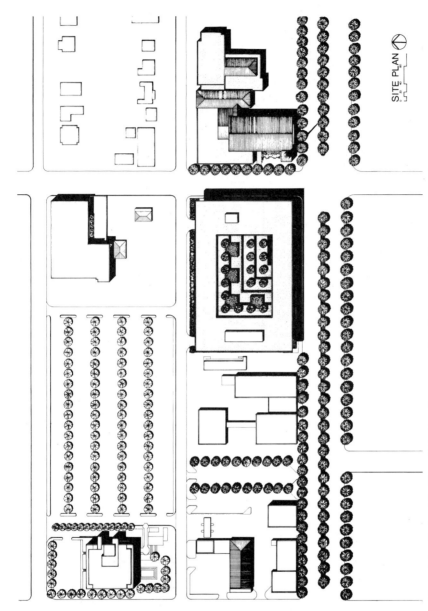

Figure 3.1. Federal Building–U.S. Courthouse, site plan. Courtesy of William Morgan Architects.

SITE PLAN

Figure 3.2. Federal Building–U.S. Courthouse. Courtesy of William Morgan Architects.

Figure 3.3. Federal Building–U.S. Courthouse. Courtesy of William Morgan Architects.

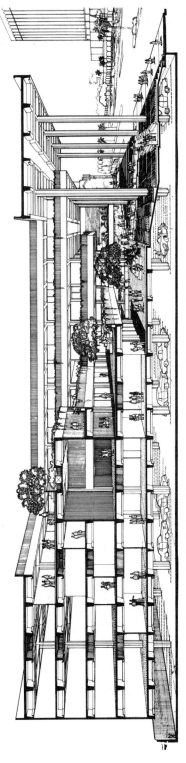

Figure 3.4. Federal Building–U.S. Courthouse, section perspective. Courtesy of William Morgan Architects.

39

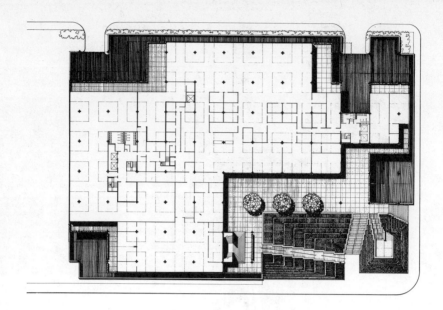

FIRST LEVEL

Figure 3.5. Federal Building–U.S. Courthouse, first level. Courtesy of William Morgan Architects.

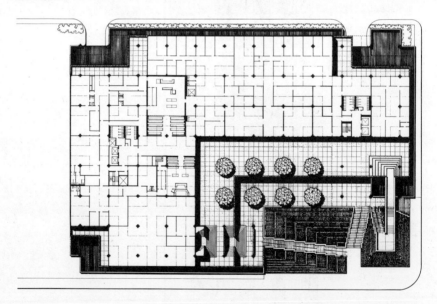

SECOND LEVEL

Figure 3.6. Federal Building–U.S. Courthouse, second level. Courtesy of William Morgan Architects.

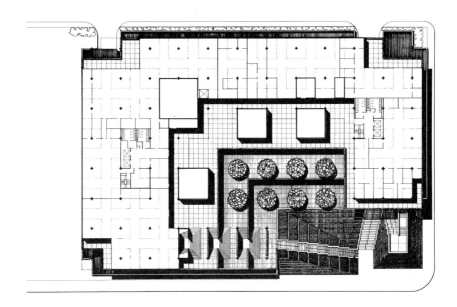

THIRD LEVEL

Figure 3.7. Federal Building-U.S. Courthouse, third level. Courtesy of William Morgan Architects.

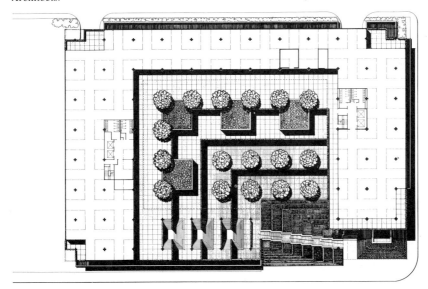

FOURTH LEVEL

Figure 3.8. Federal Building-U.S. Courthouse, fourth level. Courtesy of William Morgan Architects.

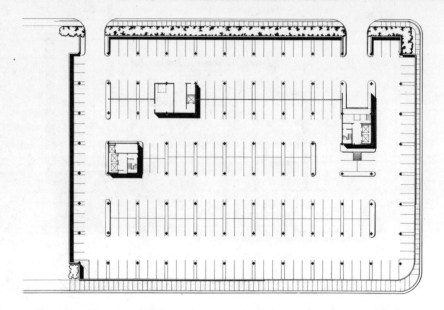

Figure 3.9.   Federal Building–U.S. Courthouse, parking level. Courtesy of William Morgan Architects.

solid, rigid block. Informality is achieved by carving out the block, making the resulting plaza and enclosing building open, airy, transparent, and inviting.

The shape of the building meets basic functional needs as well. For instance, the lofty perimeter roof provides protection from sun and rain. The perimeters of the ascending interior plazas are likewise protected by broad overhangs that are further shaded with lush vegetation. These sheltered buffer areas between the open court and enclosed portions of the building serve as vertical and horizontal circulation spaces and as entrances to the many separate governmental offices. Placement of these elements in a naturally conditioned outdoor space reduces the overall building volume that must be tempered by artificial environmental-control systems. In this case, the extension of form, a liability in most climate-rejecting buildings, is the key that permits a reduction in enclosed building volume.

The self-shading concept of the building form is likewise demonstrated in the use of envelope. All glass is shaded by the building form. All windows, which are fixed, are placed under the broad overhangs adjacent to the plaza or at the notches carved from the building's corners. The outer perimeter walls are left opaque and insulated. The extended form of the building is sufficiently narrow to allow the use of windows on only the protected side of the building facing the court.

Building volume is also reduced by the use of a structural "tree" concrete slab and column system. Cruciform columns are centered in coffered and beamed floors and roof slabs. Each "tree" canopy is 20 ft^2. Between each tree is a 10-ft beam-free chase area which contains all mechanical ducts. This innovative integration of structure and mechanical services permits a reduction of 5 ft in building height because ducts never run under or through beams. The fluorescent lighting system is also integrated into the structural system. Lighting coves are formed by attaching precast concrete ledges to the bottom of the exposed poured-in-place beams of the concrete tree system.

This discussion only touches on some of the many connections made between separate design elements in this building. From the perspectives of urban context, space planning, and energy-effectiveness, this solution finds integrity through the integration of many diverse design needs. After examining the preliminary design, the GSA design advisory panel warned other governmental review committees that "the various parts of the design interact so totally and interdependently that the project would suffer if major conceptual changes are seriously considered."[*] Another testament to the power of integrity through integration is the completion of the project for $10.8 million, 25% under the original GSA budget for a conventional building and parking garage.

As an example of energy-related envelope and form design innovation, the Federal Building–U.S. Courthouse illustrates two very important points. The first is the potential for the integration of energy-related objectives with a host of other design concerns. We contend that the combination of energy-related objectives with other significant design concerns will produce a substantially better overall solution than the isolation of energy issues as incremental improvements to a design already derived. This difference is well exemplified in Morgan's building. Instead of achieving solar protection by bolt-on solar fins, the glass was placed under artful folds in building form. In the case of solar fins, an incremental improvement brings with it an incremental construction cost without adding tangible value to the building. In the latter case, the integration of many innovations produces an overall cohesive design and, at least in the most innovative solutions, the opportunity to reduce construction cost while adding value. Although designers may collectively develop energy-related skills by studying incremental changes to climate-rejecting buildings, total dependence on applying energy-related strategies to a climate-rejecting form and envelope will only constrain overall innovation and the potential for architectural integrity.

[*]*Report of the Public Advisory Panel, Courthouse, Federal Office Building and Parking Facility, Fort Lauderdale, Florida.* November 14, 1975.

The second point demonstrated in this project is that a climate-rejecting building need not necessarily be an insulated cube to achieve energy-efficiency. The decision to use a narrow, extended building form for the Federal Building–U.S. Courthouse came from much broader, nonenergy-related design concerns. The resulting form and envelope, however, are well suited to meeting energy-use needs as well. Shade and external circulation that minimize interior volume and opaque outer walls all reduce the climatic liabilities that are usually counteracted by a cubelike form. Since heating is not a problem (as reflected in the absence of a heating plant in the design), a new balance of the element of form and envelope produces an overall design that is as effective in shedding climate-imposed loads as a cube. The number of effective energy-related form and envelope solutions for a climate-rejecting building is actually as limitless as the diverse range of client design criteria encountered in private practice.

33 West Monroe

The 33 West Monroe building (Figs. 3.10–3.14) also combines energy-related objectives with much broader design concerns. It is a 28-story, 1.1 million ft^2 speculative office tower in the heart of Chicago's Loop. The innovative use of form and envelope in this building does conserve energy, but the major driving force behind this solution is economics. With the present high costs of construction, land, and money, adequate return on investment requires solutions that add amenities to justify higher rent, yet are more economical to build than conventional designs.

Without the need for reentrants, climate-rejecting buildings with internal environmental-control systems could be much deeper and broader than their historical predecessors. Building owners saw merit in this solution type since it assured occupant comfort and permitted the use of deep-bayed, higher density, low surface-to-volume ratio buildings that have proved very profitable. The depth of a building with internal environmental control has no theoretical limit; however, the potential of constructing buildings with immense external dimensions has never been realized.

In the speculative office building market, the limiting factor on building depth is generally the ratio of perimeter offices to interior offices. This proportion is most apparent in the classic 100-ft-wide office buildings typical of most urban centers. To push such forms toward a cube for energy reasons would be in direct conflict with owner/developer concern for an appropriate number of exterior offices.

The use of three separate, stacked atriums is the key innovation of 33 West Monroe that provides amenity for tenants, lower construction cost, and energy conservation. In an earlier single-atrium office building, the architects found that many executives preferred interior offices that overlook the atrium to perimeter offices. In 33 West Monroe the center of

Figure 3.10. 33 West Monroe. Courtesy of Merrick/Hendrich-Blessing.

Figure 3.11. 33 West Monroe, section. Courtesy of Skidmore, Owings & Merrill and *Architectural Record*.

Figure 3.12. 33 West Monroe, interior. Courtesy of Skidmore, Owings & Merrill.

the office block is carved out in a fashion reminiscent of the old reentrants. These view reentrants are enclosed to make pleasant atriums that allow inwardly focusing "internal" perimeter offices. It is somewhat ironic that a variation of the reentrant, eliminated in the past for economic reasons, should reemerge for current economic reasons as in this case.

Without the atriums, 33 West Monroe would have been a 100-ft-wide, 50-story structure. With the concept of interior view offices, the building

Figure 3.13.   33 West Monroe, interior. Courtesy of Skidmore, Owings & Merrill.

became much wider, 180 by 210 ft, and covered the entire site. The same leasable area was achieved in 28 floors rather than 50.

This building shape is a major energy-conserving feature. The lower, broader building form, even with the added volume of three atriums, exposes much less exterior surface area to climate than the narrower, higher alternative. By replacing external perimeter offices with interior view offices the surface-to-volume ratio for the building is much less. The added volume of the atriums is somewhat of a liability, yet the external glazing

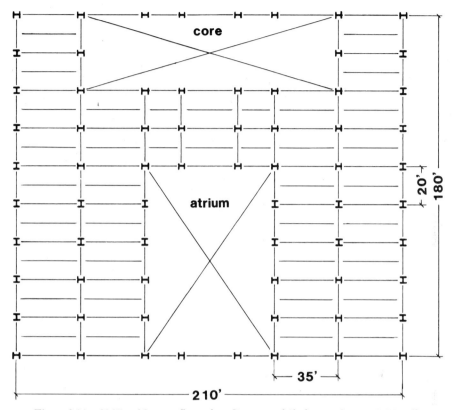

Figure 3.14. 33 West Monroe, floor plan. Courtesy of Skidmore, Owings & Merrill.

area of the atriums is far smaller than the large expanse of adjoining glassed-in offices.

Incremental change features that add to the building's efficiency include a highly insulated exterior aluminum panel skin that has a winter U-value of 0.1. Exterior glass area is also held to 38% of the exterior wall. Inside, the office lighting standard is one 2-by-2-ft deep-cell parabolic fixture per 55 ft² of area which provides electric lighting for 1.8 W/ft². Even with this low level of lighting energy, lights are still the major single energy need in the building (Fig. 3.15). To further conserve lighting energy, lighting controls are provided for each 1000 ft² of open office space and in most private offices. Turning off environmental-control equipment when it is not needed is still the single best means to conserve energy. Similarly, separate, high-efficiency variable-air-volume systems are provided for each floor to enable tenants to work at nights or on weekends without incurring the high costs of running a large central air-handling system.

Skidmore, Owings & Merrill's comparison of energy use of the all-electric 33 West Monroe and the 50-story alternative is shown in Figure 3.15.

Internal systems are held constant in this comparison. The total annual
energy use difference between the two is solely the result of form and
envelope modifications.

Figure 3.15 suggests a total annual energy savings of 20% for 33 West
Monroe. This value exceeds the 11% of total annual building energy use
attributed to envelope in Table 2.1. One reason for the difference is that
heating-related envelope loads increase as the heat of lights is reduced.
However, this increase is quite small in 33 West Monroe. The people,
machines, and remaining heat of lights offset the large majority of winter
heat loss through envelope. The architects estimate that 75% of the heating
load presented in Figure 3.15 is to temper code-required fresh air. The
remaining 25% is used primarily to warm the building to a comfortable
temperature on winter mornings.

The internal systems of 33 West Monroe are far more efficient than the
equipment used by the mid-1970s building data base reflected in Table 2.1.
As the amount of total annual energy need for internal systems decreases,
the proportion of the remaining annual total dedicated to envelope
increases. In other words, if internal energy needs are reduced, the heating
requirements appear proportionally larger. As a first simple incremental
change, or as a major break in design conventions after significant
improvements have been made to internal systems, the absolute total
potential energy savings of form and envelope changes are nearly equal.

Since the total potential Btu savings are relatively equal between
incremental and nonincremental form and envelope options, why would
one choose the more complex and difficult task of nonincremental change?
Additive incremental changes to envelope or internal systems generally
increase initial construction cost. If these options are expected to perform
more efficiently than past construction techniques, their components will

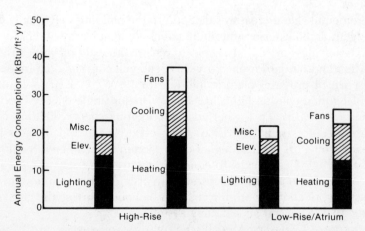

Figure 3.15.   33 West Monroe, bar graphs. Courtesy of Skidmore, Owings & Merrill.

generally cost more than the replaced components. On the other hand, nonincremental changes in form and envelope have the unique potential advantage of reducing initial construction cost as is well illustrated in 33 West Monroe.

The stacked atrium concept of 33 West Monroe cost less to build than did the 50-story alternative. The large area of window wall facing the atriums is less expensive than the exterior equivalent that must be designed to withstand wind, rain, and greater temperature differentials. Also, the shorter building form allows the use of slower, less expensive elevators.

The building's lower, broader form achieves the most significant cost reductions in structure. Foundation costs were trimmed since the building's weight is distributed over a larger area. Skidmore, Owings & Merrill estimates foundation cost savings at $1–1.5 million, not including a construction reduction time of 8.5 months. Likewise, less steel superstructure is required since the broad 28-story building has considerably lower wind loading than the 50-story structure. These lesser loads allowed the engineers to reduce superstructure poundage to 14 lb of steel/ft^2 of floor area from the 22 lb required for the 50-story alternative. This adds up to an additional $2.5–3 million savings for the new form.

Nonincremental form and envelope changes are complicated design problems, yet the reward of reducing initial construction cost makes these options very desirable. In such an approach, energy issues must be united with other design considerations. Structural cost savings are not realized solely by studying energy issues. Internal loads may be more significant in most commercial buildings. Yet, form and envelope innovations appear to be the only way to finance significant internal system improvements in projects with set construction budgets.

Another issue well exemplified by 33 West Monroe is people's response to nonincremental change. Building users, owner, and designers all benefit from the stacked-atrium concept. Tenants gain a visual amenity that modifies the scale of the building. For example, the accounting firm of Arthur Andersen & Company occupies floors 12–16 surrounding the middle atrium. This location gives a central focus to their space and a feeling of a separate building within a building. To gain these advantages, tenants give up the potentially grander views offered by the upper floors of the 50-story alternative.

Besides the obvious initial cost advantage, the design benefits the owner by drawing a specific type of tenant. As a marketing device, the atrium offers an important advantage over competing structures which, combined with lower utility expenses, reduces investment risk. The initial cost- and investment-related advantages of this scheme led owner/developer Douglas Draper of Draper and Kramer, Inc. to conclude that 33 West Monroe could launch a new generation of office building designs.

At 33 West Monroe, Skidmore, Owings & Merrill developed a relatively simple solution to a variety of complex problems: in short, the architects gained the satisfaction of reinvention. They did not invent insulation, efficient luminances, atriums, or structurally efficient broad buildings. The profound innovation is the combination of these elements. Form is molded to create an energy-efficient, more pleasant working environment for a total initial cost that is less than that of a conventional building. To this end, the architects relinquished certainty for risk, and replaced the simplicity of the conventional with the complexity of the unproven.

The Federal Building–U.S. Courthouse and 33 West Monroe illustrate additional elements of nonincremental form and envelope changes. First, in each case energy-related goals are combined with other major design issues into one problem statement. To achieve these broader design goals, one of the basic climate-rejecting capabilities discussed earlier under incremental changes is sacrificed: neither of the two preceding case studies is a minimum volume cube. In the Federal Building–U.S. Courthouse surface area was enlarged, yet the volumes of conditioned space and climate-imposed loads were reduced by using form to shade envelope. In 33 West Monroe, on the other hand, volume was increased to reduce significantly the exterior surface area exposed to climate. Volume, surface area, form, and envelope may be combined in many ways to achieve energy effectiveness and broader design goals. The result is not a compromise between energy objectives and other design needs; rather, the best innovations in form and envelope for climate-rejecting buildings would never be found without combining energy issues with other major design concerns. Ultimately, density appears to be the only significant physical limiting factor to the use of innovative form and envelope concepts.

How energy influences style is also reflected in these two case studies. Both are dramatically different in style, yet both can be defined as energy-responsive, climate-rejecting buildings. From these and many other studies that we have reviewed, we find little evidence that energy issues mandate a specific architectural style. In fact, the opposite appears to be true. As Sarah Harkness of the Architects Collaborative summarized in a discussion with us about the book:

> It (energy) can influence form and therefore influences design, but I would say that it does not influence style. A good energy solution can be of any individual style that suits yourself (sic) and also suits the particular project. We've been working with atriums recently, but if you look at the way atriums have been used from the 1800s until now, you see every type of style yet the basic design idea is the same.

The two preceding case studies also exemplify how form and envelope may be used to reduce building energy needs beyond annual consumption and peak demand. Innovative form and envelope solutions in any building type also have the potential to limit the use of nonrenewable energy and resources embodied in the materials of construction. According to architect Richard Stein, "about five years' worth of energy use goes into the building of an average one-family residence and almost ten years' worth of operating energy is required for the construction of an office building." The effective use of form and envelope to reduce the need for nonrenewable energy in commercial buildings is not limited to utility bills alone. Both the Federal Building–U.S. Courthouse and 33 West Monroe achieve substantial energy-related savings with efficient structural systems.

As shown in Figure 3.15, 10,625 Btu/ft^2 per year are saved in cooling, heating, and fan energy by the low-rise atrium concept. However, these Btu are electrical, not primary energy such as oil, coal, or natural gas. According to Stein, it takes about 3.34 Btu of primary energy to generate and deliver 1 Btu equivalent of electricity to a building site. Therefore, the low-rise atrium building comparatively saves about 10,625 × 3.34 or 35,000 Btu of primary energy per square foot per year. In effect, the structural embodied energy savings of 33 West Monroe are equivalent to 6.5 years of operating energy reductions derived by the atrium concept.

How energy is accounted for in buildings can greatly influence the problem statement and, therefore, the derived solution. Utility bills are not the only significant indicator. Embodied energy in construction, the on-line peak electrical demand capacity required for a new building, and building location in relation to occupant transportation requirements can be just as significant. Learning how to equate our collective energy savings with impacts beyond the building site is a task equally important to deriving innovative form and envelope alternatives. We are learning not only how to improve energy-effectiveness by design, but also how to account for the savings we seek and achieve.

The most significant conclusion we derive from the Federal Building–U.S. Courthouse and 33 West Monroe is that nonincremental change is an act of reinvention. Both buildings merely comprise glass, concrete, steel, luminances, and HVAC systems. The true innovation is the reorganization of these standard components into a decidedly different end product. Moreover, effective reinvention does not seem to occur only by concentrating on energy issues: in fact, the reverse appears to be true. Beyond simple incremental changes, significant energy-use-limiting strategies cannot be found unless energy issues are absorbed and intertwined with the whole of building design. For this reason, Chapters Three and Four are dedicated to relationships and principles rather than components and hard numbers. Beyond incremental change, the challenge in the design of energy-responsive commercial buildings is reinvention. The design frontier hangs at the transition point between those people who devise and test specific components and those who can transform these innovative energy-conserving components into an equally innovative total solution.

SYSTEM OPTIONS

In the commercial sector, rebalancing heating, ventilating, and air-conditioning systems, reducing lighting levels, and using computers to control heating and lighting loads can be both energy-efficient and cost-effective. Such "tidying-up" activities can yield energy savings of as much as 30 to 50 percent.

DAVID WHITE[*]

Improvements to systems usually represent a starting point for deriving substantial energy-use reductions in climate-rejecting buildings. As reflected in Table 2.1, about 89% of total annual energy need of mid-1970s office buildings occurs behind the building skin. Likewise, Figure 3.15 demonstrates that 33 West Monroe, a more energy-efficient design than the building reflected in the 1975 data base, is also dominated by internal energy needs. From our review, it appears that sealed office buildings are typically internally load dominated. This section explores the means being used to improve the energy-effectiveness of internal environmental-control systems. As in the preceding section, the discussion begins with a general assessment at the incremental change level. With this information as a base, two nonincremental change case studies are presented and assessed.

The basic objective in the design of energy-responsive internal environmental-control systems for climate-rejecting buildings is to meet or exceed the visual and thermal comfort expectations of people while requiring a minimum of nonrenewable energy subsidy. Nonrenewable energy subsidy may be expressed as annual energy use at the building site, the energy embodied in building and maintaining utility infrastructure, or the energy embodied in the materials of construction at the site.

As symbolized in Figure 3.16, all internal systems comprise four elements: an energy source, a conversion/distribution system, a system of controls, and people whose needs and desires manipulate the controls. At the incremental change level, energy-related improvements to systems typically center around this list of elements. Choices can be made to adjust the design conditions to be maintained in the building, change the controls to better reflect people's needs, improve or change the methods of conversion and distribution, or change to another energy source. Each option will be briefly discussed before case studies are presented.

Internal design conditions represent the quantitative and qualitative needs of people. To protect the health and well-being of the public, some of these design conditions are prescribed by codes. Our review of recommended design conditions from the 1950s through the 1970s indicates that quality is sought by prescribing excessive quantity. To permit easier

[*]David White, *Technology Review*, August/September 1980.

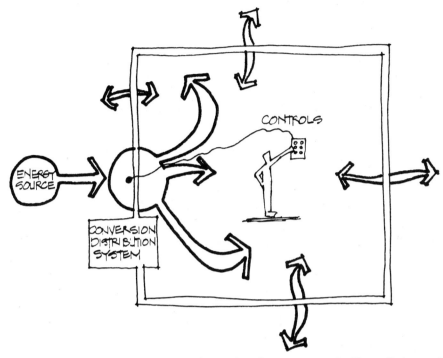

Figure 3.16. Elements of environmental control in climate-rejecting buildings. Courtesy of Steve Hogg.

compliance, codes and standards often reflect the convenience of quantitative goals.

Standards for lighting levels and comfort zone requirements used in the United States are significantly higher than comparable standards in other developed countries. In spite of a great collective effort to reduce this quantitative excess, U.S. design conditions are still the world's most restrictive. This discrepancy in standards between the United States and other countries is best visualized by comparing the 1981 Illuminating Engineering Society recommended task lighting levels, referenced in most building and energy codes, to similar standards of other countries (Fig. 3.17). Rather than addressing only the quantitative aspects of lighting and comfort levels, the designer would do well to focus on the qualitative aspects of visual and thermal comfort. In fact, the use of qualitative considerations can result in a higher degree of comfort than in past buildings while using design conditions outside the bounds of existing quantitative limits. Because lights seem to dominate the energy use of commercial buildings, the selection of appropriate lighting design conditions is very important. Care exercised in qualitative design concerns can substantially reduce lighting energy requirements. Both initial cost and energy need are affected. The number or type of fixtures can change, allowing annual

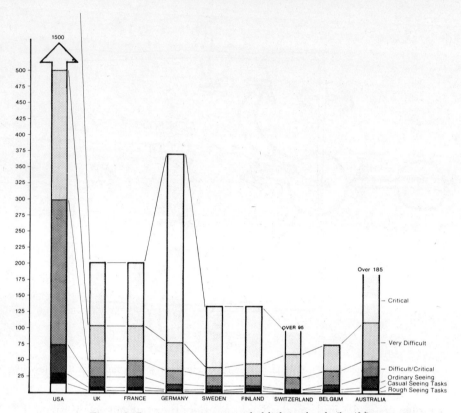

Figure 3.17. Average recommended lighting levels (lm/ft^2).

energy-use reductions for lighting and cooling, peak-demand reductions, and a shift to a smaller cooling plant. Balancing qualitative and quantitative issues in the selection of building-design conditions influences the need for environmental control and can be the most critical energy-related design decision in a climate-rejecting building.

The operation of environmental-control systems is also fundamental to energy use in a climate-rejecting building. Alternatives such as unoccupied period setbacks and changing to deadband comfort limits from seasonal design-temperature set points can have a pronounced effect on total building energy use. Deadband thermostats are finding wide acceptance—they reduce total annual energy use, peak demand, and the size of heating and cooling plants. Increasing the acceptable temperature range in a building also aids related strategies. For instance, interior building materials with high thermal capacitance can dampen internal heat gains and lose this heat through the building envelope during unoccupied hours.

Other important control options include the ability to switch off unneeded equipment and to control the time of energy use by equipment.

For instance, providing switches to turn off unused lights or to provide lower overall lighting levels for building maintenance are key conservation strategies. Although the day has passed when there was a single lighting switch per floor, and when a central HVAC system had to condition a whole building for one weekend occupant, much room for improvement still exists in convenient control strategies for commercial buildings. This type of switching and zoning will not substantially impact peak period energy use, but can reduce the annual energy needs for lighting, cooling, and heating.

Building controls that limit peak demand of electrical energy are very important conservation options. Energy codes skirt the issue, missing a potential for energy conservation on a national level at electric generating plants that we believe is significantly larger than energy conservation at the building site. Based on our sample of 3000 incrementally changed climate-rejecting buildings, three times more nonrenewable energy was saved by limiting peak demand than through conservation efforts. A tremendous amount of nonrenewable energy can be saved by preventing the need for and maintenance of new utility infrastructure.

The cost of controls that limit peak demand are often difficult to justify at the incremental change level. Such controls are not in many existing buildings and therefore always represent an additive cost. Because the motives of people do not change at the incremental change level, cost likewise must not increase. However, the increasing occurrence of utility-imposed site capacity limitations are making peak-demand control an important issue even at the incremental change level.

Project capacity limitations set peak service that a customer can receive from the supplying utility. This problem often is a function of the size of the existing electrical feeder and transformer substation available for the customer to draw down. For both this problem and that of limiting peak demand, control options can be used to selectively shut down nonessential systems during peak-demand periods. Another option is to separate the conversion of energy from the distribution of cool or warm air by using off-peak water storage. Heated or cooled water storage can reduce plant size. However, this advantage seldom equals the added expense of tanks, insulation, and extra pumps at the incremental change level.

The relationship between energy conversion and distribution systems within a building is central to the design of an energy-responsive, climate-rejecting building. As in the design of form and envelope, the best place to begin is by thoughtfully using the existing elements of environmental control to best advantage. The basic task is to find the most efficient combination of equipment suited to the selected energy sources that will maintain the building at the given design conditions.

We surmise that designers appraise conversion and distribution system options in two ways. The first is to improve the efficiency of singular components by design or selection. This process is often successful, yet does not consider other conversion/distribution systems that may be more effective over the course of a year's operation. Total system effectiveness must be judged over time under both peak-load conditions and the partial-load situations that prevail through the majority of the year. Peak-load efficiency is critical to the peak energy demand of a building. Partial-load efficiency is central to the annual energy use of the building. Partial-load efficiencies drop very rapidly in most systems and can be a major liability in a climate-rejecting building. Effectively matching system output to meet a wide range of loading conditions is the step beyond improving the efficiency of individual components.

Conversion and distribution systems are combined in this analysis because of their interrelationship. A highly efficient chiller is of little value if an inefficient distribution system is used. In a sample of 200 buildings, we found the energy needs of central cooling systems in office buildings to be divided about equally between chiller and fans. Many case studies exist that indicate that more energy is used to push warm or cool air around buildings under either full or partial loading than is initially used to temper the air.

Studying combined conversion/distribution systems raises the issue of scale. Centralizing conversion systems often increases plant efficiency and the potential benefit of options such as off-peak storage, yet increases required subsidiary fan or pump power. Remote or modular plants can greatly reduce energy needs of fans and pumps, yet tend to reduce overall conversion efficiency by using an array of smaller plants. One engineer interviewed insists that small through-the-wall air conditioners are the most effective energy-related alternative he has found for climate-rejecting office buildings. Such an alternative is not found and judged acceptable by studying the efficiency of components; rather, it is found by studying full- and partial-loading conditions, the total effectiveness of the combined conversion/distribution system, the acoustical and thermal comfort needs of people, and the initial and lifetime cost.

Alternative energy sources can be used for climate-rejecting buildings provided such sources are compatible with the buildings' nature. Internal environmental-control systems cannot exist without concentrated forms of energy. From the caveman's fire to contemporary central chiller plants, internal-energy systems use relatively small, high-energy outlets to temper much larger areas of occupied space. Large building zones can be tempered and lighted by diffusing energy through a handful of grills, registers, and luminaires. Even the use of outdoor air in an economizer cycle demands that this energy source be concentrated via high-volume fans and funneled into small cross-sectional ductwork. This need for a concentrated output through small outlets is in contrast to climate-adapted systems that use the broad expanse of envelope to distribute diffuse climatic energies directly to occupied space.

Three alternative energy strategies are most common in climate-rejecting buildings. The first is to use alternative energy as a direct substitute in conventional environmental-control processes. This strategy includes options such as photovoltaics, wind generators, and active solar heating and cooling. The challenge is to concentrate diffuse energy sources so that sufficient power exists to activate processes that typically require concentrated conventional energy sources. Although the diffuse energy source may be free, the process of concentration can be very expensive.

The second common alternative energy-source strategy is to greatly modify systems or components to work at a much lower energy level. For instance, evaporative coolers are popular in the semiarid regions of the West. This option reduces both annual energy use and peak demand by changing the means of cooling rather than finding an alternative energy source to power a chiller. The system is less powerful than a conventional chiller and often requires additional subsidiary fan and pump power, yet total annual building energy needs can be substantially reduced to about one quarter of the cost of compression refrigeration.

The third widely used energy-source strategy is to cascade conventional concentrated energy sources through a series of processes. Waste heat available from on-site industrial processes can often be used as the primary energy source for both heating and cooling occupied space. Cogeneration is another possibility where on-site industrial processes exist. In this case the fuel is first used to generate electricity and the by-product heat of that process is used for industrial purposes.

On a smaller scale, computer rooms often can provide enough waste heat to warm a whole building and heat recovery systems can be employed to salvage useful heat for service hot water from compressors or condensers. Ventilation air can also be tempered with building exhaust air. In the past, conventional energy sources were cheap and plentiful so that every energy use was from an original source. Now, however, it makes sense to extract the greatest possible work from each energy source.

The only general rule for a successful change to an alternative energy source is to use the lowest thermodynamic quality energy source that can adequately perform the intended task. This general rule requires careful selection of how the intended task should be performed as well as which energy source should power that process. Success depends upon matching systems and sources within the limits of the nature of the climate-rejecting building.

In conclusion, incremental system-related changes offer substantial energy-use reduction possibilities. As in form and envelope options, the place to begin is to use the existing to best advantage. Selecting appropriate design conditions, flexible controls, efficient conversion and distribution systems of appropriate scale, and energy sources whose thermodynamic quality appropriately match the intended use can greatly limit nonrenewable energy use in climate-rejecting buildings. Incremental system changes are highly effective because many existing buildings have excessive energy demands that can be easily reduced by emphasizing the importance of energy issues in building design. A technological breakthrough is not required to substantially improve the energy-effectiveness of climate-rejecting buildings. The solution lies in questioning the conveniences of the past in order to derive designs appropriate for today.

Nonincremental system changes address the same basic concerns as do incremental changes. The major difference between the two is the degree of energy conservation possible when the economic criteria of a proposed project are changed. As defined, nonincremental changes require the acceptance of a new motive or perceived advantage from past climate-rejecting buildings. The predominant new perceived advantage associated with innovative internal environmental-control equipment is a connection between initial construction cost and future energy-related operating cost. Beyond incremental changes, the decision to make significant equipment-related improvements involves a trade-off between paying now or paying later. Added dollars may need to be borrowed at the beginning of a project, but the operating cost savings should allow an overall positive cash flow to the owner. Since the economic circumstances of individual owners can vary greatly, the system-related decisions made regarding the trade-off between initial construction cost and future energy-related cost will also differ.

We feel this new perspective is fundamental in case studies that seek energy-related internal system improvements because past internal systems were well optimized for minimum initial cost. Adding the concern for effective energy use at both peak- and partial-load conditions requires these systems be superior to past systems. Beyond incremental improvements in equipment selection, sizing and controls, additional options add to the base cost of past systems. Such is the case in the following two examples. Both examples trade a larger initial investment in energy options for the benefits of future operating cost savings.

The two case studies are the Rocky Mountain Energy Company Headquarters (RMECH), Broomfield, Colorado, by Kohn Pedersen Fox Associates of New York in a joint venture with Johnson-Hopson & Partners of Denver, and the National Security and Resources Study Center at the Los Alamos National Laboratory, New Mexico, by Charles Luckman Associates. The RMECH represents nonincremental system changes that seek to optimize the use of conventional energy sources within a climate-rejecting building. The Study Center emphasizes the use of alternative energy sources to power internal environmental-control systems.

Rocky Mountain Energy Company Headquarters

RMECH (Figs. 3.18–3.20) is a 200,000-ft^2, owner-occupied office building located in a Denver suburb. Being in the energy business, the owners wish to exemplify the sensible use of nonrenewable energy in their new headquarters building. According to engineer Clark Bisel of the Denver office of Flack and Kurtz Consulting Engineers, the mechanical, electrical, and energy consultants for the project, the client specified that the systems selected for heating, cooling, and lighting incorporate the latest advances in energy conservation technology. The client expected these features to increase initial construction cost and requested that these options collectively have a payback period of less than 5 years.

The heating, cooling, and lighting systems of RMECH use variable modes of operation to match changing needs and climatic conditions. For example, three different cooling modes spring from one primary central system. An electric chiller and cooling tower is the primary cooling plant and removes heat from the sealed building during periods of extreme heat and humidity. An economizer cycle with enthalpy control is the second cooling mode used during cool weather. The third mode is the indirect cooling of water by evaporation in the cooling tower. In this mode, the chiller is bypassed during the milder months of the year. According to Flack and Kurtz, the annual result is a conversion/distribution system that can extract 3.5 Btu of space cooling load for 1 Btu of electricity.

Three different heating modes are available. The simplest portion of the system collects the excess heat of lights, people, and machines from internal (nonperimeter) zones and the computer room in ceiling plenums and directs this warm air to thermostatically controlled perimeter induction boxes for distribution. When perimeter heating is not necessary, or the distance between waste-heat source and point of need is too great, heat is centrally extracted with a heat-recovery chiller. From here, the heat can be diverted to distant spaces requiring heat or stored in water tanks for deferred use. An electric back-up boiler connected to the water storage completes the system. Flack and Kurtz states that this heating system delivers 4 Btu of heat to occupied perimeter areas for the expenditure of 1 Btu of electricity on an annual basis.

System management becomes important in obtaining energy efficiency through system diversity. In RMECH, a JCS-80 computer monitors internal and external environmental conditions, and also serves as an advanced fire and security protection system. The computer controls energy performance and comfort by selecting which cooling and heating system is used at any given time. The JCS-80 also sheds loads during peak periods of power use by shutting down nonessential equipment. Since the electrical peak demand charges for RMECH were predicted by Flack and Kurtz to be 48% of total annual energy cost, power management is an important energy-performance consideration of the building.

The RMECH lighting system is also variable mode and two complementary lighting systems are provided. Ambient light is generated by overhead 2-by-2-ft polished parabolic fluorescent luminaires placed on 10-ft centers.

Figure 3.18. Rocky Mountain Energy Company (RMEC) Headquarters: (*a*) exterior, (*b*) interior. Courtesy of Johnson Hopson & Partners.

Figure 3.18. (Continued)

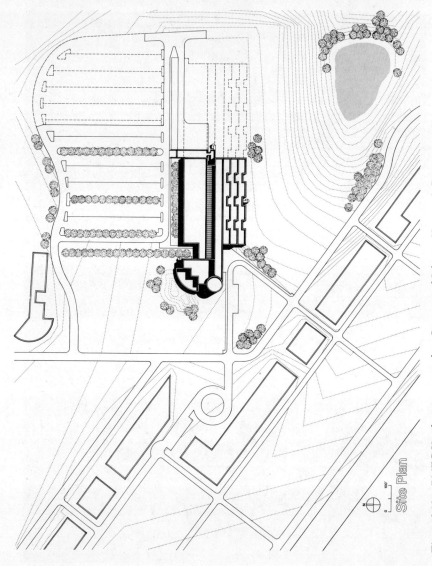

Figure 3.19. RMEC Headquarters site plan. Courtesy of Johnson Hopson & Partners.

Site Plan

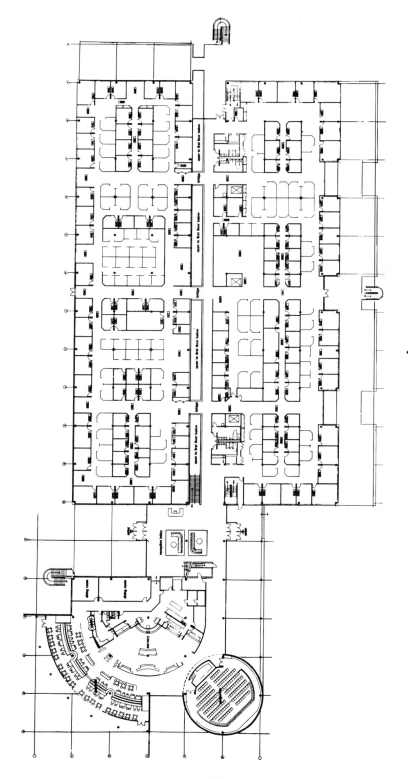

Figure 3.20. RMEC Headquarters, first floor plan. Courtesy of Johnson Hopson & Partners.

These fixtures use low-energy electronic ballast (300 mA compared to the usual 420–430 mA) and are designed to produce high-quality, wide-angle ambient lighting of 37 foot candles. A shallow direct task light with a simple prismatic lens is provided at each work station to boost lighting levels to 80 foot candles at the working surface. The combination of these lights provides a well-lit, glare-free area under peak conditions for a connected power rating of less than 1.5 W/ft² of office space. In addition to this peak-load efficiency, considerable annual energy savings are gained since each building user can control the operation of his or her own task light. Further savings are gained since building maintenance and cleaning during unoccupied hours can typically be done with only the ambient lighting system. This ability to turn off unnecessary lights not only reduces the power requirements for illumination, but indirectly reduces the annual cooling load of the building.

Decisions made for each individual system greatly influence the treatment and design of all other major systems in the RMECH. For instance, the energy-efficient lighting system reduces the annual cooling load, the initial cost of the chiller since a smaller cooling plant can be used, and the summer peak electrical demand of the building and power/needs for illumination. The same lighting system increases the annual heating load of the building to a level higher than is typical for most sealed office buildings. In this particular case, the energy-efficient lighting system shifted the building peak-demand period from a summer afternoon to a winter morning.

This degree of interaction between separate end-use systems is the single greatest difference between the design of internal environmental-control systems for residential and for commercial buildings. In a commercial building, major heating, cooling, and lighting loads commonly occur simultaneously. The proportions of these loads can also change dramatically through the daily and seasonal cycles in commercial buildings. Beyond simple incremental improvements in system design and sizing, variable mode systems that balance diverse and dynamic environmental-control needs seem to be the key to the design of energy-responsive internal environmental-control systems.

The interdependency of separate systems in commercial buildings requires that all systems be studied together. Particularly in nonincremental change solutions, either climate-rejecting buildings or climate-adapted buildings, the energy problem to be solved can change during the design process by changing the energy demands of separate systems. This fact is well demonstrated in RMECH. In a typical, nonenergy-efficient office building in this climate, lighting, cooling, and summer peak electrical demand would most probably represent prime areas for making energy-related improvements. An incremental change approach would solve these problems. Yet in RMECH, heating became a central energy need during the design process as a result of decisions to reduce the energy needs of lights, improve the efficiency of the cooling system, extend architectural form, and use electricity for heating. From the most advanced nonincremental change case studies we have reviewed, it appears that such solutions can be identified by the attempt to solve a constantly shifting energy problem. The degree of knowledge and experience necessary to tackle such a design problem is notably more advanced than that necessary to produce incremental changes.

It may at first seem that a crystal ball is necessary to perform nonincremental changes. How can an effective integrated solution be found to a constantly changing problem? The keys to such solutions seem to come in layers. At any one point, one must identify the present controlling energy need of the building. The controlling energy need is defined as the primary element (i.e., heating, cooling, lighting) that must be improved, in either an incremental or nonincremental solution, to result in substantial energy-use reductions in the building. In RMECH, the controlling energy need is illumination. Typically, the controlling energy need is the largest energy need at the start of the design process and the one that must be improved to allow the whole-building energy problem to change. When a change occurs in the energy problem of a building during design, it can raise additional, and potentially frustrating, issues. Such a change, however, also signals that significant energy-related improvements are being found.

In some building types, the initial controlling energy need may be so large that no level of improvements will substantially reduce it. However, the concept of the controlling energy need still provides a starting point and will directly influence the design of other individual systems. If the heating system of RMECH, for example, was designed before the lighting system improvements were made, the heating system would require redesigning to better perform its new task of being instrumental in controlling peak-demand costs. A similar situation would occur if one started with a cooling system design that includes off-peak chilled water storage as part of the solution. In general, fewer iterations or design steps are required if the designer simply begins with the controlling energy need of the building. Chapter Six focuses specifically on design process techniques that can be used to gain a familiarity with such design issues.

How much future technology can improve the effective use of concentrated energy sources in climate-rejecting buildings is unknown. At present, most equipment manufacturers seem more interested in improving component efficiency than in seeking new or reinvented system concepts. One interesting recent reinvention is an extension of the heat pump concept that combines two end uses into one system. This heat pump variation, shown in Figure 3.21, combines space cooling and service hot water needs into one system. Heat pump water heaters, with a coefficient of performance (COP) of approximately 2.0, can remove heat and moisture from interior air and

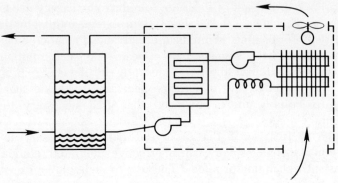

Figure 3.21. Heat pump water heater. Courtesy of Louise Morrison.

store the extracted heat in service hot water tanks. In effect, such systems allow the load of one system to become the energy source for another end use. The ability to cascade concentrated energy through a sealed building and the efficiency of performing two or more functions with one mechanical process indicate that totally integrated environmental-control systems may well be the future of climate-rejecting buildings. Past distinctions between lighting, heating, cooling, and hot water systems may soon be obsolete.

The National Security and Resources Study Center

The National Security and Resources Study Center at Los Alamos, New Mexico, (Fig. 3.22) exemplifies another task in the design of innovative internal environmental-control systems. Whereas the focus in RMECH was the effective use of conventional energy sources and systems within the sealed building, the Study Center emphasizes the collection and use of renewable energy sources to power internal environmental-control systems. Once again, the basic premise in this approach is to seek future operating cost savings by investing more in initial construction.

The Study Center has 64,300 ft² of conditioned space and was completed in 1977 at a cost of \$4.6 million. The project solar systems, which were supported by federal funding, were viewed as an experiment to derive test data on the strengths, weaknesses, and performance of commercial solar heating, cooling, and hot water systems. These solar systems accounted for approximately 9% of the initial construction cost, or a total of \$426,000 (\$6.63/ft²).

The Solar Energy Research Group at Los Alamos and the consulting engineering firm of Ayres & Hayakawa supported Charles Luckman Associates in the design of the project. The team's first goal was to derive an energy-conserving building design that limited the need for heating and

Figure 3.22. Los Alamos National Security and Resources Study Center.

cooling. Evaluated and included in the design were incremental envelope changes such as added insulation, deep window overhangs and solar fins, and the restriction of window glazing to 22% of the facade area. Control strategies were also analyzed, and time clocks were selected to control the use of ceiling lights and building fans. To conserve fan energy, a variable-air-volume system was selected as the means to distribute the solar-heated or cooled air to occupied spaces.

The solar collector array is composed of 407 prefabricated 2-by-10-ft collectors inclined at 35° from the horizontal and 13° east of south. A light paraffin oil is circulated between an expanded metal absorber electroplated with black chrome on the side facing the sun. The absorber plate is covered by a single layer of tempered water-white glass on the top, and backed by urethane foam insulation and a metal fire barrier.

The 7705-ft^2 collector array serves as the roof of the Study Center's mechanical equipment room (Fig. 3.23), visitor's gallery, and solar data room (Fig. 3.24).

The preassembled, uninstalled collector cost was \$18.45/ft^2. The collectors were used as a roof, which displaced \$9.63/ft^2 of normal roofing materials. This amount was taken as a credit by the designers in totaling the final incremental solar cost.

The solar-heated oil is pumped through a shell-and-tube heat exhanger to

Figure 3.23.   National Security and Resources Study Center, mechanical equipment room.

heat water in storage tanks. The collector outlet temperatures range from 190°F in winter to 242°F in the summer. When insufficient solar radiation is available to heat or cool, steam from an off-site generating plant is used as an auxiliary heat source.

The solar system has two basic modes of operation. Beginning around October 1, a 10,000-gal water tank stores solar-heated water for building space-heating needs. In mid-May, the system is switched to a cooling mode which uses the 10,000-gal tank to store cold water generated by chillers powered by a smaller, 5000-gal pressurized tank of solar-heated water. During 1978 and 1979, very detailed monitoring showed that the solar system contributed 76% of the Study Center's heating requirements and 97% of its cooling requirements. In total, the solar contribution represents a displacement of 20,000 Btu of the building's total load of 41,000 Btu/ft² per year. The largest remaining load is for electric lighting.

Because the solar system was installed primarily to serve as a learning tool, several added system options were included in the design to allow side-by-side testing. For instance, two chillers were included in the system to permit an energy performance evaluation. A custom-built, 77-ton

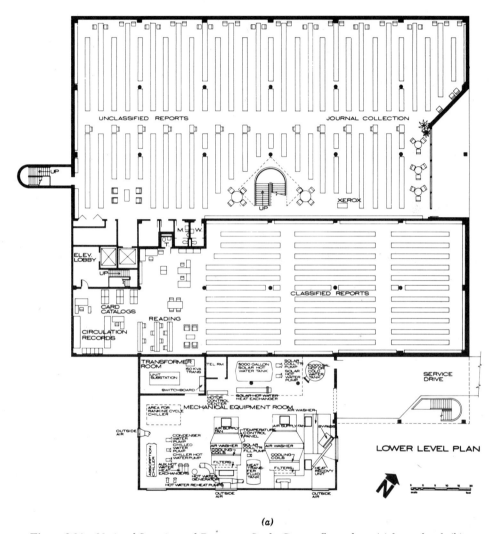

(a)

Figure 3.24. National Security and Resources Study Center, floor plans: (a) lower level; (b) middle level. Courtesy of The Luckman Partnership, Inc.

Rankine-cycle chiller built by Barber–Nichols and a less expensive, off-the-shelf, 85-ton lithium bromide absorption chiller by York were included in the design to allow a direct comparison. Measured results over the 1978 and 1979 cooling season showed the Rankine-cycle chillers electrical COP to be 3.36. The electrical COP for the absorption unit was 3.17, or nearly equivalent.

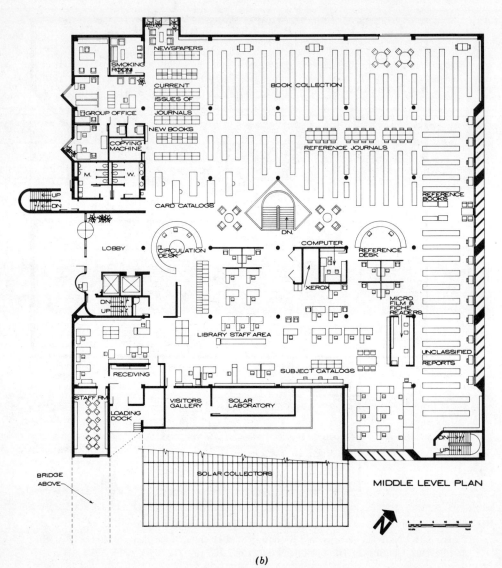

(b)

Figure 3.24.   *(Continued)*

Other experiments show that the cooling tower, which rejects heat from the chillers and also acts as a nighttime evaporative cooler to further chill water storage, actually limits the Center's air-conditioning system efficiency. In this case, the vertical pumping distance of 40 ft and the inefficient cooling tower squirrel-cage blowers required excessive subsidiary electricity. However, the design team believes that shortening the distance between tank and tower and providing propeller fans could increase the electrical COP of the nighttime evaporative cooling process to a respectable 3.0 or higher.

One of the most efficient innovations in the Study Center is a Freon heat pipe heat exchanger shown in Figure 3.25. Its basic function is as an air-to-air heat exchanger, recovering heat or cooling air from the building's exhaust air to preheat or precool incoming air. If exterior temperature is below 55°F, the unit recovers heat from the building's exhaust air. When exterior temperature exceeds 55°F, the unit is used in conjunction with a water spray to precool incoming air. Over the 2-year test period, this unit contributed 16% of the Center's heating requirements and displaced the equivalent of 11 tons of air-conditioning, or 8% of the total building cooling load.

Another major aspect of the Study Center is the architectural integration of the solar collection system with the equipment room of the building, which was the major contribution of the architect. The original design concept by the Los Alamos Engineering Department indicated collectors to be mounted in racks on the roof. The shed room on the south side at once provides a better overall architectural integration, summer shading of the south wall of the building, a very effective arrangement of the large ducting from the HVAC system, and a dual function roof. It is important to note that

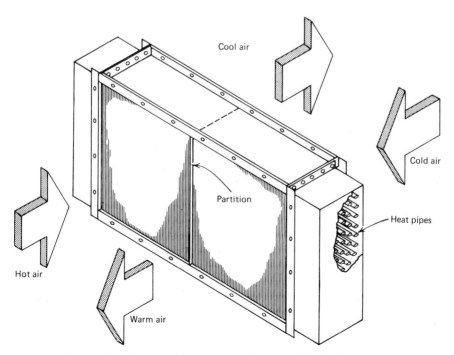

Figure 3.25. Heat pipe heat exchanger. Courtesy of Q-dot Corporation.

the equipment room is unconditioned. This means that heat loss from the piping and other systems does not add to the building's heat load requirement in summer; natural ventilation through the space provides adequate cooling. In winter the space is quite adequately heated by these heat losses with the natural ventilation openings closed off. Figures 3.26 and 3.27 show the geometry.

Although the performance of active solar space-heating and service hot-water systems has been effectively demonstrated in a variety of projects, the major cost-effectiveness issue in the Study Center was whether an integrated space-cooling, heating, and hot-water system could be competitive with efficient conventional commercial building systems. According to solar advocate Douglas Balcomb, chief technical director for the project, "The active solar cooling system does not seem to offer enough energy advantage over well-designed conventional air-conditioning to offset its complexity and high capital cost." James Hedstrom, project leader, agreed and stated, "This project doesn't show active solar cooling to be cost-effective, but I think it does move us a step closer."

We reviewed numerous active solar case studies before selecting the Study Center for presentation. That this project is not a repeatable model of success and that it is the last climate-rejecting building in this chapter are no mere coincidences. In our past experiences with active solar systems lie perhaps our most important collective lessons about the innovative use of energy in climate-rejecting buildings. These lessons not only provide ideas on the design of energy-responsive climate-rejecting buildings, but also emphasize the purpose and significance of the climate-adapted building alternative.

The initial purpose of using active solar systems was simple: reduce the nonrenewable energy needs of the climate-rejecting building by powering its internal environmental-control systems with a renewable energy source. It was a logical first attempt at using solar energy in commercial buildings since it conveniently extended the past into the future. For instance, for space heating one would replace the heat from natural gas with collectors, tanks, and a heat exchanger in the existing air-handling unit. Systems would change somewhat, but not the building nor its basic approach to environmental control. Present design conventions could be maintained while fulfilling the new energy challenge.

In some cases, such as service hot water, this substitution can work very well. Solar radiation may be a comparatively low-quality energy source, yet a system to produce 140°F service hot water need not be elaborate. The use of electricity, a highly concentrated energy source capable of magnetic induction that can rotate a motor armature for resistance heating, does seem wasteful.

In other cases, such as active solar cooling, complexity and cost can tax beyond reason the new motive of paying now instead of later. The energy

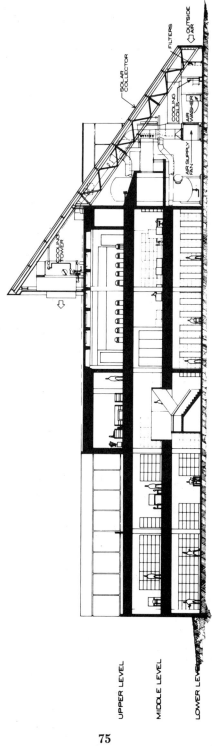

Figure 3.26. National Security and Resources Study Center, cross section. Courtesy of The Luckman Partnership, Inc.

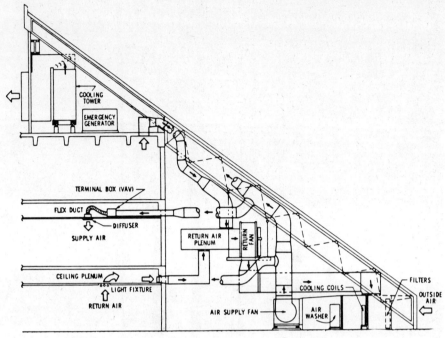

Figure 3.27. National Security and Resources Study Center, air system.

subsidy required in the manufacture of solar collectors, for example, must be considered as part of the system's total energy expenditure. There is a point where the economic or embodied energy required to fabricate a system to collect, concentrate, and store solar radiation to a level where it can mimic the abilities of concentrated energy sources is impractical. The fact remains that changing energy sources typically demands a significant change in a given system or process to reflect the abilities of the new source to fulfill a specific need. Forcing renewable energy sources of inferior thermodynamic quality to perform standard tasks in the same basic process may be more a wish to extend the past than a logical vision of a renewable energy future.

If one chooses to improve the energy needs of the climate-rejecting building rather than provide environmental control in a different way, one must accept the basic nature and limitations of this solution type and of the systems that subsidize it. It did not surprise us that the best experiment of the Study Center was the nonsolar Freon heat pipe recovery system. In every innovative climate-rejecting building reviewed, the best single improvement is consistently the one that simply makes the building a better user of concentrated energy sources.

Over the last decade, the climate-rejecting building has evolved to greater and greater degrees of efficiency. Until this trend slows down or ceases, the introduction of complex renewable-energy technologies will not be well received and may well hurt the future use of such strategies by confusing the public's perception of their value as an alternative. As the heat of lights and the accompanying need for cooling are reduced in commercial buildings, the need for low-quality heat becomes greater. Supplying low-quality heat is a function more appropriate to the abilities of alternatives like active solar systems. For these reasons, it is our opinion that options like active solar systems more appropriately represent a possible last step in the process of improving the efficiency of energy-responsive climate-rejecting buildings rather than a starting point.

We believe that the recent failures of many widely publicized energy source alternatives are due to the insistence that these substitutes power conventional systems. The value of an alternative energy source is totally dependent on the process it is expected to run. Reinvention at the level of internal systems occurs by combining new sources with new processes. Although not economically feasible, an example of this is Buckminster Fuller's experiments with using alternative energy sources to compress air which is then used to power thermal conversion and distribution systems. Until major innovations are made to systems, the task will always be merely to select an energy source whose thermodynamic quality most closely matches that needed by a particular system. In the future, the matching of an energy source with the energy use will need to be both technically and economically viable.

In conclusion, climate-rejecting buildings and their related systems or components dictate the use of certain types of internal environmental control. More than any other single factor, the basic nature of this solution type limits the range of appropriate energy-responsive design solutions. Appropriate energy-related form, envelope, equipment, and system innovations all seek to fulfill and improve this nature. As the next chapter shows, a whole new range of possible alternatives arises when the nature of the building is allowed to change.

chapter four

ENERGY-RESPONSIVE CLIMATE-ADAPTED BUILDINGS

Throughout history natural sources of energy have been utilized in an effort to provide environmental control within occupied spaces. Conventional structures have not been able to take full advantage of natural sources because of the nature of the structures themselves. . .

MEGASTRUCTURE: A NEW CONCEPT OF FEDERAL
OFFICE BUILDING DESIGN FOR THE GSA, 1975

Climatic energy sources can be used directly to light, heat, cool, and ventilate a commercial building. The sun can be used as a source of heat in the winter and a daytime light source year-round. Cooling can be achieved through natural ventilation and assorted strategies such as earth-berming and evaporation. Unfortunately, diffuse energy sources are far less reliable and convenient than the highly concentrated energy sources they replace. The daily and seasonal changes demonstrated by such energy sources require that a climate-adapted building be studied under a whole range of design conditions.

The climate-adapted building uses form and envelope to filter and distribute locally available energy sources to interior space according to the needs of the occupants. In addition, form and envelope must be designed to reject unneeded heat and repel detrimental climatic effects. The key to a comfortable working environment is balancing the impact of environmental exposure on conditioned space. In this chapter, seven case studies demonstrate how such a balance can be achieved. The studies are preceded by a general discussion concerned with contemporary issues, means, and choices related to this solution type.

The depth of a climate-adapted building is generally narrower than that of a climate-rejecting building as dictated by the limits of the penetration of light and air. The narrower the building the larger the required external surface area. The effective collection, control, and distribution of climatic energy sources may require an increase in building volume in order to use strategies such as clerestories, high ceilings, or buffer zones. Whereas climate-rejecting buildings are evolving toward a smaller skin area and volume to better use concentrated energy sources, the climate-adapted building extends form and surface area to connect a larger portion of occupied space to diffuse climatic energy sources. For these reasons, we consider the two building types to be opposites in design intent: they represent divergent solution types that follow two fundamentally different design track choices.

Energy-responsive climate-rejecting buildings can be described as a linear evolutionary change in commercial buildings. The basic objective is to maintain sameness while increasing effectiveness. Climate-adapted buildings, on the other hand, can be seen as a nonlinear design change that requires a new perception of the relationship between architecture and environmental control. Climate-adapted buildings represent a departure from the 1950s' perspective that commercial buildings are intrinsically internally load dominated. The impact of this nonlinear change on people, design, and building ownership is substantial. Typically, the degree of change requires that new perceived advantages must be found for all parties. Therefore, the design of climate-adapted buildings depends as much on the needs, desires, and motives of people as on technology.

In the pure definition of a climate-adapted building, internal environmental-control systems are totally replaced by systems comprising form, envelope, and construction materials. However, our review has found only a handful of very simple buildings, such as warehouses, that fit this definition. Very few climates and building programs will permit the exclusive use of direct climatic energies to meet all the needs of people year-round. Contemporary climate-adapted buildings are commonly a blend of climate-adaptive techniques and internal systems technology. How these contradictory design principles of the two approaches are combined to best advantage is a key design issue for most contemporary climate-adapted buildings.

The choice of environmental-control equipment in a climate-adapted building defines the trade-offs that must be made to achieve a successful hybrid solution. At one extreme no equipment is necessary. At the other end of the range of possible solutions is the climate-rejecting building that totally depends on internally serviced environmental-control equipment during all times of the year. In the transition from a pure climate-adapted building toward a climate-rejecting building, the role of form and envelope likewise shifts from opening up and adapting to climate to closing down and rejecting the influence of climate on occupied space.

Equipment can play two primary roles in a climate-adapted building solution. The first is to augment the collection, distribution, and effective use of climatic energies in occupied spaces and buffer zones. Equipment can aid in the direct use of climatic energies, or be employed to collect and store excess energies of occupied space for use at a later time when a need may exist, but the direct source is unavailable. Second, equipment can be an independent supplement to the use of climatic energies. A supplemental system can be an independent secondary or back-up system to complement climatic adaptations, or a conventional internal system for one or more environmental-control needs which may not be suitable for climatic adaptations because of climate or building program.

As an example of equipment aiding in the direct transfer of climatic energies to occupied space, fans augment the effectiveness of natural ventilation. Forced ventilation can cool a building during periods of still air when natural ventilation alone may be ineffective. If the depth of a building is limited by the penetration of air for ventilative cooling, by using forced ventilation a designer could widen the building plan. The simplest equipment-related decisions in climate-adapted buildings can greatly impact form and envelope design determinants. Form and envelope choices are directly influenced by equipment choices in the design of climate-adapted buildings.

Climatic energies are typically transient sources of energy, changing hourly, daily, and seasonally. This time-dependent variability in magnitude seldom directly matches the instantaneous need of energy in a commercial building. Interior materials and furnishings can be selected that damp climatic pulses, or supplemental systems can be employed to collect and store excess thermal energy for deferred use. An example is the storing of the excess heat from occupied space in a rock bed for nighttime use. Although such systems do augment the application of climatic energies, and are partially fueled by excess climatic energies, the result is an internal environmental-control system, which, when discharging, will be more effective in a climate-rejecting building type form and envelope.

Secondary or back-up systems can be used to supplement climate-adapted systems. For instance, the primary lighting system of the Wainwright Building was daylighting, yet artificial lighting was provided as a daytime supplement and for night occupancy. Rarely used back-up systems are designed quite differently than conventional systems in a climate-rejecting building. If used only infrequently, inexpensive systems are generally adequate regardless of their low efficiencies. For instance, one building we reviewed derived the bulk of its annual lighting and heating from the sun. Rather than investing in efficient back-up heating and lighting systems that would seldom be used, low-cost, inefficient luminaires were provided as both the back-up heating and lighting system. When systems are rarely used, initial cost is often the primary concern rather than efficiency. Instead of investing in expensive back-up systems, a designer would do better to invest in increasing the effectiveness of the primary climate-adapted system.

Conventional systems used in a climate-adapted building for one or more end uses not deemed appropriate for climatic adaptations are designed as in climate-rejecting buildings. The application of such systems to independent end uses such as service hot water is simple and direct. For interdependent end uses such as heating, cooling, lighting, and ventilation, combining conventional and climate-adapted means in one building again forces form and envelope to perform the complex and potentially conflicting roles of climate adaptor and climate rejector. In such cases, a solution that is mutually supportive of very different needs, as in the Larkin Building, must be found.

Because climate-adapted buildings often include some form of internal environmental-control strategies, to design a successful climate-adapted building one must be proficient in the design of both climate-adapted and climate-rejecting solutions. The design skills required for climate-adapted buildings build upon the significant body of skills more directly related to energy-responsive climate-rejecting buildings. For this reason, the knowledge, skills, and experience necessary to design a successful climate-adapted building are notably greater than those used to design an energy-responsive climate-rejecting building.

Although climate-adapted and climate-rejecting buildings represent two different solution types, the design of energy-responsive commercial buildings appears to follow one decision-making process. First, the controlling energy need must be addressed resulting in initial modification of form and envelope. This action will most probably affect other internal systems, yet the modification may be appropriate if the benefits gained are greater than the liabilities incurred. A technique to make such a trade-off analysis is presented in Chapter Six. The following case studies show how other designers have addressed this problem.

With this discussion as a base, case studies are presented that demonstrate the principles, means, and variations in the design of energy-responsive climate-adapted buildings. Because many factors require consideration, these issues are examined throughout the following seven case studies. The major similarity in all the case studies is that envelope is punctured to connect occupied space and climate to best advantage. The key difference is how form is reinvented to achieve this connection. To highlight these differences, the case studies are presented in three categories: Extending Form, Splitting Form, and New Forms (Fig. 4.1). The Extending Form

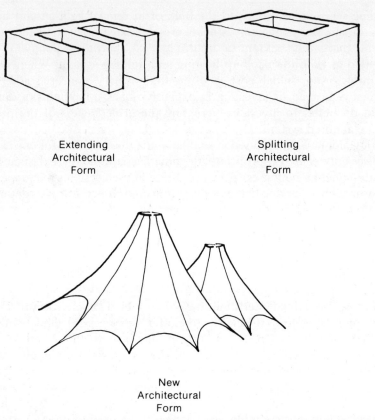

Extending
Architectural
Form

Splitting
Architectural
Form

New
Architectural
Form

Figure 4.1.   Form categories for climate-adapted buildings. Courtesy of Michael E. Doyle.

approach can be likened to the Wainwright Building where a very narrow building form allows occupied space to be directly connected to climate. In Splitting Form, as in the Larkin Building, a solid block is split in the center by adding a buffer zone. Volume is increased to reduce the external surface area exposed to climate as compared to a narrow building form. New Forms are not easily expressed as modifications to a conventional building form. These solutions break a great many design conventions in an attempt to best use direct climatic energies in combination with new materials and technologies.

EXTENDING ARCHITECTURAL FORM

The traditional way to build a department store is to construct a box, make it dark inside, light it, and then cool it off.

Owens-Corning Brochure

The simplest way to connect a greater portion of occupied space to climate is to extend form and puncture envelope. The depth of form in this approach is limited by the depth of penetration of light, heat, or air into the building. This concept is quite simple except that increasing external surface area and puncturing the envelope interferes with the defensive architectural capabilities of form and envelope, thus requiring inevitable design trade-offs. The following three case studies demonstrate how this approach can be used to derive different solutions. The first building is the Mount Airy Public Library in Mount Airy, North Carolina, designed by J. N. Pease Associates of Charlotte, North Carolina, with solar consultants Mazria/Schiff Associates of Albuquerque, New Mexico. The second building is the Baranco Pontiac dealership in Atlanta, Georgia, designed by Sizemore/Floyd Architects, of Atlanta. The third case study contrasts two Bullock's Department Stores, both in California, designed by Environmental Planning & Research of San Francisco, California, and L. Gene Zellmer and Associates of Fresno, California.

Mount Airy Public Library

The Mount Airy Public Library, Figures 4.2–4.8, is a 14,400-ft^2 building designed to hold 80,000 volumes. As an introduction to the basic techniques of adapting building to climate, the means of environmental control of this building are covered in detail.

The City of Mount Airy requested that the new facility be energy

Figure 4.2. Mount Airy Public Library. Courtesy of J.N. Pease Associates.

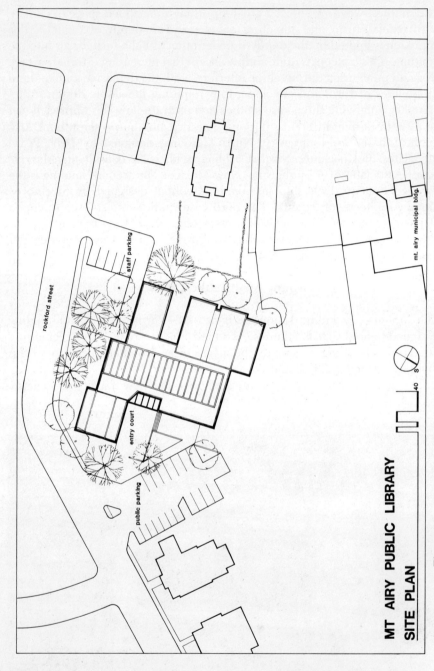

MT AIRY PUBLIC LIBRARY
SITE PLAN

Figure 4.3. Mount Airy Public Library, site plan. Courtesy of J.N. Pease Associates.

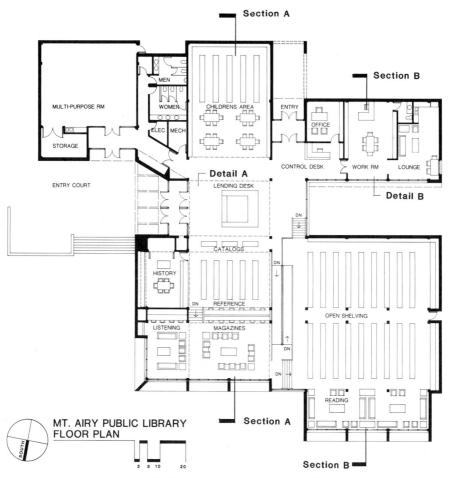

Section A

Section B

MEN

WOMEN

MULTI-PURPOSE RM

CHILDRENS AREA

ENTRY

ELEC MECH

OFFICE

STORAGE

CONTROL DESK

WORK RM

LOUNGE

ENTRY COURT

Detail A

LENDING DESK

Detail B

DN

CATALOGS

DN

HISTORY

DN

REFERENCE

OPEN SHELVING

DN

LISTENING

MAGAZINES

DN

DN

READING

MT. AIRY PUBLIC LIBRARY
FLOOR PLAN

Section A

2 5 10   20

Section B

SOUTH

Figure 4.4. Mount Airy Public Library, floor plan. Courtesy of J.N. Pease Associates.

efficient and demonstrate the effective use of solar energy in an institutional building. The building, scheduled for a 1982 completion date, was expected to cost $1.3 million, including interior furnishings, site work, and landscaping. The designers estimate that $195,000 or 15% of the total cost is directly attributed to the solar-related features of the building ($13.54/ft^2). Part of the solar-related design and construction cost of the building was funded through the U.S. Department of Energy's (DOE) Passive Commercial Buildings Program.

After performing preliminary energy-use calculations for the proposed building, the design team concluded that the lighting loads represented the controlling energy need of the building. Although secondary to lighting, heating and cooling were deemed sufficiently large to warrant considera-

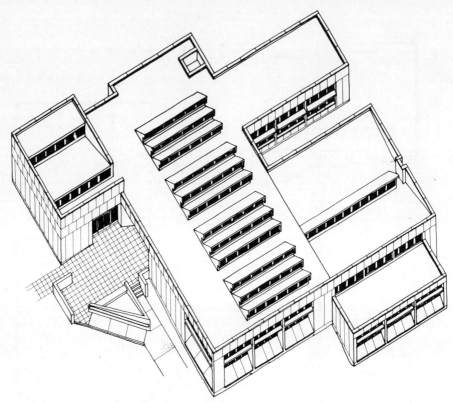

Figure 4.5. Mount Airy Public Library, axonometric (SW). Courtesy of J.N. Pease Associates.

tion of alternatives as well. Service hot water needs were found to be minimal, yet the client requested an active solar system for this end use for demonstration purposes.

Because the building would be used primarily during daylight hours, the choice was made early in the design process to use natural light to the greatest possible extent. To complement the daylighting strategies, apertures were made responsive to the seasonal needs of heating and cooling as well. Daylighting apertures are placed for proper light collection and distribution and sized and oriented to collect winter solar heat, to shade direct solar gain in the summer, and to provide swing-season cross-ventilation.

The need for daylight penetration to most of the occupied space resulted in a narrow building form comprising a series of winglike spaces that radiate from the main lending desk. According to the designers, "the lighting requirements and temperature comfort levels were carefully studied and were influential factors in organizing the interior spaces.

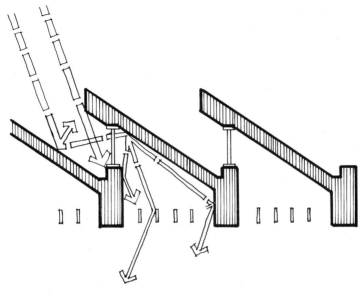

SUMMER

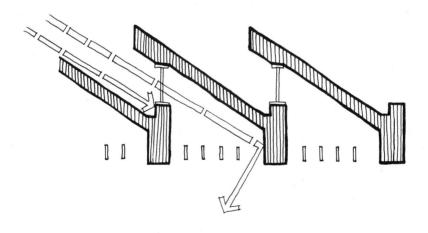

WINTER

Figure 4.6. Mount Airy Public Library, sawtooth roof section. Courtesy of Debra Berger.

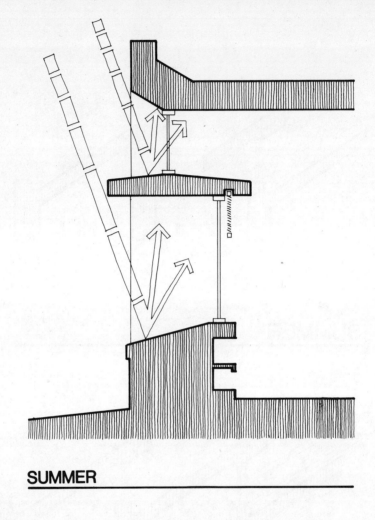

SUMMER

Figure 4.7.   Mount Airy Public Library, light shelf. Courtesy of Debra Berger.

Reading areas and other tasks requiring higher lighting levels were strategically located under clerestories [in the sawtooth roof] or light shelves placed along the southern edge of the building. Each 'wing' was used as its own daylight fixture."

The primary daylighting apertures of the building are illustrated in Figures 4.6 and 4.7. To provide daylight to the majority of interior spaces, view windows with light shelves and a sawtooth roof with clerestories are used extensively. Rather than using conventional windows, the design team decided to use an indirect daylighting scheme in order to achieve a better balance of light distribution and brightness ratios. According to project

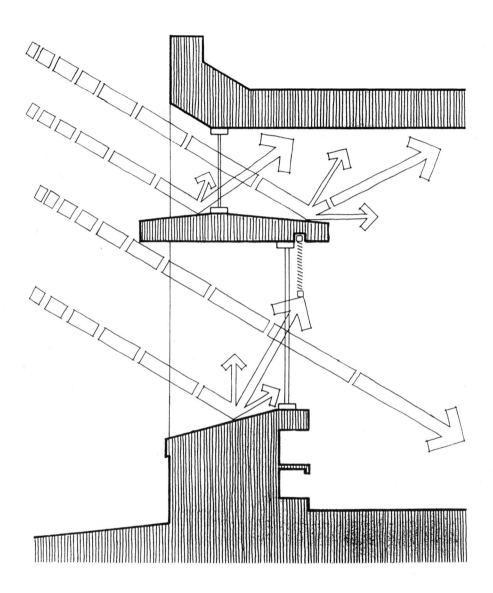

WINTER

south glazing: reading room

Figure 4.7. (*Continued*)

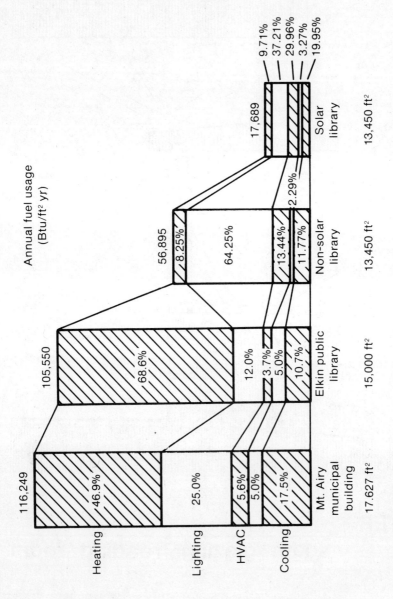

Figure 4.8. Mount Airy Public Library, energy-use estimate. Courtesy of Mazria/Schiff Associates.

architect Gary Morgan, the daylighting effect desired was "a soft, pleasant light in a space where most people will be surprised not to find artificial lighting." By bouncing window and clerestory light off white, light-diffusing ceiling surfaces, a softer distribution of light is achieved than possible with a more conventional window.

The daylighting apertures are also designed to function as passive heating elements during the winter months. The extended form and punctured envelope can be a liability in winter months, yet orientation of the lighting apertures can offset this problem by selectively admitting more radiation during cold periods. Eighty percent of all the glass is vertical and oriented slightly to the southeast to capture direct solar gain from the low morning winter sun. These same apertures are designed to shade the glass from direct sunlight during the summer, allowing only reflected light to enter the building. In this fashion, the amount of solar light and heat that enters the building is consistent with the seasonal needs for heating and cooling.

To stabilize the interior temperature of the building, large areas of high thermal capacitance materials, including the poured-in-place columns and beams which support the sawtooth roof, are left exposed to the internal environment. The majority of the floor area is quarry tile over concrete. The inner portion of the exterior walls are 12-in.-thick concrete block, grouted solid and plastered. The heat-storage capacity of the building is designed to damp the day-to-day pulselike nature of direct gain winter heating and absorb a portion of daytime summer heat gains for release during unoccupied hours. The design team also found that the indirect, even distribution of solar gain for lighting purposes is highly compatible with the need to dispense solar heat gain over large areas of high-mass internal finishes. Both heat and light use the same basic internal distribution technique in this building.

The internal-heat capacity design is closely tied to the thermal controls of the building. Programmable thermostats are set to 68°F during occupied winter hours and set back to 50°F at night. During much of the heating season, stored solar heat will meet most of the nighttime setback temperature requirements. However, since the library opens at 8:00 a.m., before significant winter solar gains can occur, the mass does provide an auxiliary heating liability for the early morning warm-up to 68°F. Until internal or solar gains can recharge the mass surfaces to 68°F, some auxiliary heat will be needed to perform that task. This trade-off is very common in the design of climate-adapted buildings. It is typically expressed as the difference between a lightweight, insulated, thermos-bottle building that can thermally recover very quickly, versus the high-mass building that can delay and damp thermal input and loads, yet is very slow in recharging. Both have advantages and disadvantages. Deciding which is best for a given project influences the number, size, and orientation of solar apertures and the control strategy of the building.

In addition to window shading, natural ventilation provides cooling during mild weather. The southern light-shelf windows and conventional northern elevation windows are operable and permit cross-ventilation. Also, exterior walls are covered by white granite quarried in Mount Airy. The light color and thermal capacitance of the granite reflect solar gains and damp solar-imposed temperature differentials between the walls and the inside. Added building shade is achieved by carefully siting the building among existing 40–50-ft-high trees located along the north, west, and east sides of the building.

On a yearly average, daylighting strategies are expected to meet all but 2 hours of the daily lighting requirements. To complement the natural lighting system, both the light-shelf windows and the overhead clerestories include a cove that contains inexpensive, bare-bulb fluorescent fixtures. When needed, these fixtures provide indirect general lighting by bouncing the artificial light onto sloped areas of the white ceiling. Task lights are also provided in reading areas and at the upper shelf of each stack. Most of the artificial lighting is also controlled from the lending desk to ensure that the system is turned off and on according to need.

The back-up heating and cooling system is simple and similar to residential systems. Since the extended building form with operable windows increases the infiltration rate, mechanical ventilation is not required and the heating and cooling system need only operate upon demand. Five rooftop heat pumps ranging in size from 5 to 7.5 tons are placed near the zones to be served. Separate units allow selective operation of each according to need. For instance, a separate unit for the multipurpose room allows that space to be conditioned only during periods of use. The heat pumps are also designed to use outside air directly whenever conditions permit.

As shown in Figure 4.8, the all-electric library is expected to use about 17,300 Btu/ft^2 per year under average climatic conditions and occupancy patterns as measured at the building boundary. To assess the energy savings represented in the design, the team analyzed the energy performance of the same building without clerestories, light shelves, quarry-tile floors, overhangs, and the solar domestic hot water system. They also reduced the insulation to that required by code. This nonsolar building required about 3.2 times more energy on an annual basis. Peak-demand requirements were not assessed by the design team since the building would not be billed such a charge.

The extension of architectural form as the means to connect inside to outside requires a comparative increase in exterior surface area. The difference between this approach and that of collapsing form in a climate-rejecting building is best illustrated by comparing the library to the Los Alamos Study Center. The external-surface-area-to-gross-floor-area ratio of the Study Center is about 0.6. The same ratio for the library is 2.1. One would expect the Study Center ratio to be smaller since it contains 4.5 times more floor area. Both buildings have a glass-area-to-total-external-wall-area ratio of about 0.25. In fact, both buildings use 3400 ft^2 of glazing. However, since the Mount Airy Public Library is only 22% as large, the glass-area-to-gross-floor-area ratio is 4.5 times larger. Whereas the Study Center conserves energy by reducing glass and wall area, the Library reverses that trend at the beginning of the design process and expands surface area and the use of glazing. This difference is the reason that the climate-rejecting building and the climate-adapted building represent extremes in the range of possible design solutions. These alternatives offer two distinct and different design tacks. The two solution types represent choices with divergent and even contradictory purposes.

Puncturing an envelope is very much like designing multimode, high-efficiency HVAC and lighting systems: the replacement elements are expected to perform better. The punctured envelope aspects of the Mount Airy Public Library are well-represented in Figures 4.6 and 4.7. Where a flat roof or narrow window wall once existed there is a new three-dimensional element. These elements perform better, and more often than not, they cost more. Even simple changes such as operable sash add to the cost of envelope over past conventions. The Mount Airy Public Library incremental initial solar cost of $195,000, on a square-foot basis and adjusted to inflation, is actually 26% more expensive and therefore more energy intensive than the Los Alamos Study Center active solar system. The concept of using climatic energies directly and in the simplest form does not in itself ensure the best possible solution. A climate-adapted building can provide superior quality and comfort; yet, a workable system is not enough by itself. In terms of either invested dollars or embodied energy, climate-adapted innovations must produce the most from the least.

Although the cost of extending form and puncturing envelope will be more as compared to that of a sealed cube, a climate-adapted building will not necessarily cost more than a climate-rejecting building. However, to keep total costs down, extras added to form and envelope must be counterbalanced by cost reductions elsewhere. Budgetary trade-offs are the key. For instance, if a boxlike building is to be finished with expensive materials to project a certain image, perhaps the same goal can be achieved by using an extended climate-adapted form sheathed with less costly finishes. We have found that optimizing structure is the most common budgetary trade-off in the design of an energy-responsive commercial building. In either a climate-rejecting or climate-adapted building, this approach does not increase total building budget yet still permits the addition of extra energy-related strategies. The Fort Lauderdale Federal Building–U.S. Courthouse and 33 West Monroe both allowed for initial cost reductions while conserving energy by increasing structural efficiency in a manner compatible with energy goals. The same is possible for climate-adapted buildings. With increased performance demanded from form and envelope, the construction of these elements must be made very cost-effective.

Baranco Pontiac

The Baranco Pontiac dealership building, Figures 4.9–4.13, is an example of a climate-adapted building with energy-related strategies similar to those of the Mount Airy Public Library. Daylighting is used year-round. Winter direct-gain solar heating and ventilative swing-season cooling are used in conjunction with high-heat-capacity interior finishes. The back-up equipment is likewise simple and direct. Yet the building was designed to meet the lowest possible budget for this building type: $27/ft^2 including site work. The building actually cost less to build than the "low average" cost as determined by the Dodge Construction System Cost Index. The attainment of that economic result is the focus of our review of this case study.

Baranco Pontiac is a 9700-ft^2 sales office and showroom for an Atlanta automobile dealership. According to Mike Sizemore, the first design goal was to reduce the volume of conditioned space which results in a reduction of both construction cost and annual energy cost. The 4600-ft^2 showroom was designed as a conditioned outdoor space. The simple building section was designed to face south, inviting direct solar gain during the winter. The roof was designed to shade during the summer. An earth berm on the north

Figure 4.9.   Baranco Pontiac. Courtesy of Sizemore/Floyd.

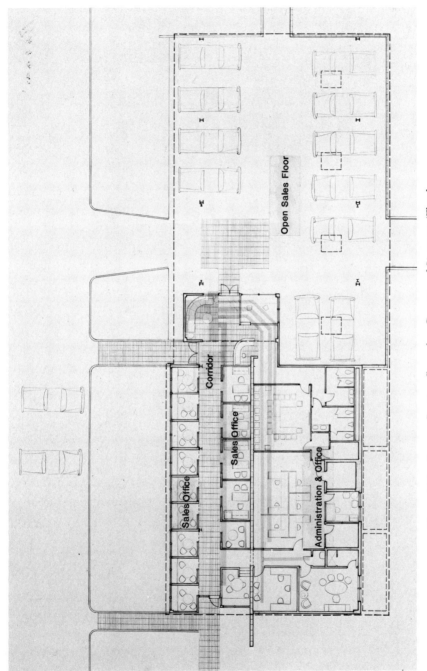

Figure 4.10. Baranco Pontiac, floor plan. Courtesy of Sizemore/Floyd.

95

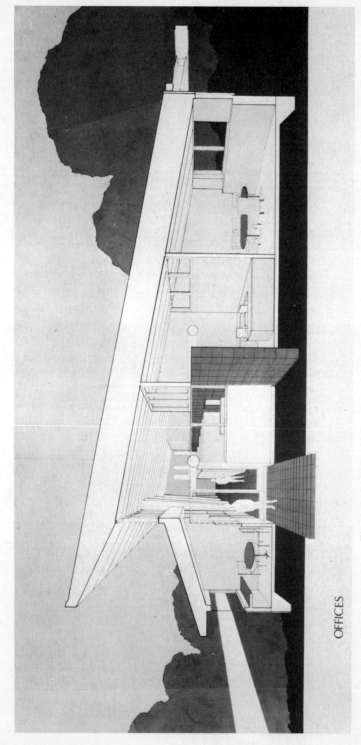

OFFICES

Figure 4.11. Baranco Pontiac, section. Courtesy of Sizemore/Floyd.

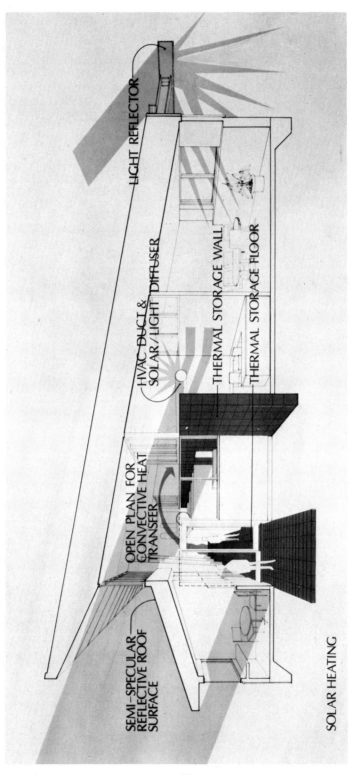

Figure 4.12. Baranco Pontiac, heating section. Courtesy of Sizemore/Floyd.

LIGHT REFLECTOR

HVAC DUCT & SOLAR / LIGHT DIFFUSER

THERMAL STORAGE WALL

THERMAL STORAGE FLOOR

OPEN PLAN FOR CONVECTIVE HEAT TRANSFER

SEMI-SPECULAR REFLECTIVE ROOF SURFACE

SOLAR HEATING

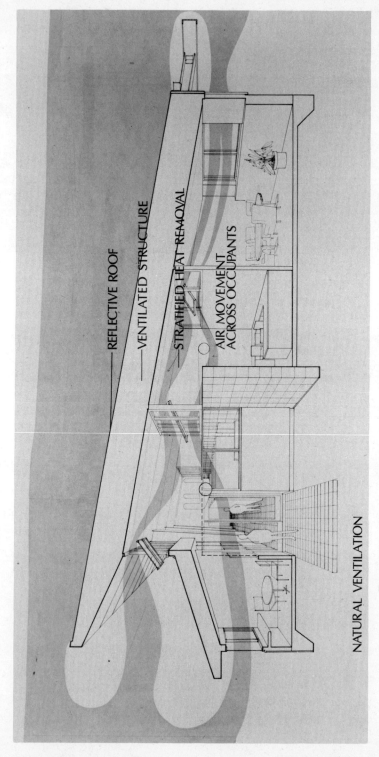

REFLECTIVE ROOF

VENTILATED STRUCTURE

STRATIFIED HEAT REMOVAL

AIR MOVEMENT
ACROSS OCCUPANTS

NATURAL VENTILATION

Figure 4.13. Baranco Pontiac, natural ventilation section. Courtesy of Sizemore/Floyd.

side of the building restricts the entrance of cold air in winter, yet allows southerly cross-ventilation in the summer. During daytime hours, the conditioned outdoor space is naturally illuminated. By achieving adequate environmental-control conditions in the showroom area without completely enclosing it, the designers eliminated the cost of walls and glazing.

The second cost-saving feature of the building was the selection of a pre-engineered building system for structure. According to Sizemore, the basic building profile was first established to meet the spatial goals of the project. During design, an INRYCO pre-engineered building of the same form was developed. Using this structure and exterior skin significantly contributed to the building's reduced cost.

The pre-engineered building complements other design goals as well. The white metal skin, used for walls and roof, reflects solar gains and gives the building high visibility in a competitive business location. The same white metal skin is used on the underside of the roof in both the showroom and sales office to maximize the use of ground-reflected light to achieve soft, high-quality daylighting. According to Sizemore, the main qualitative advantage of this building compared to similar conventional structures is this spectacular daylighting which provides a relaxing work environment.

This case study underscores the importance of recognizing the need to make a building more energy efficient than past designs, yet cost-effective. Climate-adapted buildings need not reproduce all elements of a conventional building. New possibilities, such as using outdoor conditioned space, allow the development of alternatives with inherent advantages over standard space-conditioning methods. In addition, Baranco Pontiac demonstrates the possibilities for cost reduction when form and envelope are linked with structure in the early stages of the design process. As in the case of climate-rejecting buildings, integrating energy issues with broader design concerns can only increase the potential for arriving at cost-effective architectural solutions of integrity.

Bullock's Department Stores

To clarify further the cost issues associated with climate-adapted buildings and to reinforce the importance of integrating energy-related issues with broader design concerns, this section concludes by discussing two innovative Bullock's Department Stores. The two stores are in the Oakridge Mall, San Jose, California, and the Fashion Island Mall, San Mateo, California. The San Jose store (Figs. 4.14–4.16) was designed first and served as a small-scale experiment for the innovations embodied in the San Mateo store. Together, the two case studies illustrate the roles of risk and reinvention in the design of energy-responsive commercial buildings.

The major driving force behind both projects was a highly motivated and supportive client, Paul Heindrick, Chairman of the Board of Bullock's

Figure 4.14.   Bullock's Oakridge Mall Department Store, San Jose. Courtesy of Environmental Planning & Research, Inc.

Northern Division. Heindrick stated, "Bullock's has a responsibility to challenge the traditional ways of doing things and to explore new techniques with a view to possible breakthroughs in the area of department store construction and merchandising methods." His original directive to the design team had three priorities: the store must conserve energy, it must be innovative and visually exciting, and it must incorporate new merchandising concepts and techniques. In short, the design team was charged with integrating energy, architecture, and merchandising into an overall innovative solution that addresses the contemporary challenges of the retailing business.

According to the San Jose project architect, Virgil Carter, AIA, the general design track selected for the first store was to reverse the trend of "building huge, fully enclosed black boxes, then pumping them full of artificial lighting, which requires vast amounts of energy for cooling." The major marketing concept was to develop a parklike atmosphere with small trees and hanging plants to enhance the appearance of the merchandise and counteract the impersonal quality often associated with a large retail store. Central to this idea was the soft glow of daylight through a teflon-coated fabric roof membrane. The filtered daylight has correct color balance and, therefore, permits true color rendition of the merchandise. The column-free space creates an open market effect without the discomforts of rain, noise, and humidity. Streetlike pole lighting combined with indirect lighting bounced from the ceiling reinforces this effect at night.

Figure 4.15. Bullock's, San Jose, interior.

Faced with limited design schedule and budget, the client decided to treat the Oakridge building as a small-scale experiment with the thought of applying the experience gained to a future store. Risk was undertaken in the context of a controlled experiment. The resulting prototype is a somewhat conventional design with a 96-by-160-ft-wide opening that comprises about one-third of the roof area of the two-story structure. The punctured area is covered with a double layer of teflon-coated fiberglass material separated by an airspace of 2–4 in. and supported by a pair of diagonally intersecting cross arches. This roof configuration has a light transmittance of about 7%, and on a clear day can flood the merchandising area with 550 foot candles of natural light.

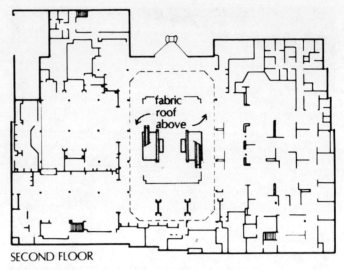

SECOND FLOOR

Figure 4.16. Bullock's, San Jose, second floor plan. Courtesy of Environmental Planning, & Research, Inc.

While the replacement of a third of the roof area with a translucent cover may appear to be a simple incremental change, the impact on energy, lighting, building systems, interior planning, code, insurance, and economics are significant. The simple elimination of the dropped ceiling required new prototypes for display cases, accent lighting, power servicing, and a redesign of most other attendant building systems. The integration of the interior merchandising with the new building shell demanded a change in nearly all the conventions of merchandising display and store construction.

Since the major energy-related goal was to reduce artificial lighting needs, the departments with the highest lighting requirements were placed under the fabric roof section. These departments include Housewares, Gifts, and China. A 3000-ft^2 test area is also included under the fabric roof. Merchandise is rotated from other departments to this area to gain experience and test sales under natural light. New modular display units, an integrated floor power system, and a space frame grid to support artificial light fixtures complete the area.

In the Oakridge store, the cost of the 15,000-ft^2 roof modification exceeded conventional construction by about $115,000. In addition, about $20,000 was added to the finishing cost for the prototype display and servicing connections under the fabric roof. The net annual operating energy savings in the first year of operation was about $18,000. Based on these numbers, the design team estimates a payback period of less than 10 years.

The design team expected that the Oakridge store, as a small-scale prototype, would have a relatively high first cost. They paid a premium for combining a conventional roof structure and fabric structure in the same building. To lower overall risk, an added 30 tons of steel was required to frame the roof opening to receive the fabric structure and to permit a return to a conventional roof if the marketing scheme proved unsatisfactory. The design team concluded, however, that on a larger scale, lower initial cost would be possible due to the lower weight of a total fabric structure compared to conventional building systems. This reduced weight can allow for cost reductions in roof and floor assemblies, walls, and foundations.

Since its opening in late 1978, this store has provided Bullock's with valuable experimental data on the use of daylighting in merchandising. As summarized by Carter, this experiment dispels the notion of retailers that daylight has no value in displaying merchandise. The public's response has been enthusiastic, and the store has been successful in attracting customers in the fiercely competitive San Jose market. Sales in the departments under the fabric roof are reportedly about 10%–15% higher than in similar stores with conventional structures.

Based on this sales experience and the possibility of reducing cost in a larger scale application of the fabric roof scheme, Bullock's decided to encase 70,000 ft^2 of its new San Mateo, California, store in fabric. This store, shown in Figures 4.17–4.19 was completed in December 1981 for a cost comparable to that of a conventional two-story department store. According to Heindrick, "Although it is impossible to precisely quantify the effect natural lighting has had on sales receipts, we felt the fabric roof had benefitted sales by creating an exciting physical environment for shopping and improved color rendition of the merchandise. So, while our decision to

Figure 4.17. Bullock's Department Store, San Mateo. Courtesy of Russell Abraham.

Figure 4.18.   Bullock's, San Mateo, interior. Courtesy of Russell Abraham.

go with a larger fabric roof on the San Mateo store was easily cost-justified by energy savings alone, the good experience we'd had with sales in the San Jose store was a major motivation for our decision."

Examining these two case studies raises two very interesting points. First, a conventional structure fitted with a climate-adaptive feature appears to be less cost-effective than an innovative structure. That the San Jose store, a modified conventional structure, is less cost-effective than the San Mateo store reinforces the conclusions drawn from our collective learning experience. Small changes to conventional forms and envelopes, such as

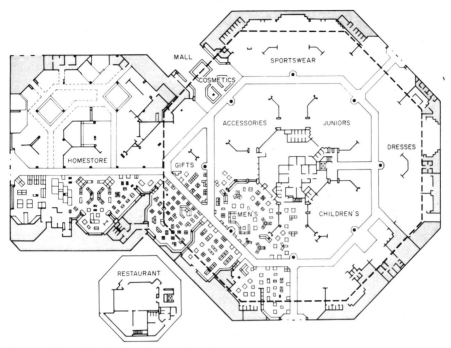

Figure 4.19. Bullock's, San Mateo, floor plan. Courtesy of *Architectural Record,* L. Gene Wellmer Associates, and Environmental Planning & Research, Inc.

narrowing the depth of a building or replacing fixed windows with operable sash, are typically an initial cost liability. Aside from alleviating this cost burden with trade-offs in other design elements, the only way we have found to reverse this trend is to switch to new materials and construction techniques suited to new purposes. Climate-adapted buildings may reflect age-old environmental-control techniques, but the success of such alternatives seems to be linked to the latest advances in structures and materials. These advances do not spring from the needs and problems of conventional construction practices, but from the refound potential of adapting buildings to climate.

The second point well illustrated by these two Bullock's stores is that reinvention is driven by the needs of people more than by the capability of technology. Our collective technological base is very large and dwarfs what we know about matching environmental-control alternatives with other design goals. If the resolution of energy-related construction issues lies with uniting them with the whole of building design and construction, it is time to pay careful attention to people's motives and perceived advantages. Once these social goals are defined, reinvention will have a purpose beyond merely replacing the existing.

SPLITTING ARCHITECTURAL FORM

The use of the large enclosed court permits the building to develop a large perimeter, with its advantages of access to daylight and view, without suffering an increase in building energy consumption.

Site 1, OFFICE OF THE STATE ARCHITECT, STATE OF CALIFORNIA

Because most contemporary climate-adapted buildings combine internal and external environmental-control subsystems, form and envelope are required to perform the functions of climate rejector and climate adaptor. This issue is often central in the design of such structures. One common solution to this problem is the multiple environmental-control perimeter approach shown earlier in the Larkin Building. In this approach, the building mass is split from within by adding volume at the center. In effect, two or more narrow building forms are made that are connected by an atrium. The atrium serves as a climatic filter and buffer, leaving the new extended forms protected. The intent is to increase the proportion of occupied space that is connected to climate without incurring the increased surface-area liabilities of a long, narrow, extended form. The resulting building form represents a compromise incorporating both climate-adapted and internal systems.

Three case studies illustrate the concepts and principles of architectural buffers in climate-adapted buildings. The first study is the Gregory Bateson Building (Site 1), Sacramento, California, designed by former and present California State Architects Sim Van der Ryn and Barry Wasserman, with Scott Matthews, Peter Calthorpe, and Bruce Corson. The second case study is the Shell Oil Company Woodcreek Office Complex, Houston, Texas, designed by Caudill Rowlett Scott (CRS). The third case study is Princeton Professional Park, Princeton, New Jersey, designed in joint venture by Harrison Fraker Architects and Short and Ford Architects, Princeton, New Jersey.

Gregory Bateson Building

The Gregory Bateson Building, Figures 4.20–4.25, was the first contemporary climate-adapted commercial building. It was designed in the mid-1970s, when most designers associated energy conservation in large commercial buildings with delamping and more insulation. According to Scott Matthews, "at this time there were some signs of distaste for the 'bunker' school of energy-conserving design. Many of the early buildings had compact forms and minimum glass area. In our ignorance of what was, and what was not, possible, we turned in the opposite direction—exploiting 'big building-ness" to introduce features that would not only reduce energy

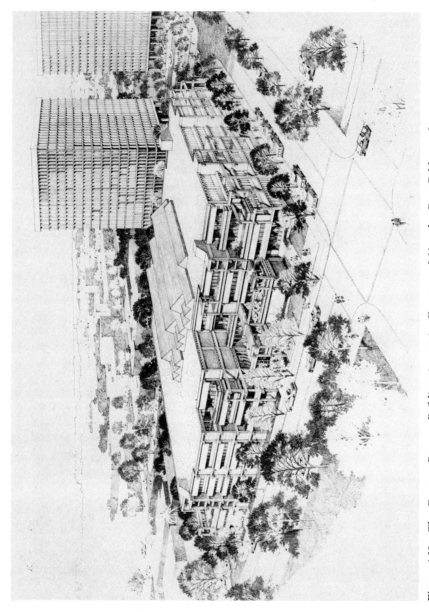

Figure 4.20. The Gregory Bateson Building, isometric. Courtesy of Van der Ryn Calthorpe & Partners.

Figure 4.21. The Gregory Bateson Building. Courtesy of Kathy Kelly.

Figure 4.22. The Gregory Bateson Building, atrium. Courtesy of Kathy Kelly.

consumption, but also contribute to a stimulating work environment." The Bateson Building was the first contemporary large office building that broke with the tradition of climatic isolation as the means to conserve energy. In our collective learning experience, this project represents a major milestone in the history of environmental-control systems for commercial buildings.

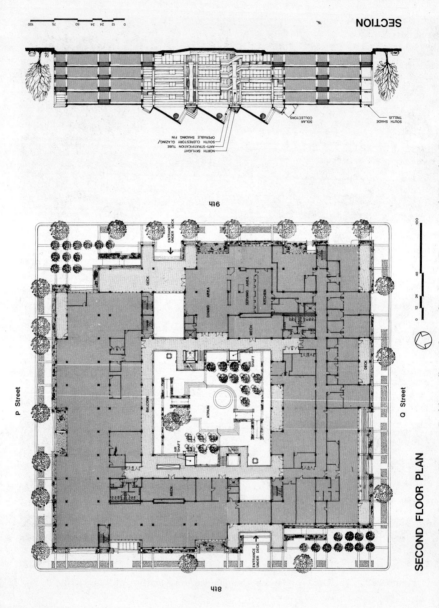

SECOND FLOOR PLAN

Figure 4.23. The Gregory Bateson Building, floor plan and section. Courtesy of Van der Ryn Calthorpe & Partners.

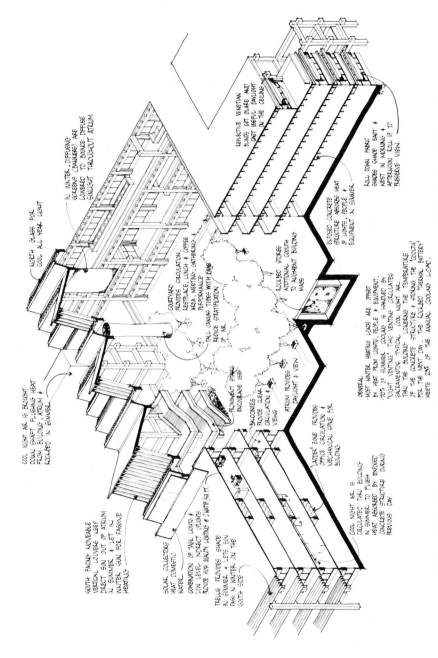

Figure 4.24. The Gregory Bateson Building, section isometric. Courtesy of Van der Ryn Calthorpe & Partners.

111

Energy Consumption Comparison

Site 1-A's energy efficient design will result in its requiring less than 20,000 Btu/ft²yr off-site energy (64,000 Btu/ft² yr raw source energy). This represents 34% of the average consumption of a similar building having no energy conserving design features beyond those required by California's Non-Residential Energy Design Standards; and only 13%–15% of the average consumption of large State office buildings constructed prior to 1973.

Site 1-A Energy Consumption

The percentage contribution toward Site 1-A's total energy demand is shown below for each of the major systems serving the building:

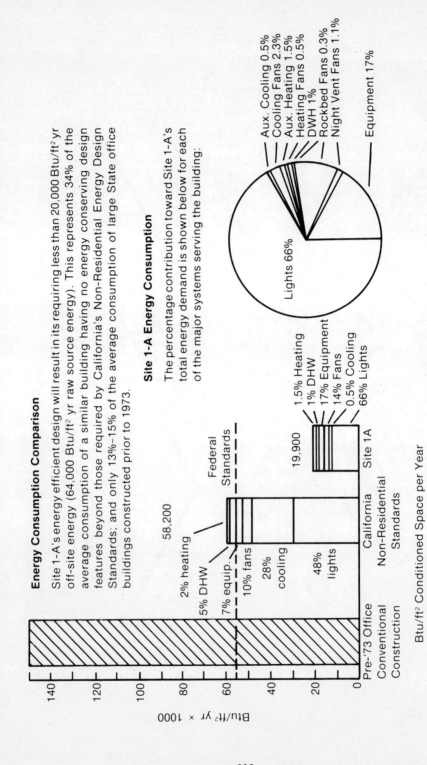

Figure 4.25. The Gregory Bateson Building, annual energy-use estimates. Courtesy of Van der Ryn Calthorpe & Partners.

The four-story, 267,000-ft^2 government office building was intended as the first of a series of 12 new state facilities to be built in California. In addition to budget constraints, the two primary goals in this building program were to establish a humanistic approach to design for institutional buildings and to conserve nonrenewable resources. In the Bateson Building, it is often difficult to distinguish which of these two goals were more central to any individual design innovation.

Access to view was the foremost determinant of form in the Bateson Building. The designers placed a priority on providing the occupants with a view to improve their well-being and increase their productivity. Access to view requires a narrow building form. This was achieved in the Bateson Building by splitting the building from within and adding a large 144-by-150-by-75-ft-high atrium to the center of the squarelike building footprint (Fig. 4.23). In this design, the maximum distance between occupied space and window is 40 ft, with the average distance about 15 ft.

The atrium is the major energy-related innovation that differentiates this building from previous case studies. It serves as a source of heating, cooling, and lighting, as well as a protective buffer space for the surrounding large expanse of building. This space is capped by a sawtooth roof with extensive south-facing glazing to capture winter solar radiation. This winter direct gain, diffused by movable fabric banners hung from the ceiling, floods the atrium with light and heat. Because the atrium is connected to the building's air-handling system, excess heat can be passed to the rest of the building or stored for deferred use in two rock beds located under the atrium floor.

In the summer, the south-facing glazing in the sawtooth roof is shaded. North-facing skylights permit the penetration of diffuse light from the northern sky. Since the summer nighttime ambient air temperature in Sacramento falls about 25°F below the daytime high, the atrium and rock beds are flushed with this night air to precool the thermal mass. The air-cooled rock beds offset 20% of the cooling load of the office spaces.

The Bateson Building atrium is used in a fundamentally different way than is the Larkin Building atrium. In the Larkin Building, office space opened into the atrium resulting in one large volume for thermal conditioning. This approach works well in situations where daylight penetration is desired and the atrium itself is used as part of the working environment. In the Bateson Building, as with most contemporary climate-adapted buildings with an atrium, a thermal break of partitions and windows is between the two environments. This system permits the atrium to act as a thermal buffer space. Atrium temperatures are allowed to float, conditioned only by selective exposure to climate and proximity to the conditioned offices. In the first half-year of operation, the Bateson Building atrium temperature has maintained a level halfway between the office temperature and the exterior ambient temperature.

By assigning spaces that serve transient functions to the atrium, the volume of the building conditioned to normal standards is reduced. Energy is also conserved because the office walls are exposed to the benign environment of the buffer. With thermal breaks, the sole use of natural space-conditioning, and extended comfort limits, this space becomes the architectural equivalent of a mechanical system deadband control strategy. Properly designed, such spaces can stay within bracketed comfort conditions without mechanical assistance.

As in many of the preceding climate-adapted building case studies, properly oriented glass, shading devices, and exposed internal thermal mass are incorporated into the Bateson Building for natural heating, cooling, and lighting. One major difference is the extensive use of nighttime air to cool the building's thermal mass in the summer. A variable volume ventilation system is used to purge heat from the mass surfaces during unoccupied hours. This system permits the exposed structure to absorb the radiant and convective heat gains of people, lights, and office machinery during the following day. About 75% of the building's cooling load is offset by this direct night venting of office space thermal mass.

Access to view and daylighting have common design requirements. Both were enhanced in the project by selecting higher than normal transmission glass for the windows. Terraces, step-backs, and reentrant corners were designed into the exterior facades to protect the glass from unwanted solar gains and to provide greater opportunities for exterior views. This geometric variety also reduces the scale of the structure—a design goal since the site bridges residential and commercial districts.

In this unique building, daylighting was perceived more as a qualitative feature than as a guarantee to energy conservation. No contemporary precedent had been set. Would the building occupants be motivated to turn off artificial lights and voluntarily use only daylighting when conditions permitted? No one knew the answer to this in the mid-1970s, and since the budget would not allow automated lighting controls, daylighting was treated conservatively. For instance, all cooling load studies for the building assumed full use of the 2 W/ft^2 task-ambient electric lighting system during all occupied hours. Daylighting model studies were performed, yet the final selection of daylighting as a building strategy was largely a result of the aesthetic appeal of a daylit office environment.

The conservative use of daylighting in this project is exemplified in the use of space at the atrium/building boundary. This zone is used primarily for circulation. Office space in this area would have a greater energy-conserving potential since it has a higher lighting load than corridors. However, the design team believed that the public would better accept daylight in circulation space, and felt it more likely that artificial lights would be turned off in the corridors. As shown in the next two case studies, this space-planning approach misses a major opportunity in an atrium design as demonstrated by experience gained over the last 7 years.

The Bateson Building is a good example of the potential of a climate-adapted building to add volume and quality to design while achieving both the humanistic and energy-related design goals of the project. The building is predicted to use 20,000 Btu/ft^2 per year as measured at the building boundary. It was also built for the original budget of \$60/ft^2 (in 1978 dollars) without requiring a variance for energy-related features. This economic achievement results from an original budget that reflects construction costs of quality rental office space and from the economic trade-offs made during design to keep structure and finish costs low. The Bateson Building was constructed for a cost comparable to the conventional office space the state now leases from developers. The state expects the new building to pay for itself in 8 years by saving the cost of leasing the same amount of space from the private sector. It is also anticipated that \$30–60 million in taxes will be saved in energy costs over the life of the building. It goes against intuition, but it appears that adding volume to a building for both qualitative and energy-related purposes does not necessarily mean that a building will cost more.

Woodcreek Office Complex

Climate-adapted buildings have unique qualitative advantages that make them more than mere substitutes for past design conventions. In the design of the Shell Oil Company Woodcreek Office Complex, Figures 4.26–4.31, a stimulating and pleasant working environment was the major design objective. Woodcreek houses 2200 employees, many of whom perform highly technical functions such as geological oil exploration surveys. Providing an office environment that would help attract and retain a quality technical staff in a highly competitive employee market was the primary design goal, a goal well suited to the versatile nature of climate-adapted buildings.

According to Jess Johnson of ARCO, "When you want to tame a wildcat, the best thing is to give him what he is wild for: trees, lakes, views, a short commute, and a good office facility." Shell started by selecting a 90-acre wooded site in a west Houston suburb. Since about 80% of Shell's employees live in this part of town, commuting time is reduced and the congestion of downtown traffic is avoided. Shell requested that the parklike atmosphere of the site be retained, and that a maximum number of private offices with an outside view be designed into the project. Additional design goals were to accent and allow individual identity for major operational units and divisions, space planning flexibility to meet changing needs, and energy efficiency.

Figure 4.26. Shell Woodcreek. Courtesy of Mark Scheyer (of Caudill Rowlett Scott).

The complex was divided into seven buildings, each containing a separate corporate unit or division. The requirement of private offices with views led the design team to devise studies that would achieve that goal. A narrow building section with a single office on each side of a central corridor allowed the greatest number of exterior views. Yet energy efficiency demanded a more compact architectural form. From this dichotomy sprang the idea of using an atrium. The final form breaks the extended double-loaded corridor form into three pieces and wraps these sections around a skylit atrium. The triangular form allows more of the existing trees on the site to be preserved. In this design, 60% of the offices have outside views with the remaining 40% looking toward the lushly landscaped atrium. The atriums also become the focal point for each major operating unit or division housed in that building.

Once again, a connection was made between the design requirement of access to view and the energy-related advantages of daylighting. Beyond incremental improvements to the HVAC systems, daylighting was selected as the major means to limit nonrenewable energy use in the project.

In addition to the atrium, three types of spaces are daylit at Woodcreek: outer perimeter offices, inner offices overviewing the atrium, and the

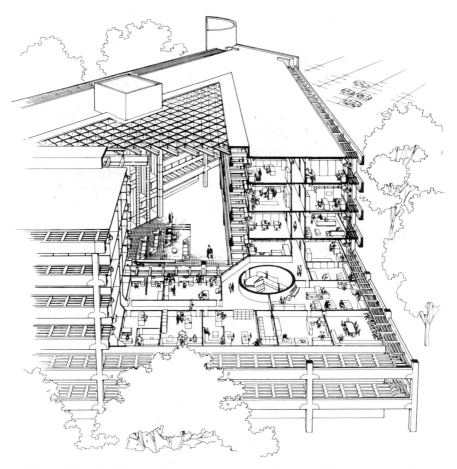

Figure 4.27. Shell Woodcreek, section perspective. Courtesy of Communication Arts.

double-loaded corridor that runs between the two. The large need for cooling in this climate demanded careful control of solar gains before daylighting benefits could be realized. To shade the exterior glass, structure was extended 6 ft beyond the enclosing envelope. This exposed structure, infilled with a trellis, shades the majority of the exterior glass throughout the year. Diffuse light penetrating the shading devices is bounced into the office by a light shelf placed above a view window. Above the light shelf, clear glass allows deeper penetration of daylight into the office. The view window is tinted glass, which adds useful daylight to desks placed near the window while controlling the brightness ratios within the offices.

The light shelf is also designed as an enclosure for the HVAC distribution ductwork and outlets. Assigning these services to the exterior perimeter of

Figure 4.28.   Shell Woodcreek, atrium. Courtesy of Richard Payne (of Caudill Rowlett Scott).

the offices eliminates the need for a suspended ceiling. In the offices, the structural concrete Ts are left exposed and painted white. A floor-to-ceiling height of 11 ft 10 in. permits the use of the window above the light shelf and promotes deeper daylight penetration. This design also permits greater flexibility in future space planning alterations.

The increased floor-to-ceiling height also allows a high window to be placed between office and corridor. Daylight spilled from the offices on both sides illuminates the corridors.

The atrium view offices are daylit via the skylighted roof. The window and light shelf configuration, as well as the structural extension, are the same in these offices as in the exterior design except that all glass is clear and the trellis is not used. Since double-loaded corridors are used, the inner offices are not removed from the atrium by circulation space as in the Bateson Building. However, the 6-ft structural extension in the atrium does reduce

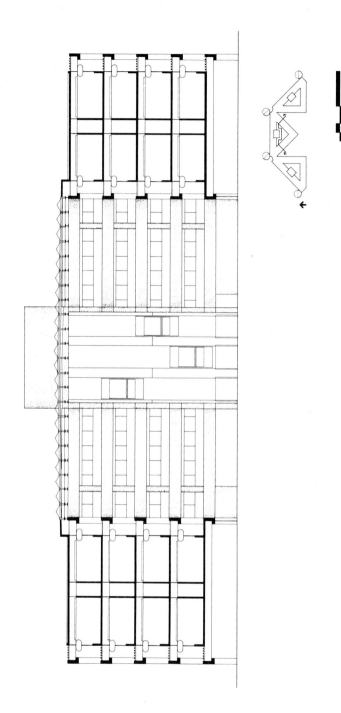

Figure 4.29. Shell Woodcreek, section through atrium. Courtesy of Caudill Rowlett Scott.

119

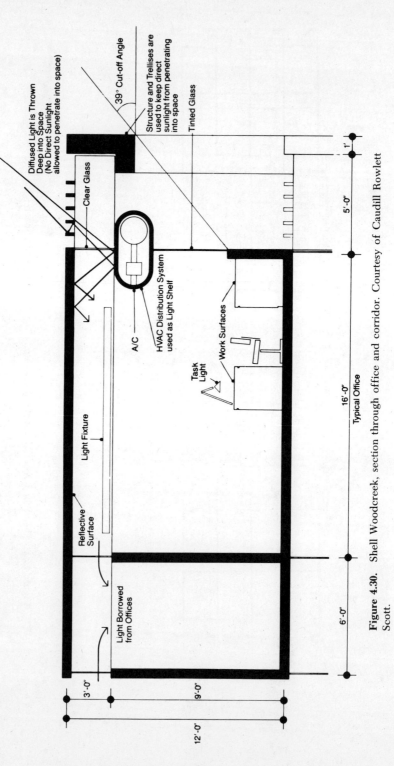

Diffused Light is Thrown Deep into Space (No Direct Sunlight allowed to penetrate into space)

Clear Glass

39° Cut-off Angle

Structure and Trellises are used to keep direct sunlight from penetrating into space

Tinted Glass

A/C

HVAC Distribution System used as Light Shelf

Work Surfaces

Task Light

Light Fixture

Reflective Surface

Light Borrowed from Offices

1'

5'-0"

16'-0"

Typical Office

6'-0"

3'-0"

9'-0"

12'-0"

Figure 4.30. Shell Woodcreek, section through office and corridor. Courtesy of Caudill Rowlett Scott.

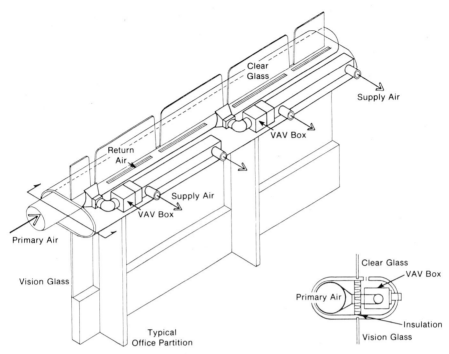

Figure 4.31. Mechanical distribution system isometric. Courtesy of Caudill Rowlett Scott.

the daylight received by the inner offices. The lower atrium offices receive only moderate amounts of daylight, yet enough to serve ambient lighting needs on typical days.

Because creating a pleasant working environment was a primary design goal, the qualitative aspects of daylighting were of great concern to Shell and the design team. To study employee acceptance, and to evaluate the energy-conserving aspects of the daylighting design, a full-scale mock-up of an office module was built at the CRS offices. Outdoor testing under different light conditions and variable orientations demonstrated that for most of the year little or no artificial illumination would be necessary in exterior offices for ambient lighting and for general tasks such as reading. The reaction of Shell employees was also positive. The quality of light in the mock-up was found to be superior to normal office lighting. John Sealey, general manager of corporate real estate for Shell Oil Company, stated, "From a humanistic standpoint this was a bonus, since better lighting made it easier for all our people to work."

The daylighting scheme of Woodcreek is augmented by desk lamps and indirect fluorescent ambient lighting suspended from the exposed ceiling. The artificial lights, as well as the temperature of each individual office, are controlled by the occupant with a wireless electronic device similar to a garage-door opener. Shell wanted individuals to have control over their own environment, with the assumption that such responsibility contributes to the willingness of each person to conserve energy. This strategy is in sharp contrast to the belief of some designers that lighting control should be taken away from people and switched automatically.

Shell Oil Company would not disclose the project construction budget, but it was probably liberal. Added costs for daylighting features and the high-efficiency HVAC system were attributed to amenity and easily absorbed within the original construction budget. As summarized by Sealey, "Our economic staff worked out a formula: every 10,000 Btu per square feet per year we saved would justify an additional cost of $1 per square foot. However, after comparing Woodcreek to comparable buildings constructed at the same time, we are unable to find any measurable cost premiums attributable to the energy-efficient design." Sealey also states that it is a widespread misconception that energy-efficient buildings must be more expensive. Although we share his opinion, we do recognize that starting with a liberal budget greatly enhances the chances of achieving this design goal.

The all-electric systems of Woodcreek are expected to use 33,000 Btu/ft^2 per year. CRS claims that this figure is half that of other energy-efficient office buildings in Houston, and one-third to one-quarter the cost of average construction. Based on these very relative numbers and the economic criteria of the Shell staff, energy-related features at Woodcreek have an investment value of $3–9/ft^2 to Shell Oil Company.

As demonstrated by Woodcreek, climate-adapted buildings can provide new design possibilities beyond the conventional systems they replace or supplement. Construction budgets often lead to a reduction in the size and qualitative aspects of contemporary commercial projects. With the addition of climate-adapted features, however, volume and amenity can be added to a project and be justified both in terms of initial construction costs and energy-related costs. Climate-adapted buildings, as an alternative means to provide environmental control, can directly support the two most prevalent design goals: an appealing, inviting environment and acceptable cost.

Princeton Professional Park

The emphasis in the preceding two case studies was on the basic means, economics, and qualitative aspects of splitting architectural form. The last case study in this section suggests the design possibilities that exist beyond these fundamentals. Princeton Professional Park (PPP), Figures 4.32–4.39, balances and extends nearly all techniques discussed to this point.

Like the Mount Airy Public Library, PPP was supported by the DOE Passive Commercial Buildings Program. The 64,000 ft^2 of leasable office

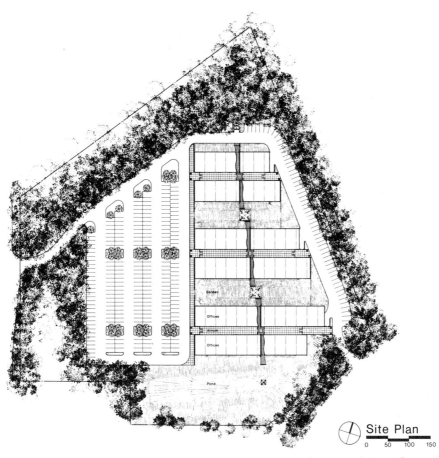

Labels in site plan: Garden, Offices, Atrium, Offices, Pond, Site Plan, 0 50 100 150

Figure 4.32. Princeton Professional Park, site plan. Courtesy of Princeton Energy Group.

Figure 4.33. Princeton Professional Park model. Courtesy of Princeton Energy Group.

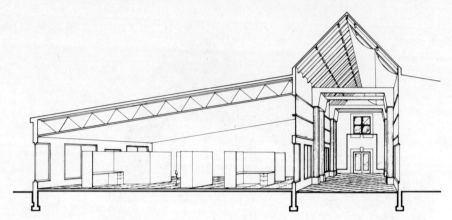

Figure 4.34. Princeton Professional Park, section perspective. Courtesy of Princeton Energy Group.

Figure 4.35. Princeton Professional Park, axonometric. Courtesy of Princeton Energy Group.

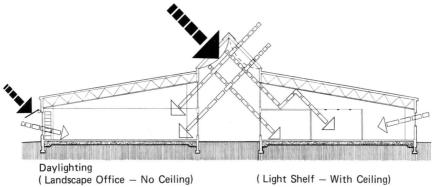

Daylighting
(Landscape Office — No Ceiling)   (Light Shelf — With Ceiling)

Figure 4.36. Princeton Professional Park, daylighting section. Courtesy of Princeton Energy Group.

space in the project is contained in three separate buildings. Because many of the innovations in this project go beyond calculation, monitoring the building will be the only way to judge the potential value accurately. The PPP bridges professional practice and building research.

Analysis of form provides a good starting point for appraising the innovations of PPP. Five major form-related concerns are balanced against each other in a refreshingly simple solution. These concerns are the trade-off between extending and compacting architectural form, the use of plan and form to encourage user acceptance of climate-adapted strategies, the adaptation of internal form to the distribution and circulation of climatic energies within occupied space, the adaptation of form to innovative internal environmental-control systems, and the reduction of structural and envelope cost to permit energy-related investments elsewhere. As separate topics, each of these issues represents challenges of noted complexity; yet PPP integrates all of these concerns into one simple solution.

The external surface-area-to-floor-area ratio of PPP is reduced by using a central circulation atrium in each building. However, 3 one-story buildings are hardly a compact solution. Since density was not a major issue for the project, one- and two-story form alternatives were considered by the design team. The one-story approach was selected to reduce the initial cost of the building shell. The two-story alternative would cost more for ramps or elevators, and would require either noncombustible construction materials or some form of mechanical separation to meet the fire code. Rather than choosing form based on energy-related factors alone, the team balanced extending and compacting form according to cost. This structural cost-balancing exercise is fundamental to the design of all cost-effective energy-responsive commercial buildings.

The areas between the 3 one-story buildings are separated from the street and parking lot by a garden trellis facade punctured with porticoes and

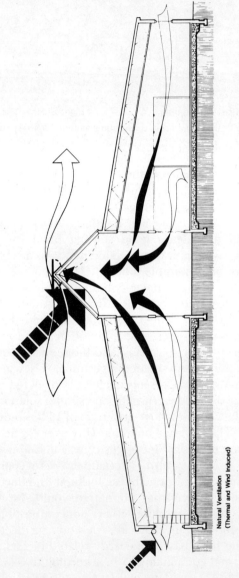

Natural Ventilation
(Thermal and Wind Induced)

Figure 4.37. Princeton Professional Park, natural ventilation section. Courtesy of Princeton Energy Group.

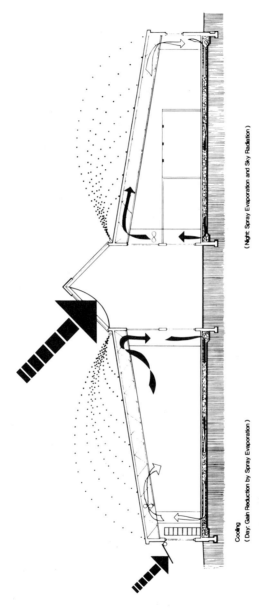

Cooling
(Day: Gain Reduction by Spray Evaporation)   (Night: Spray Evaporation and Sky Radiation)

Figure 4.38. Princeton Professional Park, cooling section. Courtesy of Princeton Energy Group.

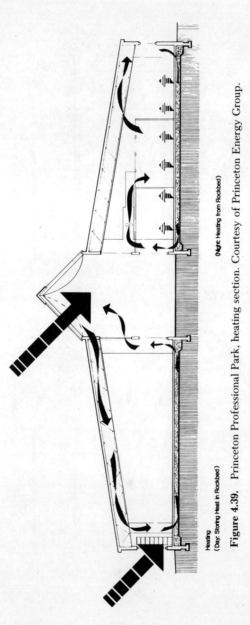

Heating
(Day: Storing Heat in Rockbed)

(Night: Heating from Rockbed)

Figure 4.39. Princeton Professional Park, heating section. Courtesy of Princeton Energy Group.

gates. These gardens provide tenants with an attractive view and encourage the use of strategies such as natural ventilation. Climate analysis by the design team showed that natural ventilation could meet all cooling requirements from April through June and from mid-September through October. By separating the source of ventilation air from the noise and dust of streets and parking lots, the design team increased the likelihood of tenant acceptance of this simple yet highly beneficial energy-related alternative.

The one-story form alternative also permits greater flexibility in directing and distributing light, air, and heat within the building. Each building joins two 45-ft-deep office sections to a central atrium. The atrium serves as a buffer zone, a source of daylight, and a control device to expel, recirculate, or store excess heat. A continuous ridge vent along the top of the triangular atrium glazing permits expulsion of warm air when necessary. Since this vent is at the highest point in the structure, a stack effect aids natural ventilation and pulls air from the offices into the atrium.

In the winter, excess warm air in the atrium can be recirculated to occupied space or drawn down into rock beds beneath the office floor. These inexpensive horizontal rock beds are charged by a finger-type air manifold that permits better distribution of heat across the entire slab. The excess heat radiates through the office floors at night and maintains the nighttime setback temperatures in these spaces.

Internal form is likewise central to the effective distribution of daylight to occupied space. The atrium serves as the primary daytime source of light to the first row of offices adjacent to that space. Motorized thermal curtains control the admittance of solar light and heat in the atrium according to need. Window-related strategies are used to daylight the first row of offices along the exterior perimeter of the building. These two strategies leave a 15-ft strip down the center of each wing that still requires access to daylight.

As illustrated in Figure 4.36, two daylighting alternatives are available for this central zone. Both depend on the slope of the roof that rises toward the atrium. The first alternative assumes the tenant will opt for full-height office partitions and a suspended ceiling. In this case, reflective materials between the suspended ceiling and upper sloped roof act to bounce atrium light into the cavity. This light penetrates the suspended ceiling through translucent prismatic panels placed over the central office zone.

The second alternative assumes the tenant will use an open office plan. In this case the central offices are illuminated through high clerestory windows placed adjacent to the atrium. Both of these central zone daylighting strategies would be impossible on the lower floor of the more compact two-story building form. Compacting and extending form must be balanced according to both offensive and defensive environmental-control opportunities. In this solution, form anticipates system-related opportunities and vice versa.

We find the use of form in the PPP project unique because it is also adapted to innovative internal environmental-control systems. Although the internal cooling system of this project is not a direct application of climatic energies to occupied space, form is central to the system. During the hot and humid summer months, two cooling strategies are used. The first strategy is a roof spray system. At about 15-min intervals, water is sprayed evenly over the metal roof. An intermittent spray permits complete evaporation. Peak exterior surface temperatures can be lowered below 100°F with this system. According to the design team, this option nearly pays for itself by reducing the peak cooling capacity required of the conventional back-up systems.

The metal roof and spray system also provide a means to purge heat from the rock beds during summer nights. Evaporative and night sky radiant cooling can reduce the temperature of the metal roof to about 60°F. A plenum created between the/metal roof and the insulated lower panels connected to the lower cord of the wooden roof joists permits the circulation of air past this cool surface. If the system works as predicted, the rock bed can be cooled to approximately 65°F, making the office floors a daytime internal heat sink. When the building is closed during hot and humid weather, return air from the offices can circulate through the rock bed for precooling. If required, the precooled air can be further conditioned by standard heat pump packages placed in each 1000-ft^2 office module. The only added expense of this system is the airtight sealing of the plenum boundaries. This heat-rejection technique and natural ventilation are estimated to reduce the PPP cooling energy needed by 90%.

Larry Lindsey of The Princeton Energy Group, the energy consultants to the project, states, "This design asserts that radiant and evaporative heat rejection from building surfaces can be more effective, even in not-so-promising climates, than current building practice implies. The bases of this assertion are primarily theoretical, and their verification or modification by empirical feedback is a major opportunity offered by the PPP project." We agree, and suspend evaluation of the system in a relatively humid climate until DOE-supported monitored data are available. Yet, it is not this individual cooling strategy that is significant but rather the integral use of form for both direct climate adaptation and new internal systems. The PPP project indicates new possibilities for internal systems as form is changed to respond to climate. That new forms can lead to new internal system innovations suggests that we have only begun to understand the range of solutions that are possible by adapting form to climate.

Besides reducing the cost of construction by selecting the one-story form, the design team also reduced initial cost in design development by standardizing construction components. All roof joists are identical. The envelope is constructed of two modular sections: one for atrium walls and one for exterior walls. According to architect Harrison Fraker, AIA, "All the wood framing components were constructed in assembly line fashion at a nearby lumber yard and trucked to the site. Each building was enclosed in only four days: two days to place all walls and two days to erect and enclose the roof." Simplicity and reduced construction time lowered the initial cost of the building shell.

In addition to integrating many diverse design concerns into one simple architectural form, PPP also innovatively addresses very restrictive economic criteria. The owners, Princeton Professional Park, A Limited Partnership, are a group of local investors with experience in small office park projects. The last project by the group was built for $37/ft^2 (1980 dollars). The owners stipulated that any cost above this base budget must produce a large return.

The stipulated base construction budget for PPP represented the lowest cost for office developments in the area. However, economic advantages were uncovered by the design team by appraising the energy needs of the owners' previous project. The utility cost of that project, paid by the owners, is $2.07/ft^2 per year. The primary incentive offered the owner for exceeding $37/ft^2 was the reduction of utility expenses in exchange for higher mortgage payments. Beyond this exchange, three additional motives or incentives were acceptable to the owners. First, much of the added construction cost would be attributed to energy-related equipment that qualifies for 5-year accelerated tax depreciation. Second, each lease would have an allowance for utility cost 30–50¢/ft^2 per year higher than predicted performance. If the project performs as estimated, this would be a profit to the owner. If a tenant's utility cost exceeds the allowance, there would be no liability to the owner as the tenant would pay the extra cost as a penalty. This arrangement at first seems one-sided. However, the tenant does benefit since the utility allowance is about half that required in leases for comparable properties in the area. This lease arrangement also motivates both parties to conserve energy. The owner is motivated to repair and maintain equipment to insure the highest return on the energy-related investments. Tenants are motivated to conserve energy in order to stay within the allowance and avoid added penalties.

The third owner incentive to exceeding rock-bottom construction cost is financing. Substantial reductions in utility-related operating cost were perceived as an advantage by the owners in gaining permanent financing. Also, the attractiveness of the design adds value to the project and provides a marketing advantage that will keep vacancies low.

The final construction cost of PPP is expected to be $53/ft^2 of leasable office space. In 1980 dollars, this is about $44.5, or $7.5 over the base target. Although PPP costs more to build than a nonenergy-conserving structure, depending on actual performance, it may cost less from the outset to own. The owners accepted the energy-related cost increases of this building because these expenses represent a superior investment. This poses a very interesting question: is it more important to reduce construction cost or to reduce the risk and cost of acquiring and owning a building? In this case, initial construction costs are higher yet the building can be appraised as a superior investment. At this point in time, there is limited correlation between initial construction cost and cost of ownership or the rate of return. Financial criteria for a project will directly influence design criteria and the potentials to limit the use of nonrenewable energy. How to convert and appraise incremental energy-related costs to cost of building ownership is shown in Chapters Six and Eight.

PPP is a prime example of a climate-adapted building. It integrates a host of complex energy-related challenges in one simple solution. In addition, it suggests future possibilities in the integration of external and internal environmental-control systems, building ownership and use, and architecture.

NEW FORMS

A large enclosed structure . . . comes closest to allowing the use of natural sources for maintaining the environment. Utilization of solar energy through the roof as a heating medium and use of the earth as a stabilizing heat sink can create conditions within the space which minimize the extremes of nature and provide minimum fluctuations.

MEGASTRUCTURE: A NEW CONCEPT OF FEDERAL OFFICE BUILDING DESIGN FOR THE GSA, 1975

In some ways, the case studies presented in this chapter can be perceived as modifications to a conventional climate-rejecting building. It is common to explore the new as an extension of the existing. The transitional process associated with an innovation is often more central to the adoption of that innovation than the product itself. Designers learn of the new—what it is and how it can be used—by associating it with the known. For this reason, we have employed descriptive terms such as puncturing envelope and extending or splitting form. These terms express both the modification of the climate-rejecting building and a description of the basic nature of specific contemporary climate-adapted buildings.

Although this chapter reviews a host of design innovations, we feel that designers and architects have only begun to realize the wide range of possible solutions in the design of energy-responsive commercial buildings. Distinguishing the past from the future seems to be central to uncovering these additional possibilities. How far will the solutions of the near future diverge from the conventions of today? Although predicting the future is a difficult exercise, nearly all the case studies in this chapter are stretching the conventional to new limits in an attempt to simultaneously solve a great many interconnected contemporary design challenges.

GSA Building

The last case study of this chapter is not easily defined as a modification to a climate-rejecting building because it breaks many design and construction conventions. The purpose of presenting this case study is twofold. First, the example represents how the principles of climate-adapted buildings can be used to generate totally new solutions to the design of envelope and form. We define new forms as reinventions that are not easily described as modifications to the existing. The second purpose of this case study is to summarize the design principles of climate-adapted buildings as applied in a bold and contemporary way.

In 1975, the General Services Administration (GSA) commissioned Building Sciences, Inc. (now Parsons and Bankhedges of Baltimore, Maryland) to lead a team of experts to investigate new design concepts to the construction of federal office space. The objective was to design a pleasant working environment that provided economy in construction, operation, and maintenance and allowed substantial energy conservation over existing GSA-managed facilities. The concept was also to allow economical, short-term, space-planning modifications and long-term, low-cost, building expansion capabilities.

As a basis for design, the team was asked to use an existing GSA building program for a 350,000-ft^2 office facility to be located on a site in suburban Denver, Colorado. An additional programmatic requirement was that the building would expand to 500,000 ft^2 10 years after the initial construction phase. This program provided a degree of realism to the theoretical study. Yet, the GSA specifically requested that the concept derived by the team be amenable to other building sizes and climates.

The proposed solution to this problem is shown in Figures 4.40–4.43. It is a building within a building and three major elements dominate the design. The first is a large, all-encasing outer envelope. The second is the highly differentiated and extended inner envelopes that contain the office space. The third is the buffer space formed between the two envelopes. This double-envelope approach establishes two unique environmental-control zones within the building. The outer envelope is designed to filter and balance climatic exposures to produce a relatively benign environment within the buffer zone. The inner envelopes are extended climate-adapted building forms. Since the outer envelope establishes a very favorable luminous and thermal environment for the inner envelopes, the inner envelopes can have a very large surface-area-to-office-floor-area ratio. The outer envelope is just the reverse, having a very low surface-area-to-floor-area ratio. Joining these two forms to make environments in series represents a very innovative approach to the application of the principles of climate-adapted buildings.

The outer envelope of the GSA building is capped by a three-layer

Figure 4.40. GSA Building, model. Courtesy of Parsons and Bankhedges.

Figure 4.41. GSA Building, model. Courtesy of Parsons and Bankhedges.

Figure 4.42.   GSA Building, model. Courtesy of Parsons and Bankhedges.

pneumatic clear span roof. Under the roof area, the site is cut down approximately one story. Removed earth is pushed to the perimeter to form earth-bermed outer walls and the roof is stretched across the building with steel cables anchored into the berms with concrete deadmen.

The major innovation of the pneumatic solar roof is its ability to control the amount of solar light and heat that is admitted. The roof is divided into cells. The upper and middle membrane of each cell is divided equally between translucent material and reflective material (Fig. 4.43). The reflective portions of the membrane can be jointed or separated by pressurizing or evacuating air in the cell to control the amount of solar radiation admitted to the internal buffer. About 85% of the heating needs of the building are offset by direct solar heat gain. The reflective portions of the roof cells, in the closed position, are not totally opaque and permit 10% of incident solar radiation to enter the buffer zone. Therefore, on a clear day when heating is not required, 300 foot candles of daylight will reach the lower floor of the buffer zone with the cells in the closed position. The result is year-round availability of daylight in accordance with the climatic circumstances and thermal comfort needs of occupants.

The outer envelope of this design, termed the "sky" by the design team, expands the concept of an atrium from an intermediate or infill environmental-control device to a total building enclosure. As described earlier, an atrium is an alternative to extending form for connecting a greater proportion of occupied space to climate. The advantages are a decrease in the area of envelope exposed to the extremes of climate and the addition of building

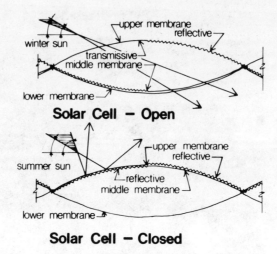

Figure 4.43.   Pneumatic roof with solar cells. Courtesy of Parsons and Bankhedges.

volume that is both an inward-focusing space and a defensive and/or offensive environmental-control device. The GSA design capitalizes on these advantages by encircling the building with the atrium. Since the concept is used on a grander scale, the benefits derived are likewise proportionately higher. A bubblelike shape encloses a large volume within a small area of exterior skin. The ratio of outer envelope area to office space floor area is only 0.55 for this building, comparable to that of the mid-rise conventional building used for comparative purposes by the GSA. This case study is a prime example of a building that uses significant climate adaptations within a building shell which is comparable in outer surface area to the climate-rejecting envelope it replaces. Once again, a major principle of climate-adapted buildings is that volume may be added to a building in order to connect occupied space to climate while at the same time limiting the surface area left vulnerable to the extremes of climate.

The open areas under the canopy are landscaped in a parklike setting and include small gardens, walkways, and exhibit space. Small clusters of inner buildings are dedicated to separate government agencies and are arranged around a central pedestrian mall. The mall serves as a public street and facilitates visitor and interagency circulation. In effect, each agency becomes a "shop on Main Street," a design feature that encourages public contact.

Environmental conditions within the buffer zone are balanced by varying many interconnected features. The admittance of solar radiation is controlled at the roof. The large expanse of exposed earth in this scheme is a useful heat sink for excess solar radiation and internally generated heat. The vertical height between earth and roof permits the collection of heat toward the top where it can be expelled or recycled according to need. The high thermal capacitance of the earth and the exposed concrete structure of the inner envelopes dampen buffer zone temperature variations. The designers estimate a very modest 7°F day-to-night temperature swing in the winter within the buffer zone because of these elements. This thermal mass also permits night air flushing when appropriate to precool these surfaces for use as a daytime heat sink. Precooling the buffer zone rather than the inner offices directly yields the same thermal advantages, yet avoids potential problems such as dust collection on work surfaces and equipment. Lastly, the extensive landscaping within the open area permits evaporative cooling, a very useful strategy in semiarid climates such as Denver. Collectively, the selective control of these features permits a high degree of comfort that is responsive to a great many combinations of external conditions and internal needs.

As in the Bateson Building, energy is conserved via buffer zone by assigning support and amenity functions that allow greater deadband comfort design conditions to the less precisely controlled atrium. The expanse of volume in this design beyond specific programmatic needs is not a major energy-related liability since it is conditioned primarily by locally available renewable energy sources. Climate-adapted buildings can often justify an increase in building volume in the pursuit of overall project cost reductions.

The inner envelopes are designed as long, extended forms, much as in the Mount Airy Public Library. Based on a 30-by-30-ft bay, these structures are liberally punctured to permit access to buffer zone light and air. Natural light penetrates to all levels of the three- and four-story inner buildings through light-wells and strategically placed step-backs and reentrants. The inner buildings are totally separate from the outer structure, permitting sufficient area for the addition of 150,000 ft² of office space.

Since these buildings are contained within a weather-tight environment, interior construction materials can be used. The column-free buffer zone allows office space to be vertically and horizontally distributed freely according to functional requirements and need for climate adaptation. Since the buffer zone is a total environment, light and air can be accessible to work areas from any direction rather than just one or two as in previous case studies.

The GSA building may be a unique architectural form, yet the forms of the inner buildings are a direct extension of previous form principles used in climate-adapted buildings. To use climatic energies, past conventional building forms had to be extended or split into elements of smaller depth. The inner forms of the GSA building shatter the conventional office building box into a myriad of pieces. This alternative is only reasonable in the mildest of climates or, as in this case, where climate is neutralized by design.

Conventional lighting and HVAC back-up systems are provided within the innermost environments to ensure year-round visual and thermal comfort. This equipment should be used infrequently and requires only modest capacity since climate balancing will offset all but the greatest climatic extremes.

In 1975, the GSA prototype was estimated to cost $22.3 million. A comparable six-story conventional office block was estimated to cost $21.5 million. This 4% initial cost liability is partially due to the fact that the prototype was designed to accept the future 150,000-ft² expansion within the initial outer envelope. To add the same amount of space to the control building, three additional stories would need to be added at a cost of $13.8 million. The infill addition to the prototype would only cost $3.3 million. These construction cost savings, added to the dollars saved in energy costs, amount to a projected 30-year total savings of $36.2 million for the prototype: a total greater than the entire construction cost of both phases of the project.

The innovative application of the basic design principles of climate-adapted buildings in the GSA study building make it a thought-provoking case study. We are not suggesting that future buildings need exhibit these same innovations. After all, we are not even certain that suburban office parks will be a part of our future. Yet, of the innovative new form solutions we have reviewed, this study is not only the boldest, but also the 'clearest expression of the elements of climate-adapted design in an unconventional form. Form, envelope, structure, volume, cost, and building use may be distinctly different between a climate-rejecting and a climate-adapted building, yet the potential for new and effective solutions appears to be the exciting reward for challenging the conventions of today.

CONCLUSION TO THE RANGE OF POSSIBLE SOLUTIONS

As extremes in the range of possible solutions, the climate-rejecting building and the climate-adapted building represent two distinctive choices to providing environmental control in commercial buildings. The climate-rejecting building has particular form, envelope, and equipment design objectives. The climate-adapted building uses these elements in a contradictory way. The climate-rejecting building emerged in the 1950s and changed the major need of environmental control in commercial buildings from counteracting the extremes of climate to offsetting self-imposed internal loads. Contemporary climate-adapted buildings reverse that trend from being internally load dominated back to being envelope or climate dominated.

Deciding which type of environmental control is to be provided is a key choice in the design of energy-responsive commercial buildings. A host of second order choices are established by this choice. More often than not, the best solution mixes elements of both solution types. However, successfully combining elements of both into one design demands that the advantages and disadvantages of each be understood.

To the best of our knowledge, there is no decisive energy-related advantage to either solution type. Beyond personal choice, the only major difference between the two solution types that can influence selection is the issue of density. The tighter one must pack people, the less opportunity one has to extend form, surface area, and volume.

Perhaps the most significant factor in successful solutions of both types is the integration of energy-related issues with other design concerns. The best energy-related goal of a project is the derivation of architecture appropriate for the 1980s rather than the design of energy-responsive buildings. Intent, motive, and advantage are the keys; structure, materials, and components are only a helpful list of some of the means. Resolution is achieved when energy issues are absorbed into architecture. Reinvention is the state of the art in the design of energy-responsive commercial buildings.

chapter five

THE RANGE OF POSSIBLE DESIGN APPROACHES

There cannot be an elegant solution to a misstated problem.

RICHARD RITTELMANN, AIA

The first three chapters of Part One highlight the key principles associated with unique energy-responsive commercial building solution types. The major issue not addressed to this point is how to determine needs and isolate alternatives most appropriate to a specific project. This chapter covers the major energy-related design approaches used by the buildings industry on a conceptual level and focuses on key issues associated with the success of any energy-related design approach or process.

We define a successful energy-responsive design as any solution that meets the intended energy-use goal and design intent of the project without ignoring simpler, less expensive or energy-intensive means to achieve the same end. The difference between success and failure is not usually a technical problem: the most common failure we have observed stems from an earnest attempt to meet misperceived energy-related needs. From the many case studies we reviewed to prepare this book, we feel that the way a designer first perceives the problem to be solved controls nearly all solutions. This first perception sets the design process, guides design decisions, and serves as the basis for the justification of the final design. If this first perception is awry, so is the solution. Understanding energy use in a contemporary commercial building is a prerequisite to finding appropriate alternatives.

During a 1981 AIA National Convention workshop, we tested 250 architects and engineers on their intuitive understanding of the energy needs of a conventional commercial building. Each participant was given a data sheet describing a one-story office building in Pittsburgh, Pennsylvania. The data sheet defined the lighting and HVAC systems; building size, shape, and orientation; glass type; insulation thickness; infiltration rate; number of occupants; schedule of use; and the local utility rate structure. In a questionnaire on the back of the data sheet each participant was asked to estimate the building's total annual energy use, peak demand, and cost, as well as the annual energy use, peak demand, and cost of specific end-use systems such as heating, cooling, lighting, and hot water.

The building used in the survey had a total annual energy cost of 60¢/ft^2 of floor area. The majority of respondents estimated the cost to be twice that figure. Only 8% of the responses put the annual cost in the range of 40–80¢/ft^2.

The controlling energy need for the sample building was lighting: 56% of annual cost was for lighting, 22% for heating, and 17% for cooling. Heating dominated the estimates of the respondents as the major energy need of the building: 36% identified heating as the biggest energy-related cost need, 30% selected lighting, and 29% identified cooling. The questions on the questionnaire elicited a puzzling mix of answers. Neither a clear perception nor a common misconception of the energy needs of this building was revealed from the questionnaires. Plotting the answers gave a random pattern, much like firing a shotgun at graph paper.

Had the same group been asked to estimate the depth of a structural member in one of the base building's 25-by-25-ft structural bays, we are quite certain that the answers would have been spread closely around true member depth. Architects and engineers do not yet have the intuitive sense or experience about energy use in commercial buildings that they have for other elements of design. For this reason, we believe that when designers rely on intuition to appraise the energy needs of a given project, the odds are very high that they will fail. Until experience and knowledge is gained in this area, a clear process or method must be used to identify energy-related problem-solving issues.

In this chapter two major topics are addressed. In the first section, case studies are covered to illustrate the conceptual differences of two energy-related design approaches. These conceptual differences are important to understand since the design approach used for a project will directly influence the solution that is found. The last half of the chapter focuses on the use of numbers in energy-related design approaches. Specifically, the unit of measure selected to appraise energy-related numbers will also alter the perception of the problem that is to be solved for a given project.

INCREMENTAL CHANGE DESIGN APPROACHES

Energy-related design methods, like solutions, can be split into two categories: incremental change methods and nonincremental change methods. The primary difference between the two is the degree of change from the conventional. Incremental change methods begin with a conventional building that is appraised and modified. This method identifies how, when, where, and why energy is used in a specific design and indicates where specific improvements can be most beneficial to that building. Nonincremental change methods explore new means to provide environmental control. These means are seldom simple extensions of the conventional, so merely studying the energy-use patterns of an existing building is of limited value. The intent is to find new means to avoid the energy problems of a conventional commercial building rather than to fix or solve those problems directly.

In this section, two case studies demonstrate the advantages and disadvantages of incremental change design approaches. The first building is from the AIA/Research Corporation report *Life Cycle Cost Study of Commercial Buildings.*[*] The second example is from a DOE-funded report undertaken by The Ehrenkrantz Group of New York entitled *Cost Benefit Analysis of Passive Solar Design Alternatives: New Office Building/ Temperate Climate.*

The simplest way to identify energy-related improvements is to first design a building, appraise the energy-use patterns of that design, and then evaluate the benefit of component or system options that can improve the base design. These options can be evaluated individually or in combination. Value is derived by comparing the before and after energy performance and economic influence of each alternative. The most effective options can then be selected and incorporated into the final design.

Such an approach is exemplified in the AIA/RC report *Life Cycle Cost Study of Commercial Buildings*. This report was funded by DOE as a portion of the work related to the proposed Building Energy Performance Standards (BEPS). The purpose of the report was to identify the minimum yearly energy needs and minimum life-cycle cost of three incrementally improved commercial buildings, and to determine if a predictable relationship exists between these two variables. (No such relationship was found.) One of these three buildings, a 100,000 ft² office building in Denver, Colorado, is a good example of the incremental change design approach.

The Denver Building study began by appraising the energy-use patterns

---

[*]AIA Research Corporation (with Hanscomb Associates, Inc. and Syska & Hennessy Engineers, Inc.). December 1979. "Energy Performance Standards for New Buildings." *Life Cycle Cost Study of Commercial Buildings*. Draft Final Report. Prepared for U.S. Department of Energy, Office of Conservation and Solar Energy and Office of Buildings and Community Systems.

of an actual building that was designed and constructed in 1977. The AIA supported the original design team of Brooks Waldman Associates and engineers Beckett, Harman, Carrier & Day, Inc., in performing two studies. The first study was a redesign of the original building to maximize energy efficiency within the original owners' program, site, and cost constraints. The second study had the same objective, yet first costs were permitted to increase according to best life-cycle cost advantage.

The procedure used in these studies reflects how most architectural and engineering firms first introduce energy-related considerations into the design process. The first step is to study either the proposed design or a similar building. In the Denver Building study case, the original building was used (Fig. 5.1–5.6). Some form of energy analysis is performed to isolate the amounts of energy used by each subsystem and to establish a total building base energy-use figure for later comparisons. The energy needs of the original Denver Building were generated with the computer code AXCESS and are shown in Table 5.1 (DEO1). The next step is to make a list of possible beneficial options. By reappraising the energy performance

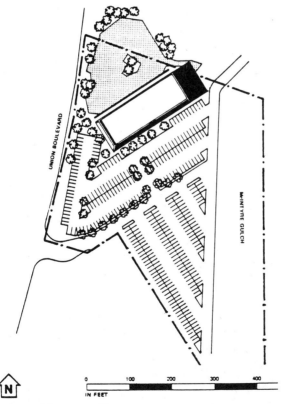

Figure 5.1. Original Denver Building, site plan. Courtesy of AIA/Research Corp.

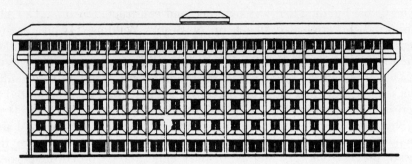

Figure 5.2. Original Denver Building, elevation. Courtesy of AIA/Research Corp.

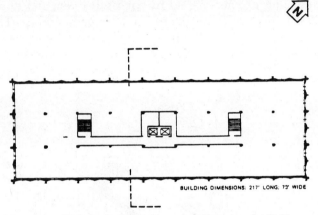

BUILDING DIMENSIONS: 217' LONG; 73' WIDE

Figure 5.3. Original Denver Building, floor plan. Courtesy of AIA/Research Corp.

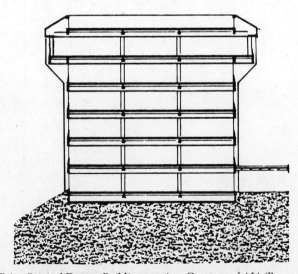

Figure 5.4. Original Denver Building, section. Courtesy of AIA/Research Corp.

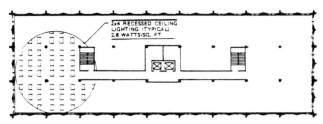

Figure 5.5. Original Denver Building, lighting layout. Courtesy of AIA/Research Corp.

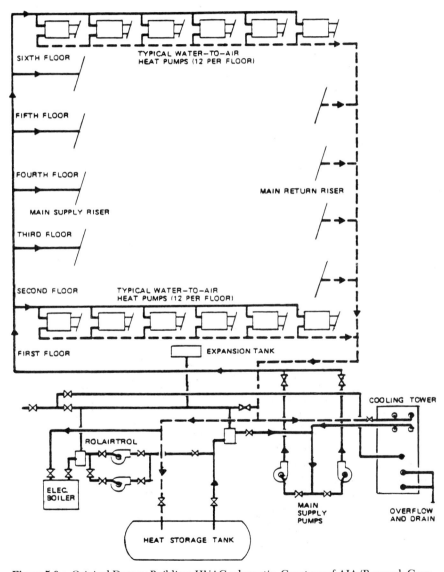

Figure 5.6. Original Denver Building, HVAC schematic. Courtesy of AIA/Research Corp.

TABLE 5.1. AIA/RC STUDY—COMPARISON OF DESIGN ENERGY
PERFORMANCE, DESIGN ENERGY CONSUMPTION, AND
DESIGN ENERGY BUDGET FOR THE DENVER OFFICE BUILDING

	DEP[a]	DEC[b]	DEB[c]
DE01 original building			
Electric	49.4	152.2	109
Natural gas	53.4	137.0	109
DE25 redesign of DE01			
(with corrected data)			
Electric	26.5	81.6	109
Natural gas	29.0	72.0	109
DE30 redesign (DE25) plus			
3 zone daylighting			
Electric	24.5	75.5	109
Natural gas	27.2	65.2	109
DE54 redesign (DE25) plus			
dimming daylighting			
(DE31), deadband thermostat			
(DE40), and hot			
water storage (DE45)			
Electric	20.4	62.7	109
Natural gas	22.4	54.7	109

[a]Design Energy Performance in thousands of Btu/gross ft^2·yr measured at the building line.

[b]Design Energy Consumption with weighting factors to reflect cost differences in energy sources.

[c]Design Energy Budget from NOPR, November 1979 (proposed BEPS).
"Electric" stands for an all-electric building.
"Natural gas" stands for natural gas for DHW and space heating; the rest of the building is electric.

NOTE: Natural gas efficiencies of the appliances were determined by the design teams and differed for each building. The efficiency used for the Denver Building was 70%.

of the building with each option, a designer can then determine if energy-use reductions are derived within the economic criteria of the project.

The first Denver Building exercise, called the Redesign Building, assessed numerous conservation and alternative energy options. Since economic motives did not change, the appropriate options were those that used existing elements of design to best advantage. As shown in Figures 5.7–5.11, the team modified the facade to permit solar shading, switched to a more efficient task-ambient lighting system, and selected a central HVAC system with off-peak storage that is more effective in this particular design. The energy-conserving potential of sound professional practice is well-demonstrated in this study: the Denver Redesign Building (DE25) cuts in half the total annual number of Btu used at the site.

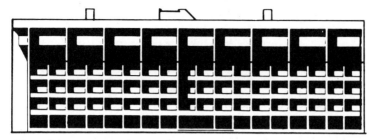

Figure 5.7. Denver Redesign, elevation. Courtesy of AIA/Research Corp.

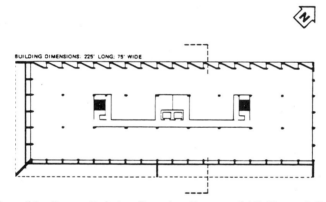

Figure 5.8. Denver Redesign, floor plan. Courtesy of AIA/Research Corp.

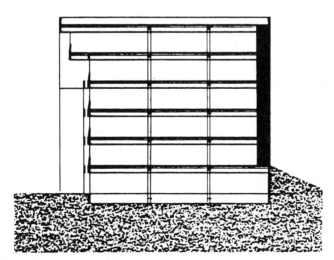

Figure 5.9. Denver Redesign, section. Courtesy of AIA/Research Corp.

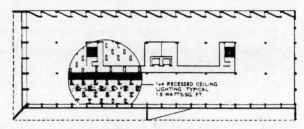

Figure 5.10.   Denver Redesign, lighting layout. Courtesy of AIA/Research Corp.

From the performance data listed in the report, it is difficult to evaluate separately the specific value or contribution of each of the above alterations. However, additional information supplied by authors Joe Derringer and Lehry Mehta indicates that 65% of the total energy reduction is attributed to the lighting system (this includes a reduction in cooling energy). Less than 10% of total energy-use reduction is attributed to the envelope modification, with the remaining 25% being a result of the HVAC system redesign.

The Redesign Building (DE25) was used by the team as a new base building in the second part of the study. The intent was to see how efficient the building could be made if the economic criteria were altered from a first cost concern to one of life-cycle cost. Once again, a great many alternatives were assessed. Even though initial costs were permitted to rise, the law of diminishing returns prevented the use of expensive options. As the energy needs of a commercial building are incrementally improved, fewer Btu remain to be saved, and the less cost-effective expensive energy-related alternatives become. The three options that appeared attractive were deadband thermostats, perimeter daylighting with automatic dimming controls for the electric lighting system, and additional hot water storage that recovers heat from the refrigeration cycle. As shown in Table 5.1, these additional strategies (DE30) reduced total energy needs by 20% from the Redesign Building base level.

The AIA study is extremely valuable because of the many alternatives tried and documented. Although the objective in the incremental change design approach is to isolate the feasible alternatives, important insights can be gained into the energy needs of commercial buildings by examining the options that failed. For instance, the four alternatives presented in Table 5.2 are all related to insulating the envelope. The energy savings derived from these options is negligible. A close look at such options reveals that they do not address the major causes of energy use, which lie elsewhere. At first, incremental change methods isolate useful options through the process of elimination. Once an architect or engineer gains experience in such a technique, the effectiveness of various alternatives becomes more apparent, requiring fewer runs and deadends. Incremental change methods are

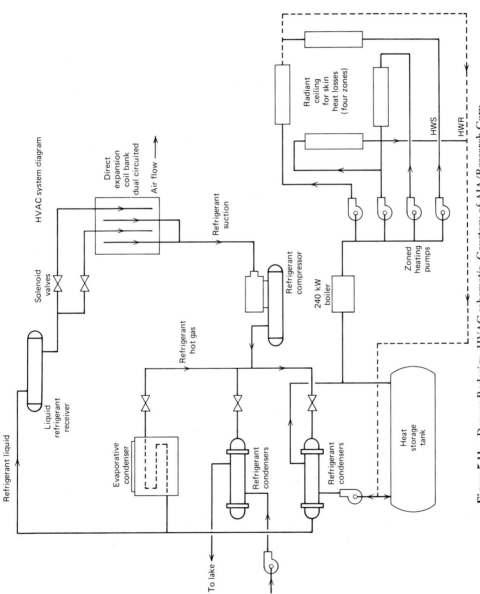

Figure 5.11. Denver Redesign, HVAC schematic. Courtesy of AIA/Research Corp.

TABLE 5.2. AIA/RC STUDY—DENVER BUILDING REDESIGN ENVELOPE EXPERIMENTS

Design Strategy Description	Area (ft²)	Heating and Cooling[a]	HVAC (Aux.)[a]	HVAC (Aux.)[a]	Lighting[a]	Domestic Hot Water[a]	Other[b]	Total[a]	Percentage of Base
DE35 redesign (DE25) plus increased roof insulation	102,990	7,182	756	1,296	14,790	1,397	987	26,408	(100)
DE36 redesign (DE25) plus doubled wall insulation	102,990	7,258	756	1,313	14,790	1,397	957	26,471	(100)
DE37 redesign (DE25) doubled wall insulation (DE36) moved to the exterior wall surface	102,990	6,903	761	1,336	14,790	1,397	970	26,157	(99)
DE38 redesign (DE25) plus insulating drapes	102,990	7,287	753	1,321	14,790	1,397	957	26,505	(100)

[a] In Btu/gross ft²·yr.

[b] In Btu/gross ft²·yr; includes elevators, escalators, general exhaust fans, etc.

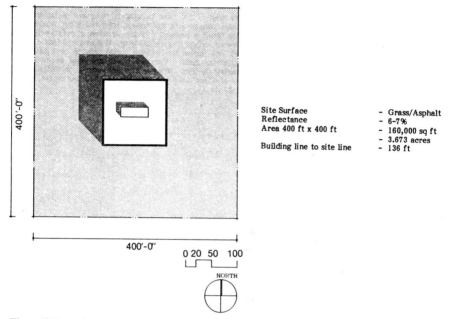

Site Surface   − Grass/Asphalt
Reflectance   − 6-7%
Area 400 ft x 400 ft   − 160,000 sq ft
                                    − 3.673 acres
Building line to site line   − 136 ft

400'-0"

0 20 50 100

NORTH

Figure 5.12.   Ehrenkrantz study, site plan. Courtesy of the Ehrenkrantz Group of New York.

generally only necessary as part of a learning process or for demonstrating to a client the comparative value of specific energy-related options.

Regrettably, strategies such as electric-demand limiters and passive solar thermal techniques were not included in the AIA study since the AXCESS computer program could not model, these options. In contrast, the Ehrenkrantz study illustrates how the incremental change approach can assess climatic adaptations to a conventional building. The purpose of this study was to isolate the benefits of passive technologies applied to a conventional office building. As in the AIA study, the report on the study begins by defining a base building (Fig. 5.12–5.18). The systems, form, and

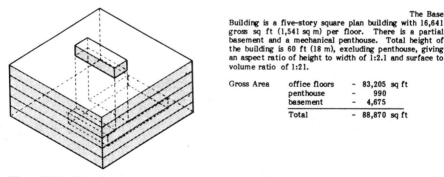

The Base

Building is a five-story square plan building with 16,641 gross sq ft (1,541 sq m) per floor. There is a partial basement and a mechanical penthouse. Total height of the building is 60 ft (18 m), excluding penthouse, giving an aspect ratio of height to width of 1:2.1 and surface to volume ratio of 1:21.

Gross Area   office floors   − 83,205 sq ft
               penthouse   −   990
               basement   − 4,675

               Total   − 88,870 sq ft

Figure 5.13.   Ehrenkrantz study, isometric. Courtesy of the Ehrenkrantz Group of New York.

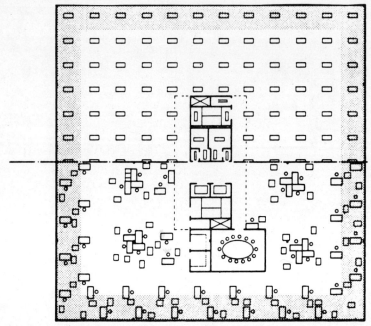

Figure 5.14.   Ehrenkrantz study, floor plan. Courtesy of the Ehrenkrantz Group of New York.

envelope were selected to represent an energy-conserving building in a
New York climate. The energy needs and construction cost of this base
building were then determined as presented in Tables 5.3 and 5.4. All costs
are per net square foot. Energy needs are expressed in Btu at the building
site per energy type, and in dollars per on-site energy cost. A list of options
to be tried on the building was also developed as shown in Table 5.5. Each

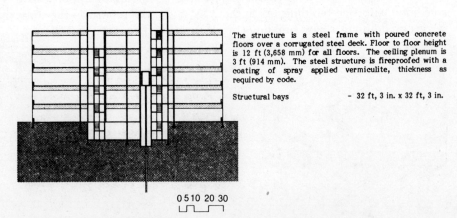

The structure is a steel frame with poured concrete
floors over a corrugated steel deck. Floor to floor height
is 12 ft (3,658 mm) for all floors. The ceiling plenum is
3 ft (914 mm). The steel structure is fireproofed with a
coating of spray applied vermiculite, thickness as
required by code.

Structural bays   – 32 ft, 3 in. x 32 ft, 3 in.

0 5 10 20 30

Figure 5.15.   Ehrenkrantz study, section. Courtesy of the Ehrenkrantz Group of New York.

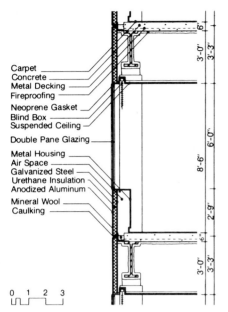

Carpet
Concrete
Metal Decking
Fireproofing
Neoprene Gasket
Blind Box
Suspended Ceiling

Double Pane Glazing

Metal Housing
Air Space
Galvanized Steel
Urethane Insulation
Anodized Aluminum

Mineral Wool
Caulking

The wall of the base building is composed of insulated metal panels with continuous insulated glass windows. This "skin" is connected to the structure at points only to prevent excess thermal bridging. It is assumed that a fan coil unit under the window would provide heat to the perimeter zone. Venetian blinds are used as interior shading devices. Window lites are secured to the panels by resilient neoprene gaskets at their perimeter and mullions.

Figure 5.16. Ehrenkrantz study, wall section. Courtesy of the Ehrenkrantz Group of New York.

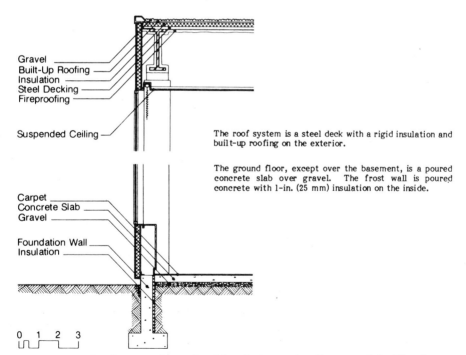

Gravel
Built-Up Roofing
Insulation
Steel Decking
Fireproofing

Suspended Ceiling

The roof system is a steel deck with a rigid insulation and built-up roofing on the exterior.

The ground floor, except over the basement, is a poured concrete slab over gravel. The frost wall is poured concrete with 1-in. (25 mm) insulation on the inside.

Carpet
Concrete Slab
Gravel

Foundation Wall
Insulation

Figure 5.17. Ehrenkrantz study, roof and foundation section. Courtesy of the Ehrenkrantz Group of New York.

153

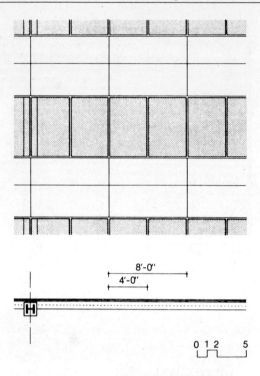

The wall panel system is expressed on the elevation as
continuous wall and window bands around the building.
Panels of clear anodized aluminum have a reflective
metallic surface. Windows are clear insulating glass and
are joined with neoprene gaskets. All four elevations are
identical.

Opaque wall to window ratio is 50% (1:1).

Glass and wall are on the same plane; there is no shading
on the windows.

Glass area	– 15,480 sq ft total
Opaque wall area	– 15,480 sq ft total
Total wall area	– 30,960 sq ft

Figure 5.18. Ehrenkrantz study, elevation/window layout. Courtesy of the Ehrenkrantz
Group of New York.

modification was then analyzed by computer to determine the energy-use
reduction and changes in first cost and life-cycle cost.

Figures 5.19–5.23 are example results from the study. In general, envelope-related strategies that defensively or offensively counteract the extremes of climate were very disappointing. Perimeter daylighting, Figure
5.23, is the only alternative that made a substantial impact on the building's
energy use. This option produced a 20% annual energy-use cost reduction. In
terms of the added initial cost of daylighting as an investment, the expense
of this option represents a 67% internal rate of return for the building owner.

TABLE 5.3. COST SUMMARY

Item	$/net ft²	Total Cost ($)
1. Site	2.35	213,703
2. Substructure	2.64	131,279
3. Structure	11.72	849,356
4. Exterior wall	4.67	338,559
5. Glazing	3.57	258,509
6. Roofing	0.68	49,569
7. Doors, frames and hardware	0.26	18,608
8. Fireproofing	0.54	38,939
9. Stairs and railings	0.59	43,050
10. Interior partitions	0.09	6,409
11. Finishes	4.07	294,797
12. Toilet partitions and accessories	0.21	15,426
13. Venetian blinds	0.24	17,750
14. Vertical transportation	2.50	180,820
15. Plumbing	0.26	18,627
16. HVAC	5.96	432,000
17. Electrical	7.95	575,773
Total	48.91	3,543,180

TABLE 5.4. ENERGY CONSUMPTION SUMMARY

Item	Btu	Gal	kWh	$	%
Heating	1,184	8,457		3,806	7.8
Cooling	568		166,422	8,321	17.0
Lighting	1,503		433,420	21,371	43.7
Fans and pumps	406		118,957	5,948	12.2
Domestic hot water	286	2,044		920	1.9
Office equipment	404		113,438	5,975	12.2
Elevators	133		38,969	1,948	4.0
Total	4,484	10,501	883,266	48,889	

Energy consumption/net ft² = 61,891 Btu/ft².

TABLE 5.5.   EHRENKRANTZ LIST OF ALTERNATIVES

1	*Site*
1.1	Orientation
1.2	Ground reflectance
1.3	Berming
1.4	Shading
1.5	Wind breaks
2	*Outside of Wall*
2.1	Horizontal overhang shading
2.2	Vertical fin shading
2.3	Horizontal and vertical shading
3	*Wall*
3.1	Opaque wall/low mass
3.2	Opaque wall/medium mass
3.3	Opaque wall/high mass
3.4	Opaque wall/exterior absorptance
3.5	Opaque wall/vented walls
3.6	Opaque wall/Trombe walls
3.7	Opaque wall/setback
3.8	Glazing
3.9	Vented windows
3.10	Window/wall ratio
3.11	Beam lighting
4	*Roof*
4.1	Roof construction
4.2	Roof absorptance
4.3	Water-cooled roofs
4.4	Skylights
5	*Interior*
5.1	Insulating shutters
5.2	Blinds
5.3	Photoelectric light controller
5.4	Structure mass
5.5	Interior planning
5.6	Core location

When an option fits the nature and needs of the base building, an easily recognized energy-related improvement will be evident. Finding energy-related alternatives via the incremental change approach is not a matter of splitting hairs. The difference between workable and unnecessary options is typically so large that this approach can be used very early in the design process with very simplified assumptions about the base building.

There are two primary limitations to incremental change methods and

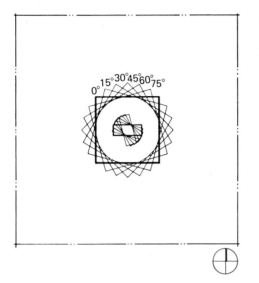

The base building is assumed to face the four compass orientations and is labeled as 0° from south.

To test effects of changing orientation, the base building is rotated in 15° increments to reach a maximum shift of 75°.

Since all four elevations on the base building are the same, a rotation of 90° or more is equivalent to alternatives already tested.

EHRENKRANTZ BUILDING EXAMPLE: ORIENTATION OPTION

Benefits Data	Units	Degrees from South		
		30°	45°	60°
Investment Tax Credit at 10%	$	0	0	0
Energy Tax Credits	$/yr 0	0	0	0
Straight Line Depreciation at 0 yr schedule	$/yr	0	0	0
Salvage Value in year 30	$	0	0	0
Energy Savings:				
Heating	$/yr 0	$29.00	$26.00	$36.00
	Gallons/yr	64.4	57.7	80
Cooling	$/yr 0	$58.00	$15.00	—
	kWh/yr	1160	300	—
Lighting	$/yr 0	0	0	0
	kWh/yr	0	0	0
Mechanical (fans, pumps, central plant)	$/yr 0	$53.00	$38.00	$23.00
	kWh/yr	1060	760	460
Total	$/yr 0	$140.00	$79.00	$59.00

Figure 5.19. Ehrenkrantz study, rotation of the building. Courtesy of the Ehrenkrantz Group of New York.

two very important advantages. The greatest drawback to this approach is the extensive number of computer runs that may be required to try a long list of options. Undirected, the incremental change approach is a lengthy process of elimination. However, this process can be alleviated if the base building energy needs are presented so that the causes of energy needs are highlighted rather than the amount of energy used by individual pieces of equipment. Identifying the major causes of energy use of a building defines its specific nature. These methods select viable options without wasting time or money on identifying inappropriate alternatives. Stating the energy

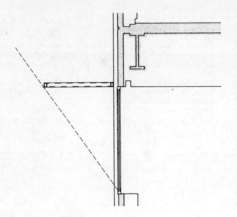

The window area of the base building is shaded by a single overhang, 1, 2, and 3 ft (305, 610, 914 mm) wide.

The overhangs are prefabricated with 4-in. (102 mm) wide metal strips attached to a metal frame. The spaces between strips allow hot air usually trapped below the overhang to escape without transmitting its heat to the interior. Only the low winter sun is able to pass between strips.

Shading devices are tested one elevation at a time, with resulting energy changes calculated for the total building. Only selected combinations of shading devices and elevation orientations are tested.

All shading alternatives are compared to the base building design with no shading.

EHRENKRANTZ BUILDING EXAMPLE: OPTION—3-FT OVERHANG ON THE SOUTH ELEVATION

	Units	South
COST INCREASE DATA:		
Construction	$	$32,547
	%	.92
	$/net sq ft	$0.45
Maintenance	$/yr 0	0
Insurance	$/yr 0	$65.10
Property Tax	$/yr 0	0
Replacement Period	Yrs	40
BENEFITS DATA:		
Investment Tax Credit at 10%	$	$325.00
Energy Tax Credits	$/yr 0	0
Straight Line Depreciation at 40 yr schedule	$/yr	$815.00
Salvage Value in year 30	$	0
Energy Savings:		
Heating	$/yr 0	-$125.00
	Gallons/yr	-278
Cooling	$/yr 0	$527.00
	kWh/yr	10,540
Lighting	$/yr 0	0
	kWh/hr	0
Mechanical (fans, pumps & central plant)	$/yr 0	$258.00
	kWh/yr	5160
Total	$/yr 0	$660.00

Figure 5.20. Ehrenkrantz study, overhangs. Courtesy of the Ehrenkrantz Group of New York.

needs of the base building in a way that suggests what types of options can be most helpful can greatly reduce this limitation to incremental change methods. Such a technique is presented in Chapter Six.

The second limiting factor in this approach is that all feasible options are direct responses to the energy needs of the base building. Incremental change studies only indicate solutions that can improve the base building. Not even considered are the great number of possible alternatives if the nature of the base building itself is changed. This is not a limitation in the retrofitting of an existing building: the base building is generally the existing

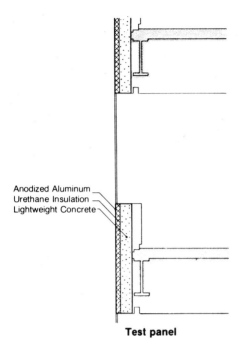

Prefabricated panels of lightweight concrete are tested with 1, 2, and 4 in. (25, 51, 102 mm) of insulation located on the outside of the panel. Insulation is covered with anodized aluminum skin for exterior finish.

Outside insulation alternatives are tested with double glazing of clear glass and compared to the base building's low mass sandwich panel of 3-in. (76 mm) insulation.

Anodized Aluminum
Urethane Insulation
Lightweight Concrete

Test panel

EHRENKRANTZ BUILDING EXAMPLE: OPTION—2-IN. POLYURETHANE OUTSIDE INSULATION

	Units	Total
COST INCREASE DATA:		
Construction	$	$1928
	%	.05
	$/net sq ft	$0.027
Maintenance	$/yr 0	0
Insurance	$/yr 0	$3.86
Property Tax	$/yr 0	0
Replacement Period	Yrs	40
BENEFITS DATA:		
Investment Tax Credit at 10%	$	$193.00
Energy Tax Credits	$/yr 0	0
Straight Line Depreciation at 40 yr schedule	$/yr	$48.00
Salvage Value in year 30	$	0
Energy Savings:		
Heating	$/yr 0	-$13.00
	Gallons/yr	-29
Cooling	$/yr 0	$58.00
	kWh/yr	1160
Lighting	$/yr 0	0
	kWh/yr	0
Mechanical (fans, pumps & central plant)	$/yr 0	$38.00
	kWh/yr	760
Total	$/yr 0	$83.00

Figure 5.21. Ehrenkrantz study, increasing wall insulation. Courtesy of the Ehrenkrantz Group of New York.

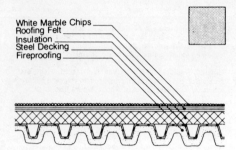

White Marble Chips
Roofing Felt
Insulation
Steel Decking
Fireproofing

White marble chips on roofing felt are tested as a low-absorptance roof cover.

The roof design is the same as on the base building.

The absorptivity of marble chips is assumed at 45%, as compared to the base building absorptivity of gray gravel of 60%.

EHRENKRANTZ BUILDING EXAMPLE: OPTION—LOW ABSORPTANCE ROOF COVER

	Units	Total
COST INCREASE DATA:		
Construction	$	$2,582
	%	.07
	$/net sq ft	$0.04
Maintenance	$/yr 0	0
Insurance	$/yr 0	$5.16
Property Tax	$/yr 0	0
Replacement Period	Yrs	20
BENEFITS DATA:		
Investment Tax Credit at 10%	$	$258.00
Energy Tax Credits	$/yr 0	0
Straight Line Depreciation at 15 yr schedule	$/yr	173[a]/667[b]
Salvage Value in year 30	$	0
Energy Savings:		
Heating	$/yr 0	-$3.00
	Gallons/yr	-6.7
Cooling	$/yr 0	$15.00
	kWh/yr	300.00
Lighting	$/yr 0	0
	kWh/yr	0
Mechanical (fans, pumps & central plant)	$/yr 0	$9.00
	kWh/yr	180.00
Total	$/yr 0	$21.00

[a]Years 1 through 15

[b]Years 20 through 30

Figure 5.22. Ehrenkrantz study, low absorptance roofing material. Courtesy of the Ehren-krantz Group of New York.

building in such a case. However, when one is designing a new building, immediately deciding upon a particular base building actually defines the appropriate types of options. For this reason, the incremental change method is often called the new building retrofit approach.

The greatest advantage to incremental change methods is the very significant potential energy-use reduction that can be achieved with little change in professional practice and building design. The simplicity and

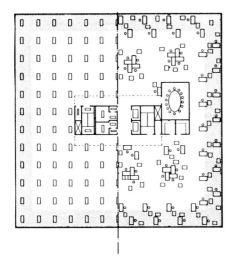

Perimeter artificial lighting is controlled by an automatic photoelectric light dimmer system.

The controlled zone is 10 ft (3,048 mm) and one fixture deep.

The system is designed to dim or switch off artificial lighting when good lighting levels are available from daylight penetration through windows. Each zone is controlled separately.

The computer simulation assumes a venetian blind in the down position whenever direct sunlight falls on the window area.

The base building has no photoelectric system.

EHRENKRANTZ STUDY EXAMPLE: OPTION— PERIMETER DAYLIGHTING WITH PHOTOELECTRIC CONTROLLER

	Units	South[a]	East[a]	North[a]	West[a]	Total[b]
COST INCREASE DATA:						
Construction	$	$2,847	$2,816	$2,945	$2,798	$11,780
	%	0.08	0.08	0.08	0.08	0.33
	$/net ft²	$0.039	$0.039	$0.041	$0.039	$0.16
Maintenance	$/yr 0	0	0	0	0	0
Insurance	$/yr 0	$5.69	$5.63	$5.89	$5.60	$22.81
Property tax	$/yr 0	0	0	0	0	0
Replacement period	yrs	20	20	20	20	20
BENEFITS DATA:						
Investment tax credit at 10%	$	$285.00	$282.00	$295.00	$280.00	$118.00
Energy tax credits	$/yr 0	0	0	0	0	0
Straight line depreciation at 15-yr schedule	$/yr	190[c]/735[d]	188[c]/727[d]	196[c]/760[d]	188[c]/721[d]	785[c]/3040[d]
Salvage value in year 30	$	$750.00	$750.00	$750.00	$750.00	$3,000
Energy savings:						
Heating	$/yr 0	−$122.00	−$167.00	−$275.00	−$176.00	−$740.00
	gal/yr	−271	−371	−611	−391	−1,644
Cooling	$/yr 0	$483.00	$469.00	$337.00	$513.00	$1,802
	kWh/yr	9,660	9,380	6,740	10,260	36,040
Lighting	$/yr 0	$1,923	$1,946	$1,949	$1,948	$7,766
	kWh/yr	38,460	38,920	38,980	38,960	155,320
Mechanical (fans, pumps & central plant)	$/yr 0	$238.00	$215.00	$124.00	$228.00	$805.00
	kWh/yr	4,760	4,300	2,480	4,560	16,100
Total	$/yr 0	$2,522	$2,463	$2,135	$2,513	$9,633
LIFE CYCLE COST/BENEFIT DATA:						
Discounted payback	yrs	1.75	1.78	2.11	1.73	1.89
Internal rate of return	%	72.17	71.44	61.66	72.97	67.73
Net present value	$	$98,002	$95,681	$82,438	$97,697	$373,414

[a] Option applied to this zone only.

[b] Option applied to all zones.

[c] Years 1 through 15.

[d] Years 20 through 30.

Figure 5.23. Ehrenkrantz study, perimeter daylighting. Courtesy of the Ehrenkrantz Group of New York.

directness of sound professional practice belies its value. Our collective learning experience consistently shows that energy needs and peak demand of contemporary conventional buildings can be easily halved compared to buildings of the mid-1970s. Although options do exist that can further reduce energy needs beyond this level, the degree of change required is often large for energy savings that are proportionally smaller than the savings first derived by simple incremental improvements.

The second advantage to incremental change methods is the educational experience derived from the approach. Energy has not been a significant design concern in the past. Until this issue is better understood, intuition has a limited role to play in solving energy problems. Incremental change methods ensure success at this level by testing options within the context of interconnected environmental-control systems as they would perform throughout an annual period. Working with incremental change approaches also allows the designer to develop a familiarity with energy-related issues necessary in the implementation of nonincremental change approaches.

NONINCREMENTAL CHANGE METHODS

Nonincremental change methods differ from the preceding examples since the designer assesses the advantages of different solution types rather than assumes improvements are to be made to a given base building problem. The designer starts by isolating the type of building most suitable for the project by exploring alternative whole-building solution types. For instance, both of the last two case studies identified perimeter daylighting as a very useful option. Conventional building forms were never intended to be daylit; in fact, they evolved away from the use of that alternative. If perimeter daylighting is useful, then perhaps a nonconventional building form could capitalize on this benefit to a greater degree.

Nonincremental change solutions represent a leap to new concepts and solutions that are not direct extensions of the conventional. The skill necessary to find such solutions is notably greater than that required to develop incremental changes. To envision innovative solutions, a designer must understand the controlling and major energy needs of conventional commercial buildings, and how these needs interact, as well as understand the principles, advantages, and disadvantages of alternative means of environmental control. Even with this knowledge, intuition must still be restrained and all alternatives must be tested to determine their true value.

The early design experience of the Tennessee Valley Authority (TVA) Chattanooga Office Complex illustrates the basic sequence of nonincremental change methods (Fig. 5.24 and 5.25). TVA instructed the design team to advance the state of the art in energy-conscious building design while emphasizing a sensitivity to human needs, the urban context, and environ-

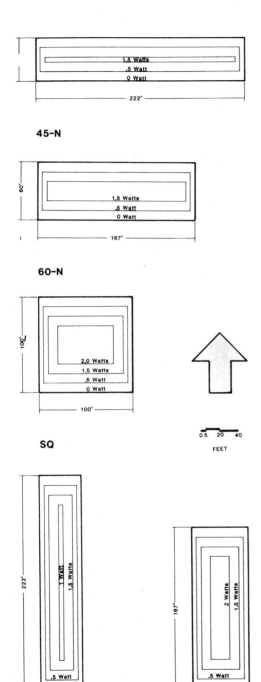

45-N

60-N

SQ

FEET

45-E

60-E

Figure 5.24. TVA, five alternative building configurations. Courtesy of Van der Ryn Calthorpe & Partners

163

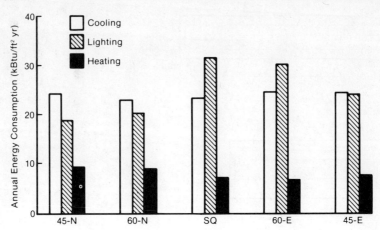

Figure 5.25. TVA, source energy comparison of the five configurations. Courtesy of Van der Ryn, Calthorpe & Partners.

mental quality. From the beginning, the well-experienced design team strived to develop new solutions rather than to improve a conventional structure (Figs. 5.26–5.28).

Although the design team knew that expanding form and puncturing envelope could reduce the lighting load, they did not know the impact of such changes on heating and cooling loads. To better define the relative impact of variables such as climate and building use, orientation, massing, and section depth, preliminary parameter studies were performed by team members Van der Ryn, Calthorpe & Partners, and the Berkeley Solar Group. These studies were not used to evaluate the individual strategies but to define the relative importance of individual and often contradictory roles of form, envelope, and equipment.

The parameter study began by assessing the energy needs of five building configurations (Fig. 5.24). Daylighting was assumed for each configuration as were standard window and shading devices for each orientation. Along with the selection of the basic heating and cooling systems used in the buildings, these assumptions change the relative value of the different configurations. The earliest professional judgement decisions influence the results of nonincremental change experimentation. Experience is central to tempering this judgement. Reinvention requires skill and experience.

As shown in Figure 5.25, the primary energy needs of the different configurations were generated by computer. The comparative trends derived from this information by the design team are as follows:

The annual need for lighting energy is reduced as the building massing gets thinner north to south. Thin buildings with broad east-west

Figure 5.26.   TVA, atrium model. Courtesy of Tennessee Valley Authority.

elevations require more energy for lighting since they require more extensive shading devices to block the low morning and afternoon sun.

Orientation may not be significant in the earlier Ehrenkrantz building where a cube form and identical elevations are used, yet a substantial difference is possible when strategies and facade treatments are varied and climate adaptations are central to the proposed design.

The heating requirements increase as the building gets thinner. Two variables influence this fact. First, a narrow building has a larger building skin. Second, a narrow building has a greater daylighting portion than a deeper building and, therefore, a reduced heating contribution from electric lights. However, this liability is small since the need for heating energy is much less than that required for lighting and cooling.

Cooling energy need is consistently high in all configurations. The only significant pattern seems to be a slight decrease in cooling energy needed

Figure 5.27.   TVA, exterior of model. Courtesy of Tennessee Valley Authority.

in configurations with smaller external surface areas. The impact of this variation is small and counteracted by reduction in the heat of electric lights by the larger daylighting potential of the shallow buildings.

From this general analysis, the team could see that east–west elevations are a liability and that narrow forms with broad north–south elevations have a distinct advantage. Combining these considerations with many non-energy-related issues, the team developed an atrium building section to be used with a long east-west building shape (Fig. 5.26). The atrium allows access to daylight, yet counterbalances the liabilities of extended form for heating and cooling from within. As shown in this example, numbers alone do not dictate the progression from general sensitivity studies of different possible building configurations to the selection of a base building form. Solutions are not derived solely by analyses; rather, analyses can indicate the relative value of separate parameters. The final building form integrates all major design concerns. Cost, density, aesthetics, and energy performance finally can be combined only on an intuitive level through reinvention. Process is merely an aid at the nonincremental change level: it cannot directly generate a solution.

However analysis is structured to select a basic building form or nature, the result will still have many undefined issues. At this point, nonincremental changes are treated as a base building in an incremental change approach. Additional computer runs can test the advantages and disadvan-

MARKET STREET ELEVATION

Figure 5.28. TVA, elevations. Courtesy of The Architects Collaborative.

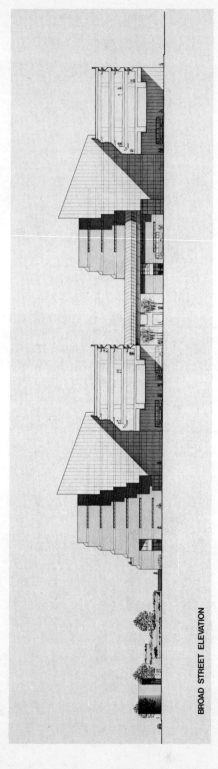

BROAD STREET ELEVATION

Figure 5.28. (*Continued*)

168

tages of a host of second-order system alternatives, just as in the incremental change method. In nonincremental change methods, the task at the schematic design level is to find an appropriate nature for the building. In design development, the task is to select, size, and detail the individual systems that provide a cost-effective and energy-responsive balance within that nature.

The most important lesson we extracted from the study of energy-related design approaches is that process serves intuition. Process is a paradox in the design of energy-responsive commercial buildings. On the one hand, the purpose of process is to explore and test that which uninformed intuition cannot accurately appraise. Yet, regardless of what information is clarified by process, the solution generated is bound by the concepts one intuitively offers to test or study. Intuition is both the problem and the key to the design of energy-responsive commercial buildings. Design approaches are a framework to inform, stimulate, and educate intuition, not a mechanistic, computerlike series of steps that guarantees that the best possible solution can be found for any project. A new framework for design that keys on the purpose of process to inform and stimulate intuition is the subject of Part Two of this book. Before that topic is started, though, we need to explore the way numbers can influence the execution of any energy-related design approach.

USING NUMBERS TO DEFINE THE ENERGY NEEDS AND OPPORTUNITIES OF COMMERCIAL BUILDINGS

A familiarity with energy end uses and their relationships within a building type can provide use guidelines for focusing the design effort where it might have the most significant impact.

"A Base Line for Energy Design," Progressive Architecture, April 1982

As suggested by the survey presented at the beginning of this chapter, designers have a limited intuitive understanding of the energy needs of commercial buildings. For this reason, energy-related approaches, aids, and techniques that inform the design team of the energy needs and opportunities of commercial buildings are very important. Invariably a major product of these tools and techniques are numbers. Perhaps the single most disputed topic in the design of energy-responsive commercial buildings is what units of measure are best to express energy-related numbers.

All case studies in this book use numbers either to express energy-related need or to quantify the benefits of proposed solutions. We have intentionally avoided emphasizing these numbers, or their comparison between case studies, since a wide variety of units of measure are used. In this section, the energy-related units of measure that are currently in use are reviewed and assessed. As is shown, different energy-related units of measure present fundamentally different information about the energy needs of commercial buildings and the benefit of proposed alternatives.

Four major energy-related units of measure are most commonly used to appraise the needs and opportunities of commercial buildings. They are (a) energy loads, (b) energy used at the building site, (c) primary or source energy, and (d) energy costs. Before examples are presented that demonstrate the different answers or conclusions that can be derived with different units of measure applied to the same basic problem, each of these four units will be defined and appraised.

Energy loads are commonly expressed in Btu and represent the heat that must be added or extracted from a building to maintain comfort design conditions. Lighting energy/needs can likewise be expressed as a Btu load by converting the electrical lighting needs from kWh to Btu. Heating and cooling energy loads do not include an appraisal of the systems that will be employed to counteract these loads. They merely state the heat extraction or addition that must be achieved at the conditioned space. Therefore, when loads are documented, the listed Btu are not considered the same as the Btu of fossil fuels or electricity that will be required to operate the heating and cooling plants and their distribution systems. For instance, if it takes 1.25 Btu of natural gas at the boiler to deliver 1 Btu of heat to the conditioned space, the building heating load will be 25% smaller than the building energy need, in Btu, for the heating system. Likewise, if a cooling plant and distribution system has a annual average COP of 3.0, then the annual cooling load for the building will be three times larger than the number of Btu of electricity required to operate the cooling system over the year.

A major advantage of energy loads as a unit of measure is that the means used to provide heating and cooling need not be identified. In effect, system design and selection become part of the problem rather than part of the statement of need. The major disadvantage of loads as a unit of measure is that far too many designers establish priorities for the individual energy needs of a commercial building with these numbers. The annual totals and comparative magnitudes of heating, lighting, and cooling loads have no direct relationship to the actual energy needs of the building. Energy loads may be far larger or smaller than actual energy needs since conventional environmental-control systems can have efficiencies of 1 or less, or COPs of 1 or more. Once again, a Btu of electricity in a cooling system might offset 3 or more Btu of excess heat in a conditioned space. On the other hand, a Btu of natural gas in a heating system might offset only a fraction of a Btu of heat that must be added to a conditioned space.

Energy used at the building site is typically expressed in Btu and assesses both loads and systems. Therefore, this unit of measure demands that both the heat addition and extraction rates and the performance of specific heating, cooling, and lighting systems be appraised. The major advantage of this approach is that the end results reflect the actual energy used at the building site to provide environmental control. If the goal is to limit the amount of nonrenewable energy used by a building, this unit of measure better reflects the challenge of the design team over the appraisal of energy loads.

There are two major disadvantages of appraising the energy needs of a building as Btu used at the site. The first disadvantage is that system assumptions must be made to generate the information, and the results will be highly influenced by these system assumptions. For instance, if one assumes highly efficient heating and lighting systems, yet includes a very inefficient cooling system in the appraisal of the energy needs of the building, then the largest overall annual energy need of the building may appear to be cooling. In actuality, the results may indicate that the major annual energy need of the building is to power the very inefficient cooling system assumed in the study. Therefore, whenever the energy needs of a building are being documented as Btu used at the site, it is extremely important to document the systems that were assumed to generate those numbers.

The second major disadvantage of Btu used at the site as a unit of measure is that all Btu are assumed to be equal. This is most definitely a matter of comparing apples and oranges. A Btu of electricity is not equal in cost or energetic value to a Btu of natural gas or fuel oil. Often it can take 3–4 Btu of natural gas or fuel oil to generate and deliver 1 Btu of electricity to a building. This is why the cost of electricity on a Btu basis is invariably higher than the cost of a Btu of fossil fuel. Expressing energy need as Btu used at the site indicates that subsidiary energy needs beyond the building site are not included in the numbers. For this reason, Btu used at the site are often termed end-use Btu.

A Btu of natural gas is often 2–4 times less costly or energy intensive as a Btu of electricity. Therefore, if a designer appraises the relative weight or magnitude of heating, cooling, and lighting end-use Btu to determine which is the most significant, and thus the one that should be the focus of energy-related design efforts, the appraisal will not reflect either total energy cost or total nonrenewable energy use. Likewise, end-use Btu do not reflect either the capital cost or the embodied energy invested in building and maintaining off-site facilities such as power plants.

End-use Btu is the unit of measure most commonly applied by professionals and energy codes, and is prevalent in the case studies of Part One. It can be a useful means to assess and present the energy needs of a building; however, we are convinced that very few designers understand the limits of end-use Btu as a unit of measure. A building that uses 40,000 Btu/ft^2 per year as measured at the site can be either a very efficient building or a very inefficient design. If all of these Btu are natural gas, the building is a superior energy-related solution. If the building is all-electric, the total energy need including subsidies beyond the site may actually be 120,000 Btu/ft^2 per year. In short, the annual energy needs of both individual environmental-control systems or of the building in total may be off by a factor of 3 or 4 when one compares end-use Btu to the actual energy required to operate a building.

Primary or source energy, as its name implies, is a unit of measure that estimates the total energy usage of a building by including energy subsidies beyond the building site. This unit of measure attempts to accurately assess the total nonrenewable energy usage of a building. As mentioned above, building energy usage, as either an annual total or as a means to compare the magnitude of the individual energy needs of separate environmental-control systems, can be different by a factor of 3 or 4 as compared to end-use Btu. The increased accuracy of a primary energy-accounting system may make it sound as if it is the best unit of measure to use. However, the use of primary energy units is questionable since there is limited agreement on the multipliers that should be used to convert end-use Btu to primary energy Btu. A respectable degree of accuracy can be achieved in deriving multipliers based on national averages. Yet individual buildings are site- or region-specific and the great many means used to produce and deliver energy to buildings in different regions is not well described in multipliers based on national averages. For instance, the majority of power generation in the Northwest is by hydroelectric plants. Using a national average multiplier to assess the energy embodied in a Btu of electricity in this region can result in an error of 200% or more.

For these reasons, we do not suggest that designers use source energy units. Source energy represents an alien language to most designers, one that does not coincide with past experience and existing knowledge like loads, end-use Btu, or energy cost. However, we feel that source energy calculations are better suited to the needs and abilities of the research community.

The last widely used unit of measure is annual energy cost. Rather than converting end-use Btu to source energy, energy cost multiplies end-use Btu by the local utility cost to express the total annual energy need and the comparative magnitude of the energy used by individual environmental-control systems. Although the conversion is by no means perfect, we have found that the relative magnitudes of the energy needs of individual environmental-control systems are nearly equal when either cost or source energy units of measure are used. In general, the cost difference between a Btu of electricity and a Btu of natural gas closely approximates the embodied energy difference between the two source types. Likewise, utility costs are regionally specific, permitting a relatively close relationship between methods of energy production and delivery and cost.

From our discussions with many building designers, it appears that most believe that end-use Btu better express energy need than energy cost. Few designers believe that energy cost has any relationship to energy use. In fact, most designers we have interviewed clearly distinguish between saving energy and saving dollars. In one way they are right. The energy needs of a commercial building expressed in end-use Btu and in annual utility costs paint completely different pictures of the energy needs and opportunities of the same building. Yet based on our wide experience in both the research and private sectors, the truth of the matter seems to be that cost typically expresses a much more accurate definition of actual energy need if the important energy subsidies beyond the building site are to be included in the analysis.

Energy cost, as a unit of measure to define the energy needs and opportunities of commercial buildings, permits many additional advantages. First, the tremendous capital and energy subsidy required to expand electric utility capacity to support a new building can be easily expressed by cost in the form of annual peak-demand charges. Few designers realize that for every dollar spent on the construction of new buildings an expenditure of about 40¢ is required by the local electric utility to support the existence of that structure. In terms of either cost or primary energy, controlling the peak-period rate of electrical energy use in commercial buildings offers a tremendous cost and energy savings potential. As mentioned in Chapter Three, our preliminary research indicates that 2–3 times more nonrenewable energy can be saved on a national basis by reducing the peak rate of electrical energy use in commercial buildings than by equivalent expenditures that focus on limiting annual energy consumption.

The lack of awareness by designers of the importance of energy-capacity issues versus energy-use issues is perhaps best shown by the fact that none of the energy-related numbers of the case studies in Chapters Three and Four include an appraisal of the rate of energy use. In fact, we identified many case studies that specifically addressed the issue of peak-demand cost, but chose not to use them in this book because designers believed it would be embarrassing to the clients to publish buildings which were more effective in reducing energy cost rather than end-use Btu.

Peak-demand charges are not a separate issue to limiting the use of nonrenewable energy on a national or global basis. The potential reward is the elimination of the capital and energy expense of building, maintaining, and operating new generating plants.

Another major advantage of energy-cost units is that energy use is invariably converted to dollars during the design process to perform cost-benefit analysis. Given an unlimited budget, reducing the nonrenewable energy needs of a commercial building is very easy. Initiating energy analysis in units of cost only facilitates the later task of comparing the cost of improvements to the economic benefit derived by the client.

To reinforce the fundamentally different results that are derived by using

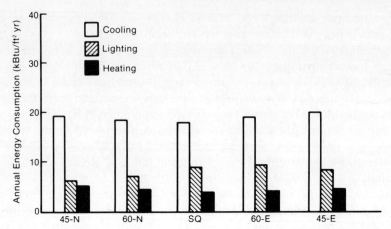

Figure 5.29. TVA, loads comparison of the five configurations. Courtesy of Van der Ryn, Calthorpe & Partners.

different energy-related units of measure, three case studies are reviewed. The first case study returns to the TVA Office of Power Building that was used to exemplify nonincremental change approaches in the previous section of this chapter. As discussed, Figure 5.25 was generated by the design team to appraise the energy needs and advantages of five building configurations. The unit of measure used in that figure was source energy. In Figure 5.29 the energy needs of the same five building configurations are presented as energy loads.

A comparison of these two figures indicates a radical difference in the definition of the primary and major needs of the buildings. For example, the total annual building energy needs by loads of design 60-E is 62% for cooling, 25% for lighting, and 13% for heating. By source energy units of measure, cooling represents 41% of the total, lighting is 46%, and heating is about 13%. If only load data were generated, a designer could well conclude that cooling is the overwhelming major energy need of the building. However, source-energy data strongly suggest that cooling and lighting are both major energy needs that require consideration if the energy needs of the building are to be significantly reduced.

A comparison of the results between end-use Btu and cost for a base building is shown in Figure 5.30. This base building comparison was generated for Baranco Pontiac, a climate-adapted case study presented in Chapter Four. Note that the largest energy needs by end-use Btu are cooling and heating, while lighting, HVAC, fans, and cooling represent the largest energy costs. By using the energy-cost data rather than the Btu site data, the designers found that daylighting and natural ventilation would be very useful alternatives for the building. These same conclusions would not have been obvious from the sole appraisal of end-use data.

Figures 5.31–5.33 represent the energy-use breakdowns of a multistory

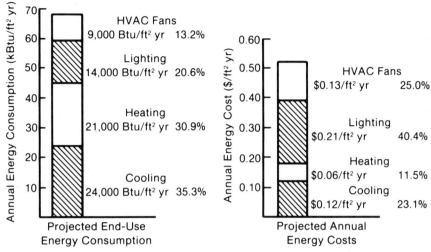

Figure 5.30.   Baranco Pontiac, comparison of building energy need by end-use Btu and costs. Courtesy of Sizemore/Floyd Architects.

office building in Pittsburgh, Pennsylvania. These figures assess building energy need as loads, end-use Btu required to operate the environmental-control systems, and costs. Two categories of information are documented. Figure 5.31 summarizes the annual energy needs of the building by consumption, or the actual use of energy by the environmental-control equipment. In Figure 5.32, information on the building peak capacity needs and cost is summarized. It is our opinion that the best means to appraise need in this building would be to combine consumption and demand costs

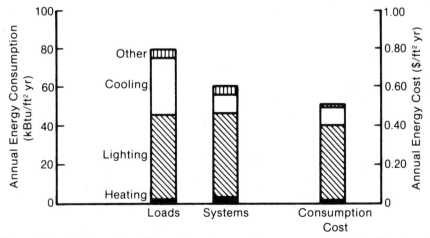

Figure 5.31.   Loads, end-use Btu, and cost comparison—consumption only. Courtesy of Sizemore/Floyd Architects.

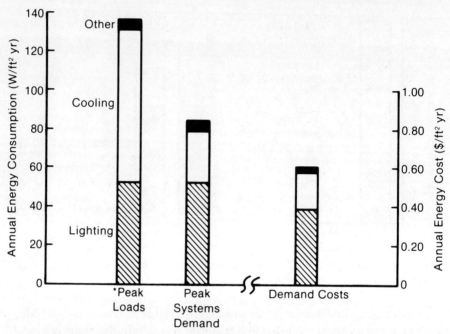

Figure 5.32.   Loads, systems, and cost comparison—peak demand only.

into one problem statement (Fig. 5.33). Yet it is not a matter of one set of units being right and all others being wrong. Each breakdown offers the designer unique information that can be important if the definition and limits of each unit of measurement are well understood.

The four units of measure discussed to this point are the most common accounting systems that the reader will encounter in literature on energy-responsive commercial buildings. However, since this book focuses on innovation and reinvention, we wish to at least mention a couple of unconventional accounting systems that appear beneficial in appraising the energy needs of commercial buildings and deriving indications of where design effort might best be applied.

One of the most informative methods we have found for breaking down energy-related numbers is the CRS method introduced in Chapter Two and illustrated in Figure 2.11. The significant improvement in this method is not in the unit of measure, but the categories into which the numbers are divided or placed. Rather than assigning energy numbers only to equipment such as cooling, lighting, and heating, the CRS breakdown also divides total annual energy use by cause. In this way interconnected relationships, such

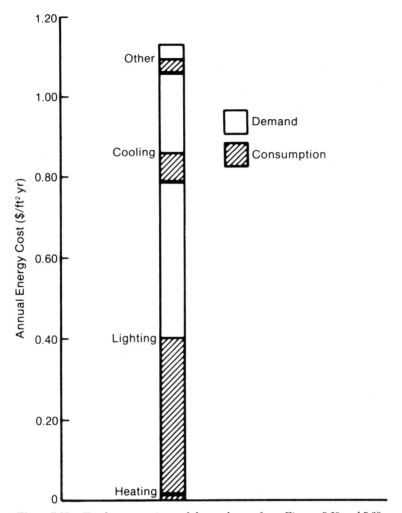

Figure 5.33. Total consumption and demand costs from Figures 5.29 and 5.30.

as the cooling energy required to offset the heat of lights, can be better visualized. Likewise, the need for heating or cooling can be assessed as a problem of heat gain or loss through the envelope, or as heat gains and losses attributed to internal loads or ventilation air. If a major reason for generating energy-related numbers is to identify the specific areas of improvement that a designer should investigate, then knowing the cause of an energy need is just as important as assigning energy use by equipment.

CRS uses the energy-cause breakdown in conjunction with end-use Btu. However, it is not difficult to visualize energy-cause charts based on loads or dollars. In Chapter Six, a method is presented that uses the concept of energy numbers by cause that includes energy cost for both consumption and peak demand.

The last example of an innovative means to assess energy-related numbers comes from Edgar Russell, Jr., Manager of Communications for the Real Estate and Construction Division of IBM. As shown in Figure 5.34, one way to appraise energy cost is in relation to the cost of constructing, financing, and operating a building for 20 years, and the direct and indirect cost of employing people to use it. In such a comparison, IBM finds that the utility-related cost of their buildings represents about 1%–1.5% of this total. We do not offer this analysis to diminish the importance of energy conservation. Rather, this single chart summarizes both the issue of energy numbers and the review of energy-responsive commercial buildings contained in Part One.

In Chapter One, we stated that innovations are resolved as wider and wider concerns are considered and the innovation is placed within the context of a complete or much larger process and product. In the case of building-related energy issues, our collective efforts over the last decade have been an intensive investigation of the energy needs of buildings and the abilities and limits of specific alternatives and components. Based on diffusion research, the study of parts and pieces always precedes resolution. Yet the most advanced energy-related case studies being generated by designers are embodying innovations far beyond the application of components. Instead, the state of the art in the design of energy-responsive commercial buildings is reinvention at the whole-building level. Figure 5.34 clarifies the challenge of reinvention in two ways. First, the purpose of reinvention is not to change the whole to adapt to the piece. Rather, the advantage of the new piece is adopted and molded to support the larger product or process.

As suggested by Figure 5.34, any energy-related improvement that reduces productivity or occupant health in the slightest is an inappropriate

A: PEOPLE (94%)

C: CONSTRUCTION COSTS (3%)

B: BUILDING OPERATING AND
   ENERGY COSTS (3%)

Figure 5.34. IBM 20-year cost breakdown for construction, operation, and use of office buildings.

solution. Conversely, an energy-related improvement that reinforces the productivity of people is a superior solution. Up until now, the theme of the book has been energy. We are still at a point where this singular focus is required. However, resolution is not solely achieved by understanding how pieces operate and the design issues associated with their use. Reinvention is equally the understanding of the whole design challenge and the transformation of pieces in an innovative way to best support the overall objectives of a commercial building design.

Figure 5.34 symbolizes the most important lesson the authors have gained from researching and writing Part One. That lesson is the constant expansion of unresolved design challenges toward wider areas of concern. Part One may not cover every possible design alternative that can be appropriate for commercial buildings, yet the track toward reinvention is clear. When in doubt, assess the problem at one or two levels of concern above the use of energy in buildings. In the end there will be commercial buildings, not energy-responsive commercial buildings.

part two

A FRAMEWORK FOR DESIGN

Introduction to Part Two

It seems to me that analysis and database and so forth are like a dictionary, whereas design ... is like prose and really good design is like music.

SARAH HARKNESS

In Part Two, the emphasis shifts from learning through the experiences of others to the presentation of a design framework that the reader can use to support the generation of successful solutions for a specific design challenge. As stated in Chapter Five and as reinforced by the above quote, a framework or process cannot directly produce a final solution. How well the mechanical tasks of process support the synthesis activity of design is the true test of the usefulness of any process. The framework presented here specifically addresses this criterion. The framework includes the most important lessons learned in Part One that address this topic. These lessons range from a base list of facts that must be assessed to avoid common design failures to the types of variables that need to be explored to support innovation and reinvention beyond existing knowledge.

The major lesson learned in Part One that has most influenced the material presented in Part Two is the importance of integrating energy concerns into the whole of architectural design. Most of the solutions presented in Part One would not have been found without expanding energy issues into the wider concerns of overall building use, design, and ownership. This trend toward whole-building solutions coincides with the Chapter One description of how innovations are modified and adopted for general use. Innovations typically begin as a singular, focused component or process. Toward resolution, innovations are modified and often reinvented to fit the progressively wider sets of concerns of later adaptors. In the end, an innovation loses its separate identity and is totally absorbed into the wider needs and concerns of a larger product or process.

The case studies of Part One clearly suggest that energy-related design issues are following a similar path toward resolution. Our very broad collective experience is forming a catalog of alternative components, concepts, and systems. Yet, as with the singular Wainwright Building issues of the elevator, the steel frame, and the architectural expression of the tall building, resolution will be achieved at a level above that of the application of singular components and concepts. This approach in the design of energy-responsive commercial buildings stresses the innovative combination and integration of building elements to suit whole-building design needs, concerns, and opportunities.

With this major lesson as a base, the purpose of the Part Two framework for design is to inform, educate, and stimulate the designer's problem-solving insights and skills (i.e., intuition) by clarifying and assessing the energy need and opportunities of specific whole-building design challenges. The intent is to present proactive energy-related information and design indicators in a format that stimulates innovation and reinvention by the reader. The means to this end is to identify and rank the significant energy-use needs, causes, and interdependent relationships of a proposed building before the building design is set. By deriving a clear statement of need and opportunity at the whole-building level, a distinctly different problem statement and design direction can be formulated than by appraising the suitability of substitute components, systems, or design concepts. At the most fundamental level of application, such an approach avoids the pitfalls of trial and error component testing. In a more advanced form, this approach permits the design team to define solutions based on whole-building needs and opportunities that at present may be beyond the direct application of our collective learning experience.

In Chapter Six, A Recommended Design Approach, the overall step-by-step method is presented and discussed. In that chapter, the emphasis is the description of the various steps and the outputs that each produces. Chapter Seven, Applying the Recommended Design Approach: Three Examples, demonstrates how the steps and outputs can be used to inform and guide the design team toward appropriate solutions. Chapter Seven also demonstrates how the use of the recommended design approach will change as the design team gains experience and skills. Chapters Eight to Ten focus on generating the specific information products that are central to the recommended design approach. Respectively, their products are building financial analysis, building energy analysis, and component energy analysis.

chapter six

A RECOMMENDED DESIGN APPROACH

You don't get good buildings from process; you get good buildings from good designers.

WILLIAM CAUDILL

INTRODUCTION

This chapter presents a design approach that can be used to integrate energy issues and facts into the overall building design process. The purpose of this chapter is to introduce and define the method and steps of this recommended design approach. In Chapter Seven, design examples are presented to clarify how these steps can be used and interpreted by the reader to define the major whole-building energy needs and opportunities of specific design challenges.

Certainly, the following design approach is not the only technique that has been or can be developed to describe and analyze the energy needs and opportunities of commercial buildings. However, this approach is based on a distinctly different premise from other techniques the authors have reviewed. This premise is that innovations beyond our collective learning experience are not only possible, but probable. As with case studies such as 33 West Monroe, the Bateson Building, and the GSA Study Building, these future innovations will result from the artful integration and combination of energy-related needs and means with new design opportunities on a whole-building level. These types of advances in the design of energy-responsive commercial buildings are not made solely by process. Rather, they are made with experience, insight, and design skills. The purpose of the design approach presented in this chapter is to present the energy needs and opportunities of whole-building design challenges in a format that stimulates innovative and reinventive design solutions by the reader. An informed designer, after all, not a mechanical process, generates superior solutions.

The recommended design approach is divided into three distinct phases reflecting different points in time in the overall building design process. The first phase of the approach, called *predesign information,* coincides with the classical programming phase of design. This phase organizes energy-related facts, clarifies energy-related criteria and goals, and defines the probable energy needs of the project in a format that clearly identifies the controlling energy need of the project and the interconnected cost and performance impact of each major element of environmental control on all others. Predesign information represents all the facts that can be known about the energy-related design challenge before the actual design exists. Predesign information tasks conclude with a decision by the design team of the best energy-related goals and opportunities for the project. These opportunities represent a "wish list" of optimum results rather than the selection of components or design concepts. Exploring the physical means that can achieve the desired results is the purpose of the next phase of the recommended design approach.

The second phase of the recommended approach is *schematic design experimentation.* As its name implies, this phase coincides with the traditional schematic design phase of the building design process. This phase begins with the definition of one or more possible environmental-control solutions that can achieve the results defined at the conclusion of the predesign tasks. Through a series of steps, these alternatives can be appraised on a preliminary basis to assess the impact of each on people, design, cost, and energy-related performance. As with the traditional activities performed at the earliest stages of schematic design, the intent is to explore basic design relationships and opportunities in preparation for the development of an actual schematic design solution. In this case, the objective is to establish relationships and opportunities between different forms, envelopes, systems, and components. The products of these efforts are designed to support the generation of a final schematic design by the designer.

The third phase assumed in the recommended approach is *design development.* With an actual design available for study, existing component optimization techniques can be applied to fine-tune the solution. Since these activities can be performed with existing energy-related design aids and techniques, the optimization tasks of design development will not be covered in detail in this chapter or in the examples of Chapter Seven. Instead, the text will emphasize the active tasks that lead to the development of an actual schematic design. At this point in our collective learning experience, the clear challenge is to define and visualize appropriate whole-building solutions. Once the key decisions are made that result in an actual schematic design, traditional reactive engineering techniques can be used to optimize that solution.

The following text is subdivided into predesign information and schematic design experimentation. In each section, the basic tasks and techniques of each phase will be presented. Since a major emphasis of the recommended approach is the presentation of key energy-related information products, a simple office building example is used to demonstrate the appearance and content of these charts and graphs. However, this example is not treated as a case study of how the recommended approach can be used. That topic is the purpose of the next chapter in this book.

PREDESIGN INFORMATION

The purpose of the predesign information tasks is to derive a clear statement of the energy-related criteria, needs, and design goals for the project. Predesign information tasks are performed during the programming stage of the overall building design process when similar facts, criteria, and goals are being defined for the whole project. Having a set format to perform these tasks establishes a bridge for communications between the different disciplines represented on the design team and constructively focuses individual team member efforts to a predetermined end.

In terms of intent and accuracy, predesign information tasks are very similar to the treatment of construction costs during the programming phase of design. Since the building design has not yet been generated, neither accurate construction cost estimates or energy-use estimates can be performed. Disregarding cost and energy-related facts until the final design is generated will typically result in failure. To insure a successful solution requires a proactive approach that establishes realistic design criteria and goals. If there are distinct energy-related advantages to the innovative combination of building elements, this knowledge is of limited use if a conventional building design has already been selected for the project under study.

PROJECT FACTS AND CRITERIA

As with programmatic cost information, clarifying the client's intent is the place to start the collection of energy-related predesign information. While facts are being collected from the client on the building's function, size, location, and character, the client's energy-related objectives for the project should also be established. More often than not, the client will express energy-related concerns in very general terms rather than as a list of well-defined goals. These general concerns are typically expressed as a need to save energy, a need to reduce utility-related operating costs, a need to meet the state or local energy code, or a need to project an energy-awareness image through the design of the building. The design team must press the client to go beyond vague expressions of intent to establish very specific qualitative and quantitative energy-related design criteria that clearly convey a means to distinguish between a successful solution and an unsuccessful solution. A failure on the part of the design team to reach clear agreement with the client on energy-related design criteria is as detrimental as trying to design a building without knowing the construction budget for the project. To prevent backtracking, now is the time to document and clearly define energy-related project criteria.

Since one of the major lessons of Part One is the benefit of expanding energy issues into wider project concerns, the only general rule for defining project-specific, energy-related criteria is to pattern them after the overall design criteria for the building. If the objective is to integrate energy issues with broader design needs and opportunities, it makes little sense to initiate the process by holding energy-related criteria separate from the needs of the project. If the major project objective is to increase the productivity of office workers, or to increase sales, or to make money, then the major energy-related objective should be to design an energy-conserving building that directly supports productivity, sales, or profits. After all, Part One demonstrates that there are a great many legitimate choices and options to the design of energy-responsive commercial buildings. One of the few decision-making tools available to designers is the comparative value of competing alternatives to meet the needs of the overall project.

Requests from the client of a qualitative nature, such as a need to project an energy-awareness image, are best incorporated into specific overall project needs. For instance, a client for a health food store could request an overall building image that reflects, reinforces, and physically expresses the lifestyle and beliefs of a targeted customer group in order to increase sales volume. As a marketing device, a building that embodies and presents a natural, back-to-basics image could represent a competitive advantage over stores housed in conventional structures. By association, a unique building that physically symbolizes a commitment to the concerns, beliefs, and lifestyle of the targeted customer will suggest that the merchandise for sale is what he or she wants. Realizing that the objective of image is increased sales and that the means to this end are the strong visual expression and reflection of the beliefs of a specific set of people, the designer can negotiate a very comprehensive description of the purpose and criteria of an energy-awareness image with the client. With such an approach, the issue becomes intertwined with marketing studies and other broader issues rather than focused on energy alone.

Qualitative energy-related design criteria must be accompanied with clearly defined quantitative criteria that specify the limits within which the qualitative results must be achieved. Beyond the collection of base facts, such as the minimum and maximum design conditions or code requirements, quantitative criteria must provide a test that can be used to differentiate clearly between successful and unacceptable solutions. Such criteria can take on many forms and are often project specific. However, one energy-related criterion common to all the case studies of Part One is economics. Project- and energy-related economic criteria are perhaps the best measurement to judge the appropriateness of any proposed solution.

Once again, if the general rule is to expand energy-related design issues into broader design concerns, energy-related economic criteria should reflect the economic criteria for the overall project. All clients perceive commercial buildings as an investment. Whether the client is the federal government that seeks to lower long-term operating cost by building rather than leasing, or a speculative developer whose interest is to build, lease, and immediately sell an office building, the decision to build or not to build a commercial building is based on the assessment of financial benefit or advantage. The broadest based energy-related economic criterion for any project is the one that matches the go-or-no-go investment criteria for the entire project. Perhaps the best description of a superior energy-responsive commercial building solution is one that meets or exceeds the qualitative project criteria while improving the client's overall project investment potential and advantage.

The key facts to collect from the client at this point of the design process are (a) how can the client financially profit from an investment in energy-responsive design, (b) what, if any, additional construction dollars is the client willing to add to the project to achieve this result, (c) what internal rate of return must the investment produce to either be competitive with alternative investment opportunities or to match the rate of return of the entire project, and (d) in what time frame does the client expect to achieve this stated internal rate of return.

Clients can profit from an investment in energy-responsive design in many different ways. For clients who will retain ownership of a building for a long term, energy-responsive design can represent a profitable investment in reduced future utility-related operating costs. If the building is to be constructed and sold in a short investment time frame, an investment advantage must be found that produces additional income for the client in the near future. This second alternative investment approach is defined and explained in greater detail in the second design example presented in Chapter Seven of this book. Additional profit motives include increased sales and the marketing or publicity value of energy-responsive design.

Determining how many additional construction dollars the client is willing or has available to invest in energy-responsive design must also be decided. In some cases, no additional money may be available. In such a case, energy-related alternatives that add to the overall project cost can only be provided through the construction cost-balancing techniques demonstrated earlier in case studies like 33 West Monroe, Baranco Pontiac, and the Bateson Building. If the client is motivated and capable of paying more now to defray future operating costs, a very specific range and upper limit of added cost must now be obtained from the client.

The internal rate of return (IRR) expected by the client on any energy-related investment is perhaps the most important fact to obtain from the client at this point. IRR defines the profit level the client expects from any investment in energy-responsive design. IRR does not include financing cost and can be specified as a before-tax or after-tax rate of return. This value establishes a profit benchmark, and allows the client to equate an investment in energy-responsive design either with the cost of financing energy-related construction cost increases or with alternative investment opportunities.

To be useful, an IRR must be accompanied by an investment time frame that defines the period in which a specific rate of return must be achieved. While most clients are aware that reduced utility operating costs will increase over the years as utility billing rates rise, and that many investments in energy-responsive design are good for the life of the building, clients consider long-term cost and benefit projections to be unreal and risky. An investment time frame acceptable to the client is typically much shorter than the life of the building. For a speculative developer, an appropriate time frame may be 3 years or less. A 5–10-year investment time frame is typical of owner-occupied buildings while 10–20-year time frames are more typical of government buildings.

The importance of collecting these facts will become more apparent later in this chapter when their use is defined and presented. Chapter Eight provides greater detail on the topic for readers not well acquainted with real estate investment analysis. The value of energy-responsive design for a specific client is greatly influenced by the availability and value of money over time to the client. Investment analysis is central to the recommended design approach presented in this chapter. It is used to both set energy-related design goals for a specific project, and to assess the financial value of all proposed energy-related alternatives.

In presenting the recommended design approach of this chapter at various conferences and seminars, we frequently have been asked why such a large emphasis is placed on financial value when the true major energy issues are pollution, health, quality of life, and the prevention of war and famine. Many well-meaning designers have been frustrated in the search for cost-effective, energy-related solutions. They feel that the short-sighted profit motives of investors limit the designers' ability to address these major social concerns. Certainly, one alternative is to legislate energy efficiency and demand a collective realization of the value of nonrenewable resources. Yet, unless the basic economic system in the United States is also changed, the design challenge will still be to find solutions that achieve energy efficiency while providing maximum value to investors.

Equating value to dollars is not a denial of the serious social implications of the limits to nonrenewable resources. Based on the examples of Chapters Three and Four, it appears that aligning investors is a far more effective approach than dismissing the personal profit motive that so greatly influences the construction of commercial buildings in this country. The study of motives and new perceived advantages is the key to finding appropriate solutions. It is our opinion that aligning social energy goals with profit motives is both a means to accelerate our collective impact on the use of nonrenewable energy in the built environment and to provide important insights for innovation and reinvention.

In these few short paragraphs, it is impossible to list or define the great number of different qualitative and quantitative energy-related design criteria that can be generated for energy-responsive commercial buildings. The importance of these early energy-related facts cannot be overstressed. If one accepts that there are numerous legitimate alternatives to the design of energy-responsive commercial buildings, and that the state of the art is the innovative recombination of existing building elements to suit new purposes, then qualitative and quantitative energy-related design criteria, when combined with the broadest whole-building concerns in a way that defines new motives and perceived advantages for people, represent seeds for design innovation and reinvention. The ultimate concern for energy issues through design is social and not technological. Beyond the application of substitute components, the design of energy-responsive commercial buildings is a result of well-defined and fulfilled social ends that use and modify technology as needed. Energy-related design criteria are not just simple project facts. Rather, they represent the key mind-set and approach that distinguish between solutions that are early incremental change learning experiences and solutions that approach and exceed the present state of the art in the design of energy-responsive commercial buildings.

BASE BUILDING GENERATION AND ASSESSMENT

As discussed in Chapter Five, the energy-use needs and causes of commercial buildings are not intuitively obvious to most building designers. Without a fair degree of experience in the design of energy-responsive commercial buildings, how one can achieve the energy-related project criteria is a matter of study and not immediately apparent. In this approach, preliminary energy-use and cost estimates should be made for the building before design alternatives are proposed. The means to these estimates are the generating and assessing of a simplified base building that reflects the general programmatic requirements of the project and the common design practices of the team.

A base building is only a starting point that permits the design team members to generate information that is outside their personal experience; it is not a solution to the problems and needs of a particular design challenge. A base building should reflect facts known about the actual project at this point of the design process, yet need not be detailed. The purpose of a base building is to inform and educate the design team about the significant energy-use needs and causes for the project, not to represent a viable solution for the client. With experience, a base building assessment step will not be necessary. However, until the energy needs and opportunities of commercial buildings become obvious to designers, a little extra study at this point of the design process is well worth the effort.

To establish a base building, certain preliminary architectural and engineering assumptions must be made. The architectural decisions are related to the programmatic requirements of the building and initial assumptions about form and the functional arrangement of spaces. The engineering decisions deal with assumptions about mechanical and electrical systems that are typically appropriate for the type of design challenge under study. Many of the assumptions can be based upon minimum requirements to meet code or on common design practices of the team. For retrofit projects, the task is simplified since the existing building can be used as the base building. A detailed description of how to generate a base building for new construction is presented in Chapter Nine.

Table 6.2 and Figures 6.1, 6.2, and 6.3 show the types of information and assumptions that must be made to define a base building. This base building was generated to reflect the building program summary presented in Table 6.1. This material may appear to be fairly comprehensive, yet is easily generated by the design team in an hour or less for most projects.

TABLE 6.1. ARCHITECTURAL PROGRAM SUMMARY

Owner-occupied corporate headquarters

Building area	10,000 ft^2
Office areas	5,800 ft^2, perimeter office (to a depth of 15 ft) open office plan in core
Conference rooms	1,600 ft^2, perimeter corner locations
Support services	located primarily in building core: these include restrooms, storage, lobby/entrance, and circulation space, 2,600 ft^2
Net/gross	approximately 0.75
Occupancy pattern	08.00–17.00 hr (plus 2 hr of cleaning at night)
Corporate tax rate	46%
Desired IRR	20% over 10 yrs

TABLE 6.2. BASE BUILDING SUMMARY

Location	Pittsburgh, flat urban site, no shading
Overall character	Slab-on-grade Light steel construction $60 \times 160 \times 12$ ft, oriented E/W 9 ft 6 in. floor to ceiling Hung ceilings and carpeting Glass area = 50% of 9 ft 6 in. floor/ceiling height
Opaque walls, roof	R-14 walls R-25 opaque roof R-4 perimeter slab insulation
Glazing	U = 0.58, SC = 0.58 Double pane glass
HVAC	Central VAV system, located on roof Perimeter baseboard heating
Electrical	2.5 W/ft^2 lighting load (occupied) 0.1 W/ft^2 lighting load (unoccupied) 0.33 W/ft^2 misc. equipment load (occupied only)
Ventilation rates	7.5 cfm/person in office areas 15 cfm/person in conference rooms
Thermal control strategy	68°F heating/78°F cooling (occupied) 55°F heating/90°F cooling (unoccupied)
Service hot water	1 gal/person/day 50°F in, 120°F out
Fuel costs	Heating oil at $1.25/gal Electricity at $0.03/kWh and $7.28/kW Gas at $3/45/MBtu
Fuel escalation rate	10%/yr

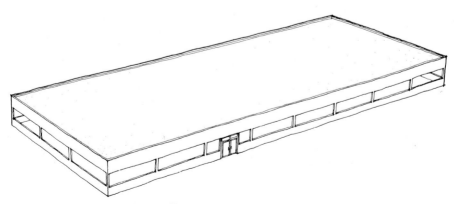

Figure 6.1. Pittsburgh office, base building. Courtesy of Michael E. Doyle.

193

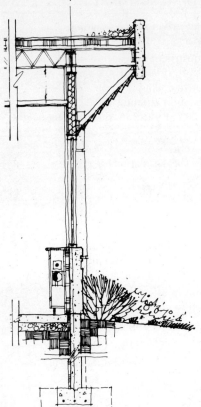

Figure 6.2. Pittsburgh office, base building wall section. Courtesy of Michael E. Doyle.

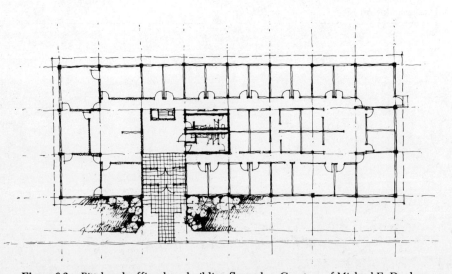

Figure 6.3. Pittsburgh office, base building floor plan. Courtesy of Michael E. Doyle.

TABLE 6.3.   BASE BUILDING, CONSTRUCTION COST ESTIMATES

	Total Cost ($)	Cost (per gross ft²) ($)	% of Total
(a) Foundations	29,897	2.98	6.7
(b) Superstructure	19,030	1.89	4.3
(c) Exterior closure	103,136	10.27	23.4
(d) Interior construction	57,154	5.69	13.0
(e) Vertical conveyance	—	—	—
(f) Finishes	25,348	2.52	5.7
(g) Plumbing	12,800	1.27	2.9
(h) HVAC systems cooling-heating 18T 99 kBtu h	54,287	5.40	12.3
(i) Electrical and lighting	50,135	4.99	11.4
(j) Site preparation	15,830	1.58	3.7
Subtotal	367,611		
(k) General contractor markup	36,767	3.66	8.3
(l) Contingencies	36,761	3.66	8.3
Total	441,133	48.92	100.00

Most decisions are made on a "best guess" basis, and represent only an agreed-upon starting point for predesign energy and cost analysis. For retrofit projects, this task is greatly simplified since the existing building can be used as the base building.

As illustrated in Table 6.3, the base building is first used to estimate project construction costs. Preliminary cost estimates are important for two reasons. First, they provide a check that insures the base building represents construction practices and means appropriate to the budget of the project. At a base building brainstorming session where all parties are aware that the intended end result is an energy-responsive commercial building, it is very common for each represented discipline to suggest high quality and expensive systems and materials. The use of large amounts of insulation, reflective glazing, high-quality energy-efficient lighting systems, and sophisticated HVAC systems at this point of the design process only load the problem if sufficient construction dollars are not available for these options. Estimating the construction cost of the base building will insure that appropriate base building assumptions are made.

The base building cost estimate is also very important in projects where additional energy-related construction dollars are not available. In such cases, investments in energy-responsive design can only be made by decreasing construction cost elsewhere on the project. The preliminary cost-estimate breakdown presents all the categories where cost balancing can be considered. As with case studies such as 33 West Monroe and the Ft.

Lauderdale Federal Building–U.S. Courthouse, major seeds for reinvention may be in foundations, superstructure, finishes, and exterior enclosure rather than in the traditional energy-related mechanical and electrical categories. Providing a complete base building construction cost breakdown puts these factors our for the design team's consideration and provides a base against which the construction cost of design alternatives can be compared as they are developed during schematic design.

While generating the cost estimate, the design team cost analyst should document any costs that are a result of base building assumptions rather than the specific programmatic needs of the project. For instance, if the team assumes a cubelike multistory form for the project where a one-story building is a distinct possibility, the cost analyst should flag expenditures such as vertical transportation, increases in superstructure, or additional code-required fireproofing. Such costs are attributed to basic architectural decisions, and their clarification before design alternatives are proposed will greatly aid the design team.

The major purpose of defining a base building at this point of the design process is to permit the team to explore the probable energy-use needs and causes of the building type under study. Rather than relying on national or regional statistical data bases that might not reflect the client's programmatic needs, the design team's current capabilities and beliefs about energy-responsive design, or the impact of additional variables such as peak-demand charges, we strongly recommend that the design team define and assess the energy-use need and causes of a base building that reflect the design challenge at hand. At some point in the future, this added design chore will not be necessary as more experience and knowledge are gained about the energy needs of specific building types in specific climates. However, the survey presented at the start of Chapter Five strongly suggests that the appropriate place to begin for most designers is with a crystal-clear definition of the major energy needs and interconnected relationships of these needs for the proposed project.

We recommend the collection and generation of four distinct sets of information to describe the energy-use needs and causes of the base building. The four sets of information are (a) utility billings and energy use of comparable existing buildings in the region, (b) total annual energy use and cost as calculated from the base building, (c) elimination parametrics and (d) design day diurnal summaries, which are called rainbow plots in this text. To better define and exemplify these information sets, each is presented in greater detail.

The analysis of energy use in commercial buildings by calculation is an evolving art. Caution should be the rule until the design team acquires sufficient experience to understand the limits of a particular building energy analysis tool or technique. To ensure that the energy analysis methods used by the design team are providing reasonable approximations of the energy needs of the base building, it is helpful to collect utility data from comparable existing buildings before energy analysis begins. Most utility companies will provide this type of information. Another source of such information is the client. The utility billings and energy use of the last school constructed in the district, or from the last office building constructed by the developer, will reflect the true annual utility cost associated with the type of building the client wants.

Another way of constructing a utility bill data base is to request past and present clients to forward copies of their monthly utility bill to your office. Richard Rittelmann, AIA, of Burt Hill, Kosar, and Rittlemann uses this tack to provide both a data base on the annual utility cost of various building types and to serve as a check to insure the environmental-control systems are performing as designed. After a year or two of actual data are collected for a building, significant increases in the use of energy in any month can be identified. In such cases, he contacts the client and arranges a field inspection. More often than not, a simple maintenance problem, such as an operable louver stuck in the wrong position, can be found.

Even if a very good data base exists on the energy needs of a particular building type in a specific climate, the design team should go the extra step to estimate the energy use for the base building. Actual utility bills will not show a breakdown of energy use for specific needs. Five analysis tools, ranging in size from manual calculation techniques to mainframe computer simulation codes, are presented in Chapter Nine. Each of these tools is capable of being used to analyze base buildings and design alternatives generated during the predesign and schematic design phases of the recommended approach. It is helpful to select the tool that will be used prior to defining the base building for the project since the input needs of each tool can be different. The energy analysis presented in this chapter, as well as in Chapter Seven, was performed using DOE 2.1A, one of the five analysis tools discused in Chapter Nine.

The first calculated information set that should be produced by the team energy analyst is a total cost and energy-use breakdown for the building as illustrated in Table 6.4. The end-use annual energy needs and cost of each environmental-control subsystem should be identified on a square-foot basis. A breakdown of energy need in end-use Btu is important for projects that must meet local or state energy codes. The cost data are important for two reasons. First, they include a clearer picture of the design challenge since both energy-use charges and peak-demand charges can be combined. Second, to make financial comparisons of future design alternatives a base annual utility cost must now be determined. We strongly recommend that the reader use total annual utility cost as the yardstick to appraise the comparative magnitude of specific energy needs for the building since cost reflects off-site energy subsidies such as electrical generation. This conversion between dollars and primary energy is indeed not perfect. Yet, based on our experience, it is much better than solely tracking end-use Btu.

The design team can gain valuable insight into the energy needs of the

TABLE 6.4. BASE BUILDING, ANNUAL ENERGY-USE ESTIMATES

End-Use	Consumption						Demand		Total Cost (Cons. + Dem.) ($/ft²)
	Elec. (kBtu/ft²)	Elec. ($/ft²)	Gas (kBtu/ft²)	Gas ($/ft²)	Total (kBtu/ft²)	Total ($/ft²)	Elec. (W/ft²)	Elec. ($/ft²)	
Equipment	0.649	0.0057	–	–	0.649	0.0057	1.195	0.0087	0.0144
Hot water	–	–	1.675	0.0058	1.675	0.0058	–	–	0.0058
Cooling	4.858	0.0427	–	–	4.858	0.0427	14.615	0.1064	0.1491
Lighting	18.967	0.1667	–	–	18.967	0.1667	28.571	0.2080	0.3747
Heating	0.613	0.0054	17.260	0.0595	17.873	0.0649	0.082	0.0006	0.0655
Total	25.087	0.2205	18.935	0.0653	44.022	0.2858	44.464	0.3237	0.6095

Notes: Cooling includes HVAC AUX.
Lighting at 2.0 W/ft² connected load.
Equipment at 0.33 W/ft².

Rates: Gas—$3.45/MBtu = $0.00345/kBtu.
Elec.—$0.03/kWh = $0.00879/kBtu consumption.
$7.28/kW = $0.00728/W

Light demand: (Assume one conference room in use at monthly peak). [(800 × 1.0) + (9200 × 2.5)] divided by 10,000 × 3.413 × 12 divided by 1000 = 0.0975.

198

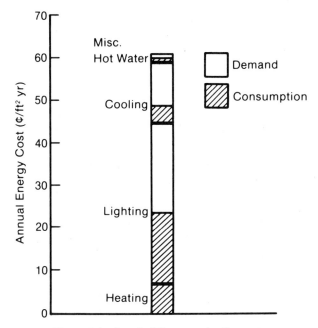

Figure 6.4.   Base building annual utility costs.

base building by studying the information in Table 6.4. For instance, the total energy use for the example base building is 44,022 Btu/ft² per year. Notice that heating and lighting are almost equal to each other and represent 41% and 43% of total annual energy use, respectively. However, a review of the total annual cost data presents a distinctly different picture. Lighting represents about 61.5% of the total annual utility cost. Heating and cooling combined represent only 35.2% of total annual cost. Demand charges at 32.4¢/ft² per year represent 53.1% of total need by cost. Demand charges are 60% of the office equipment costs, 72% of annual cooling costs, and 56% of the annual lighting costs.

In this building, when energy is needed is a greater problem than how much is used throughout the year. To clarify further the relative magnitude of the individual energy uses and needs of the base building, it is often beneficial to present the total annual cost breakdown as a bar graph as shown in Figure 6.4.

Elimination Parametrics

Elimination parametrics is an additional energy analysis technique that can inform the design team of the energy-use causes in the base building. Knowing the energy use or annual cost by equipment is of limited value, since it tells very little about what generated the need in the first place. For example, the annual energy use and the cost of the lighting system does not totally reflect the actual annual energy needed by the building for lighting purposes. The heat of lights will directly impact both the cooling and heating needs of the building. Clarifying the interdependent nature of individual elements of environmental control is the purpose of elimination parametrics.

Any energy analysis tool that can simulate the base building can also be used to appraise total annual energy need with one or more elements of environmental control eliminated from the problem. As shown in Figure 6.5, the comparison of the original base building annual utility cost to similar cost data for the base case with a specific variable eliminated from the problem provides an approximation of the total annual energy cost of the eliminated variable. Likewise, the annual cost changes in other categories such as heating and cooling will indicate how much the eliminated variable indirectly impacts these elements of environmental control.

As listed in Table 6.5, it is recommended that 10 different environmental-control elements be singularly eliminated and presented to provide a very detailed assessment of the causes of energy use for the base building. Figure 6.5 shows the annual energy cost for the example base building and for the base building with each of these 10 variables eliminated. A comparison of the annual cost totals and the changes in individual energy needs in each bar greatly clarifies the causes of energy need for this building.

By comparing the bars that represent the elimination of internal loads (no. 5) and the elimination of envelope-related loads (no. 10), whether the building is internally load dominated or envelope dominated can be quickly determined. In this example, it can be seen that internal loads dominate. If there were no internal loads, the annual energy cost for the building would be 20.7¢/ft^2 per year. Without any envelope loads, the cost would be 51.2¢/ft^2 per year. Compared to the base building data, eliminating all envelope loads would save about 9.8¢/ft^2 per year, a 16% reduction. Eliminating all of the internal energy needs would result in a 40.2¢/ft^2 per year savings, a 66% reduction in annual cost.

The elimination parametric base can also be used to clearly identify the controlling energy need of the project. An appraisal of the four internal load-related elimination parametric bars quickly indicates that the internal loads of this base building are dominated by lighting energy needs (no. 1). The elimination of lights from the building substantially reduces the annual cost of lights, plus reduces the annual cooling demand charge by 34%, reduces the annual cooling consumption charge by 27%, and increases the annual cost for heating by 28%.

Each individual elimination parametric bar informs the design team of the impact the variable in question has on all other environmental-control systems. For instance, the elimination of solar heat gains through glazing

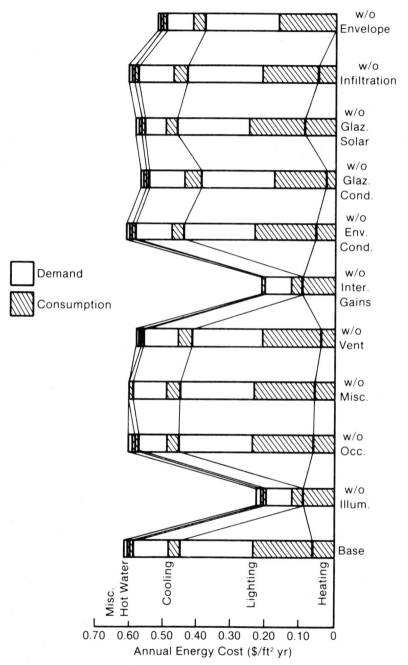

Figure 6.5. Elimination parametrics.

TABLE 6.5. ELIMINATION PARAMETRIC CATEGORIES

Elimination Parametric Category	Input Change
(1) Illumination	$W/ft^2 = 0$
(2) Occupants	occup. $= 0$
(3) Equipment	$W/ft^2 = 0$
(4) Ventilation	cfm $= 0$
(5) Internal loads (combination of 1–4)	
(6) Opaque envelope conduction	$R = 300$
(7) Glazing conduction	$k = 0$
(8) Solar gain on glazing	$Q = 0$
(9) Infiltration	$Q = 0$
(10) Envelope loads (combination of 6–9)	

(no. 8) clearly demonstrates a significant reduction in annual cooling demand and consumption cost equal to the elimination of lights. The elimination parametrics clearly show that the major need for cooling for this building is to offset the heat of lights and solar heat gains through glazing. Likewise, the elimination parametrics for this example indicate that lights and solar heat gains through glazing are the major sources of useful heat that offset annual heating cost, and that conduction heat loss through glazing is the major cause of the annual heating need.

Environmental-control elements that are both beneficial at some times during the year and detrimental at other times can also be interpreted from the elimination parametrics. For instance, the elimination of solar heat gains through glazing significantly reduces annual cooling costs, yet increases the annual heating needs. This fact informs the design team that solar heat gains through glass, if treated appropriately, could reduce energy need in both seasons.

Further insight into the use of the elimination parametrics is presented in the design examples of the next chapter. Also, more information about how to construct the charts is included in Chapter Nine.

Rainbow Plots

The last energy-related analysis products that should be generated to clarify the energy needs of the base building are rainbow plots. Rainbow plots are charts of the diurnal energy needs of the building for specific seasonal design days. The analysis of six different design days appears to be most helpful. These design days are: (*a*) winter, typical; (*b*) spring, typical; (*c*) summer, typical; (*d*) fall, typical; (*e*) winter, peak; and (*f*) summer, peak. For each design day, the plotting of eight different variables over the

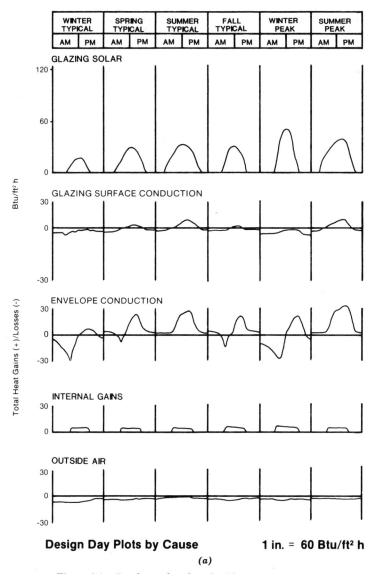

Figure 6.6. Rainbow plots for a building perimeter zone.

24-hour period is recommended. The eight variables are: (*a*) glazing, solar; (*b*) glazing, conduction; (*c*) envelope, conduction; (*d*) internal gains (occupants, equipment, and lights); (*e*) outside air (infiltration and ventilation); (*f*) total heat gains and losses; (*g*) interior air temperature; and (*h*) heat addition and extraction.

As illustrated in Figure 6.6, rainbow plots detail the cumulative hourly energy events that influence the need for energy in a building. At the

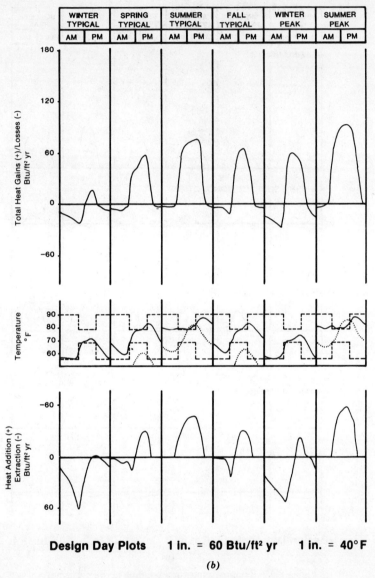

Design Day Plots   1 in. = 60 Btu/ft² yr   1 in. = 40°F

(b)

Figure 6.6.   (Continued)

simplest level, these charts indicate when peak-period energy needs are encountered in typical seasonal days and during the extreme seasonal days. The charts also define when heating and cooling is needed, which informs the design team of how alternative thermal systems and design concepts can best be used. For instance, Figure 6.6, which represents the perimeter zone of a building, indicates that the major need for heating always occurs during the first hour start-up that initiates the occupancy period of the building. Knowing this fact better prepares the design team to define the types of heating system alternatives that might be most useful for this particular project.

At a more advanced level, rainbow plots are very helpful to assess complex thermal problems. However, most designers will find that rainbow plots are less important than the elimination parametrics and may only be minimally used in many projects. With experience and further intuitive knowledge of when buildings peak in energy need, it is possible to design many buildings without using such plots at all. However, until this experience is gained, these charts should be a central part of predesign energy analysis. Typically, these charts must be generated to produce the total amount energy use and cost data. Whether they are presented to the design team or simply summarized as a list of energy-use facts is a decision the team energy analyst must make. Often a large array of rainbow plots might confuse the design team more than aid and inform it.

Further discussion of generating rainbow plots, as well as variations of this technique that produce rainbow plots for individual building blocks and zones, is presented in Chapter Nine.

Predesign energy-use data for a base building, like the base building construction cost estimates, should include an assessment by the team analyst of energy needs that are more related to the selected base building than to the design challenge at hand. For instance, if the base building included a large expanse of west-facing glazing that greatly increases the annual and peak cooling costs, and this feature was an arbitrary decision and not due to real project constraints, the design team energy analyst should clearly state this fact. Flagging such nonessential energy needs clarifies the actual energy-related design challenge of the project.

The Financial Value of Energy-Responsive Design

The next step in the recommended approach that further informs the team of the energy-related design challenge of the project is to define the financial value of energy-responsive design. With an estimate of the first-year, utility-related operating cost for the project, and with a statement of the client's investment criteria for energy-responsive design, investment analysis techniques can be used to generate a range of initial construction dollars that can be spent to achieve specific reductions in annual utility-related operating cost. As exemplified in Figure 6.7, such an output defines the net present value of energy-responsive design.

The information in Figure 6.7 is generated by assuming specific fractional reductions in total base-building annual energy costs, projecting these cost savings over the investment term the client is willing to consider by using an assumed energy-cost escalation rate, and discounting these

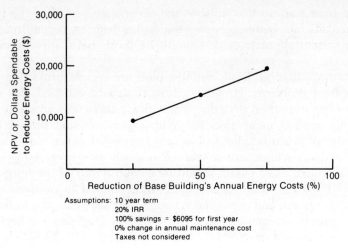

Assumptions: 10 year term
20% IRR
100% savings = $6095 for first year
0% change in annual maintenance cost
Taxes not considered

Figure 6.7.   The net present value of energy-responsive design.

future benefits by the desired rate of return of the client. By performing these calculations for three levels of energy-related improvement, say, at 25%, 50%, and 75% reduction in first-year operating costs, a graph can be delineated that relates reductions in annual energy operating cost to the number of initial construction dollars that can be spent to achieve that result. A very detailed description of how a net present value chart can be generated, and of the variations that are appropriate for different types of clients, is included in Chapter Eight.

A net present value chart can be used in two ways. In situations where the client is committed to spending additional construction dollars to invest in profitable energy-responsive design alternatives, the net present value chart clearly shows the levels of improvements that are required for various expenditures to meet the client's investment criteria. When no additional construction dollars are available for energy-related improvements, the net present value chart can be used in conjunction with cost-balancing techniques to decide where dollars saved through innovations in structure, finishes, foundations, or envelope can be best applied. For instance, 33 West Monroe had several form and envelope innovations that reduced construction cost in those specific categories. Yet, the high-efficiency lighting and HVAC systems of that building did cost more than conventional systems. Even if major construction cost advantages are found for specific portions of a proposed project, one must wisely choose where those additional dollars can be used to produce a profitable energy-related investment. A net present value chart can set the level of results that must be achieved for specific expenditures in such cases.

A net present value chart is actually the first firm energy-related design goal that has been set in this recommended design approach. This chart is the first piece of information that directly connects a specific end result with a very specific description of how it must be achieved. While the benefits to energy-responsive design are not only financial, few other design requirements can be so clearly molded into as decisive a design goal. Design goals are central to the design of energy-responsive commercial buildings. However, we have intentionally avoided traditional energy-related design goals like 40,000 Btu/ft^2 per year because these goals have absolutely no significance to most building clients and the majority of building designers. It is our opinion that the net present value of energy-responsive design is one of the very few decisive energy-related design goals that can be formulated during the earliest stages of design. As the examples of the next chapter show, this information readily indicates a clear relationship between desired results and means.

ASSESSING ENERGY-RELATED OPPORTUNITIES

Predesign information tasks end with the design team assessing the major energy-related opportunities for the project. Based on the preceding criteria, construction costs, energy uses and causes, and the range of dollars available to achieve specific annual energy-cost reductions, the team should define the types of results that would best improve the overall energy needs of the project. At this point, desired results should be emphasized rather than a list of alternative components or solutions. Identifying components first will only push the design team toward substitute alternatives rather than allow the specific consumption and peak-demand needs and causes to suggest very precise interrelated design opportunities.

How the team defines the type of results they would like to achieve depends largely on experience and skills. Less-experienced designers typically gravitate to singular issues such as the need to reduce the consumption and demand cost of the controlling energy need. At an intermediate level, designers very often list specific combined form, envelope, and systems design goals that define consumption and peak-demand results in a highly integrated way. For instance, the goal to substantially reduce annual peak-demand costs for the base building example in this chapter would lead the team to define specific interrelationships between the cooling and lighting system as well as the control of solar heat gains during the building's peak hours of electrical use. With extensive experience and a thorough understanding of the costs and abilities of a great number of energy-related design alternatives, the team could well jump to the definition of a new building nature that solves the major energy-use needs of the project by simply avoiding major energy needs through the use of a completely different environmental-control approach. A sampling of the ways energy-related design opportunities can be defined at this point in the design process is shown in the next chapter.

SCHEMATIC DESIGN EXPERIMENTATION

During the earliest part of the schematic design phase, time should be allocated for the design team to propose and test alternative environmental-control solutions. In this phase, problem definition and assessment ceases; the emphasis is on the proposal and testing of possible physical solutions. Just as the energy needs of a base building are not intuitively obvious to most designers and require some extra study and assessment, the cost and abilities of alternative environmental-control solutions may not be immediately obvious and may require controlled experimentation. The purpose of this experimentation is not the testing of final solutions; rather, the intent is to explore the abilities and cost of specific alternatives. These tests are used to inform the project designer of the relative advantages and impact on people and design of different alternatives that, in the final schematic design, may be altered and combined in various ways to achieve both the overall objectives of the project and the energy-related criteria.

PROPOSED ALTERNATIVES

Based on the whole-building results defined at the conclusion of the predesign tasks, the design team should now suggest energy-related alternatives that appear to be appropriate for the project. These alternatives can be component-specific, such as a high-quality, high-efficiency lighting system to lower both annual consumption and peak-demand costs. At the other extreme, a totally different building form and envelope could be suggested that uses daylighting and early winter morning passive heating, and that carefully controls all solar heat gains during the cooling season. Once again, the difference between incremental change and reinvention is experience and insight, qualities that can be supported by process, but not directly replaced.

The predesign information should well direct the design team toward viable options and prevent the hit-or-miss component-testing approach of the incremental change method presented in Chapter Five. However, an energetic design team may still push for the consideration of many combinations of environmental-control options. To shorten the list of options that are tested, the elimination parametrics and the net present value chart can be used to screen proposed options on the basis of cost to benefit. For instance, if a team member wishes to test how well movable exterior solar window shades reduce annual cooling consumption and demand costs, the annual cooling cost difference between the base case and the solar heat gain elimination parametric can be determined. This annual savings represents the maximum cooling cost reduction that can be achieved by eliminating all solar heat gains through glass. Taking this maximum savings

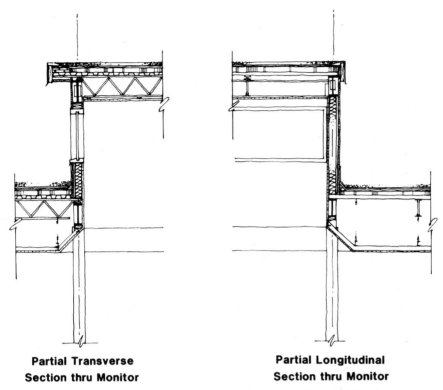

Partial Transverse
Section thru Monitor

Partial Longitudinal
Section thru Monitor

Figure 6.8.   Daylit alternative, details. Courtesy of Michael E. Doyle.

and finding the point on the net present value chart that reflects this degree of improvement, the construction dollars that can be spent to achieve this result can be estimated. If the cost of the movable shading devices readily exceeds this value, the option can be dropped from consideration.

As with the predesign base building, each alternative must be assessed in the context of whole-building energy needs. In effect, each experiment defined by the design team represents another base building. Typically, two or three new base buildings can be defined for further study.

As shown in Figures 6.8 and 6.9, simple sketches and plans can be quickly developed to test the construction costs and energy advantages of the alternate buildings proposed by the team. In this example, the team simply decided to focus maximum efforts on taming the controlling energy need of lighting. To reduce both annual consumption and peak-demand charges for the building, the team decided to experiment with the use of daylighting. Two simple daylighting alternatives were defined. One approach of using a simple two-way roof monitor to provide task illuminance to the interior of the building is shown here to exemplify the types of outputs that are generated during schematic design experimentation. A skylight alternative

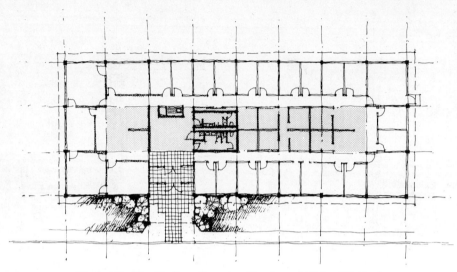

Figure 6.9. Daylit alternative, plan. Courtesy of Michael E. Doyle

to the problem is used in Chapter Nine to demonstrate the use of five different energy analysis tools to generate the information products introduced in this chapter.

EVALUATING ALTERNATIVES

For purposes of comparison, the costs and energy needs of alternative environmental-control solutions proposed by the design team should be studied in a manner similar to the techniques used for the base building. Once again, construction costs are assessed first. A comparison of base building and proposed alternative construction cost permits the incremental energy-related cost to be identified.

For the roof monitor example, existing glazing along the perimeter was assumed adequate to provide task illumination in the outer offices. However, to daylight the interior zones of the building, the roof configuration needed to be changed. Also, automated electric lighting controls were added to the existing luminaires. Both of these changes represent construction cost increases. Table 6.6 outlines the new construction cost estimate for the proposed alternative. As compared to the base case, costs have increased by about $8000.

Energy analysis for the alternative is likewise performed according to the base building techniques presented earlier. Where a new of unique component or option is included in the alternative, such as daylighting in this example, additional calculations may be required before the new whole-building annual energy-use estimate can be calculated. Chapter Ten

**TABLE 6.6.   DAYLIT ALTERNATIVE, CONSTRUCTION
COST ESTIMATES**

	Total Cost ($)	Cost (per gross ft²) ($)	% of Total
(a) Foundations	29,897	2.98	6.7
(b) Superstructure	21,170	2.11	4.7
(c) Exterior closure	114,447	11.39	25.5
(d) Interior construction	57,665	5.74	12.8
(e) Vertical conveyance	—	—	—
(f) Finishes	52,828	2.57	5.8
(g) Plumbing	12,800	1.27	2.8
(h) HVAC systems	51,515	5.12	11.5
(i) Electrical and lighting	44,841	4.46	10.0
(j) Site preparation	16,117	1.60	3.6
Subtotal	374,280		
(k) General contractor markup	37,428	3.73	8.3
(l) Contingencies	37,428	3.73	8.3
Total	449,136	44.72	100.0

addresses the topic of how one must assess special components or options that are not included in the abilities of building energy analysis tools and programs.

Determining the new annual energy use and costs for the alternative permits the design team to appraise the comparative future utility cost benefit of the $8000 investment. As shown in Table 6.7 and Figure 6.10, the energy needs of the example have been reduced by about 50%.

Whether or not elimination parametrics are generated at this point for each proposed alternative is a matter of choice. If the team wishes to understand how the daylighting option can be better utilized, or wishes to assess additional design alternatives that can be used in conjunction with the roof monitors, then the elimination parametrics should be generated. However, if the team is satisfied with the results of the alternative and wishes to stop energy-related experimentation, elimination parametrics are not generally necessary. Chapter Seven shows how elimination parametrics can be used during schematic design experimentation.

The 50% annual energy-operating cost reduction for an expenditure of $8000 is well within the financial criteria of Figure 6.7. However, now that an actual design alternative exists, a much more thorough assessment of financial value can be determined. The original net present value chart did not include factors such as income tax on operating cost savings or the effects of depreciation factors that are difficult to assess without the physical definition of an alternative. To better define the financial potential

TABLE 6.7. DAYLIT ALTERNATIVE, ANNUAL ENERGY—USE ESTIMATES

End-Use	Consumption						Demand		Total Cost
	Elec. (kBtu/ft²)	Elec. ($/ft²)	Gas (kBtu/ft²)	Gas ($/ft²)	Total (kBtu/ft²)	Total ($/ft²)	Elec. (W/ft²)	Elec. ($/ft²)	(Cons. + Dem.) ($/ft²)
Equipment	0.649	0.0057	–	–	0.649	0.0057	1.195	0.0087	0.0144
Hot water	–	–	1.675	0.0058	1.675	0.0058	–	–	0.0058
Cooling	3.702	0.0326	–	–	3.702	0.0326	11.455	0.0834	0.1160
Lighting	5.741	0.0505	–	–	5.741	0.0505	8.997	0.0655	0.1160
Heating	0.743	0.0065	19.885	0.0686	20.628	0.0751	0.055	0.0004	0.0755
Total	10.835	0.0953	21.560	0.0744	32.395	0.1697	21.702	0.1580	0.3277

Notes: Cooling includes HVAC AUX.
Demand is sum of monthly demand bills.
Lighting at 0.75 W/ft².
Equipment at 0.10 W/ft².

Rates: Gas—$3.45/MBtu = $0.00345/kBtu.
Elec.—$0.03/kWh = $0.00879/kBtu consumption.
$7.28/kW = $0.00728/W

Light demand: (Assume one conference room in use at monthly peak). [(800 × 0.75) + (9200 × 0.75)] divided by 10,000 × 3.413 × 12 divided by 1000 = 0.0307.

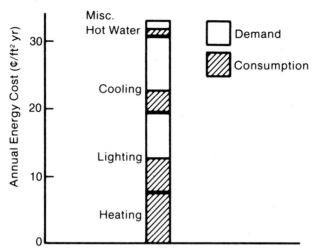

Figure 6.10. Daylit alternative, annual utility cost.

of the daylighting alternative, a complete cash flow analysis, as shown in Table 6.8, should be generated by the design team. From this analysis, the actual internal rate of return to the client for the investment in the daylighting alternative can be calculated.

How Table 6.8 is generated is reviewed in detail in Chapter Eight. In simple terms, Table 6.8 represents a spread sheet that documents the differentials in the inflows and outflows of cash to the client over a 10-year period that the investment in the daylighting alternative would produce as compared to the original base building. Note that two separate analyses are contained in Table 6.8. The first set of numbers represents a profitability analysis. The bottom line of this analysis is the differential in after-tax earnings to the client. The cash flow analysis, the second set of numbers in Table 6.8, ends with a differential in after-tax cash flow to the client. Profitability analysis reflects how the client would calculate the income produced by the energy-related investment for tax purposes. Cash flow analysis documents the real after-tax money received by the client. The difference between the two methods is the paper loss of depreciation. Presenting these two analysis methods together allows the client to see the benefits of the depreciation differential created by the energy-related increased construction costs, and indicates how the tax differential was calculated for inclusion in the cash flow analysis. Most clients will be keenly interested in the after-tax cash flow.

The financial analysis presented in Table 6.8 represents several qualities of superior investments in energy-responsive design. First, the after-tax cash flow is positive from the first year of occupancy. Another key advantage is that the positive cash flow over the 10-year term is very high for an $8000

TABLE 6.8. DAYLIT ALTERNATIVES—IMPACT OF REDUCED ENERGY OPERATING COSTS ON EARNINGS AFTER TAXES AND ANNUAL CASH FLOW

	Yr 1	Yr 2	Yr 3	Yr 4	Yr 5	Yr 6	Yr 7	Yr 8	Yr 9	Yr 10
Profitability Analysis										
Differential in energy-related operating costs	2818	3100	3410	3751	4126	4538	4992	5491	6041	6645
Differential in depreciation	(533)	(533)	(533)	(533)	(533)	(533)	(533)	(533)	(533)	(533)
Pretax earnings	2285	2567	2877	3218	3593	4005	4459	4958	5508	6112
Tax differential	(1051)	(1181)	(1323)	(1480)	(1653)	(1842)	(2051)	(2281)	(2534)	(2811)
Differential in after-tax earnings	1234	1386	1553	1738	1940	2163	2408	2678	2974	3300
Cash Flow Analysis										
Differential in energy-related operating costs	2818	3100	3410	3751	4126	4538	4992	5491	6041	6645
Tax differential	(1051)	(1181)	(1323)	(1480)	(1653)	(1842)	(2051)	(2281)	(2534)	(2811)
After-tax cash flow	1767	1919	2086	2271	2473	2696	2941	3211	3507	3833

Base assumptions:
Client: Owner of owner-occupied building.
Financier: Owner, internally financed.
Additional cost of energy-responsive building: $8000.
Reduction in energy operating costs: $2818 for the first year.

Fuel escalation rate: 10%/yr.
Depreciation Method: 15-yr straight line: $8000 ÷ 15 = $533.
Corporate Tax Rate: 46%.

Note: Parentheses indicate negative cash flow.

initial investment. Using the formula presented in Chapter Eight, the actual internal rate of return to the client is 42.6% before taxes and 25.7% after taxes.

SYNTHESIS

Whether one or five alternative designs are generated and tested during schematic design, the results of these experiments should be treated generically and comparatively. In all likelihood, additional schematic design investigations to test the overall building's needs and functional relationships will push the solution toward a distinctly different form than that assumed in the base building or in any of the energy-related experiments that were defined. As energy-related experiments that produce very positive results are found, the basic relationships between form, envelope, and systems that produce this result must be conveyed to the designer. Likewise design opportunities created by the functional and aesthetic schematic design studies for the whole building must flow back to the design team energy analyst. The final schematic design could well be daylit in this case, but the means could be dramatically changed as other design opportunities and needs arise through the schematic design phase.

In the simple example used in this chapter, the design team appraised the energy needs of the roof monitor alternative and of the skylit alternative presented in Chapter Nine. A comparison of the energy analysis results of the two design alternatives and the base building clearly defined for the

Figure 6.11.   Schematic design. Courtesy of Michael E. Doyle.

design team a very advantageous relationship between daylighting and building form and envelope.

As shown in Chapter Nine, a skylit alternative does reduce the annual energy need for lighting as compared to the base case. However, cooling and heating needs are significantly larger than those required for the roof monitor alternative. Daylighting apertures pointed toward the summer sun and away from the winter sun aggravate the heating and cooling needs of the building. With this information as a base, the team decided that the final schematic design should be daylit with the majority of building glazing oriented toward the north and south.

As shown in Figure 6.11, the team ended schematic design with a narrow building form oriented to the north and south.

CONCLUSIONS

The preceding recommended design shifts from collecting informative design data to making intuitive design decisions at several different points. We have not attempted to describe or extensively define how to go from a base building to specific proposed alternatives, or from the assessment of alternatives to the synthesis of a final schematic design. Although it is tempting to define how we personally make these connections or leaps, such a discussion would be of limited value to an audience of creative designers. The state of the art in the design of energy-responsive commercial buildings is innovation and reinvention. Although we believe the preceding approach can greatly aid the designer by organizing energy-related information and inform the designer of the significant energy uses, needs, and causes of a project, we do not suppose that the process by itself can in any way derive a final solution.

At this point in the design of energy-responsive buildings, it appears that the best way to derive successful solutions is to constantly educate designers to enable them to make better intuitive decisions. The recommended approach of this chapter can help in this regard, assuming the reader is constantly reviewing case studies like those presented in Part One in other books and professional journals. As Sarah Harkness states, "We really must . . . go back and forth; starting with the whole, taking it apart, putting it together, taking it apart, and so forth. Everthing is that way in our business." At best, the recommended design approach of this chapter can only aid in the taking-apart steps of this task. Yet, providing clarity at that level does represent an important step at this point in our collective experience.

chapter seven

APPLYING THE RECOMMENDED DESIGN APPROACH: THREE EXAMPLES

Genius is 1 percent inspiration and 99 percent perspiration.

THOMAS EDISON

This chapter presents three design examples to show how the recommended design approach of Chapter Six is applied to actual design problems. Whereas Chapter Six defines and introduces the recommended design approach, the three examples of this chapter demonstrate some of the ways the information products of the approach can aid and inform the design team of energy-related needs and opportunities.

Based on our experience with the recommended approach, it is apparent that the way the information products are used by a design team will change as designers become better informed of the energy needs of commercial buildings and the qualitative and quantitative advantages of energy-related options. To illustrate how the use of the recommended approach changes with experience, one design team is assumed in this chapter. The experience gained in each example will affect how the information products of the recommended approach are applied to the next design challenge. To begin, it is assumed that the design team has experience in incremental energy-related changes, yet does not have the level of experience required for reinvention. We believe that this middle level of application well reflects the majority of commercial building designers. Additional discussion of how the recommended approach can be further modified to fit the needs of a well-experienced design team is included in the conclusion of this chapter.

The three examples are an office building in Denver, Colorado, an office building in Pittsburgh, Pennsylvania, and a secondary school classroom wing addition in Chattanooga, Tennessee. Each case study shows how the standardized steps of the recommended approach can be applied to various building types and design challenges. By comparing the examples, one can see how factors such as climate, building function, utility rate structure, and client financial criteria can influence the search for energy-related improvements appropriate to a specific design problem. Very simple programs are assumed for all three examples to allow a greater emphasis on energy-related issues and techniques.

DENVER OFFICE BUILDING

Predesign Information

Project Facts and Criteria

The client for this project is a privately owned corporation that currently leases office space in three separate buildings. The project objectives are to build a formal yet functional corporate headquarters that lowers corporate operating costs through the advantages of real estate ownership. The client also wants an energy-efficient building to reduce annual utility-related operating costs and to exemplify the corporation's concern for energy conservation. As summarized in Table 7.1, the client's architectural program calls for 60,000 gross ft^2 of space for a construction budget of $3,100,000.

To establish energy-related project criteria, the design team asked the client for a specific minimum rate of return and investment time frame for evaluating energy-related alternatives. The client stated that additional money could be spent for energy-related improvements if the investment produced a 20% or more before-tax rate of return over a 10-year period. The client also stipulated that all such investments must not lower staff productivity or comfort.

An absolute upper limit the client was willing to spend for initial cost increases for energy-related improvements was 10% of total construction costs. However, the client stressed that such a large sum of money could be spent only if the final design could be publicized as one of the most energy-efficient buildings in the region.

The Base Building

In order to study the design challenge, the project design team generated a simple base building. This base building is only a starting point to assess issues outside of the team's present experience.

TABLE 7.1. DENVER OFFICE BUILDING, ARCHITECTURAL PROGRAM SUMMARY

Owner-occupied corporate headquarters	
Building area	60,000 ft^2
Functional units	Six divisions of equal area needs
Area breakdowns	−34,800 ft^2 of general office space −9,600 ft^2 of conference rooms; 24 in total −15,600 ft^2 support services and circulation
Net/gross	Approximately 0.75
Occupancy pattern	07.00–18.00 hr (includes start-up and cleaning)
Budget	$3,100,000.00
Energy-related financial criteria	IRR of 20% or more over 10-yr term; not to exceed $310,000 total investment

As shown in Figures 7.1–7.3, a simple six-story box was proposed. Each floor represents a separate corporate functional unit and is sized to hold the required number of offices, conference rooms, and support services. Details, such as the wall section in Figure 7.3, are considered to be typical of local conventions. A list of the base building assumptions is in Table 7.2.

Preliminary Construction Cost Estimate

With a starting point established, a preliminary construction cost summary was generated. As shown in Table 7.3, construction cost estimates were broken into standard construction elements based upon Means data with an adjustment for Denver. Since these cost estimates met the budget criteria for the project, the design team assumed that the base building systems and construction techniques reflected conventional practices for this building type and budget.

The design team cost estimator also noted that the assumed six-story base building has several cost advantages and liabilities compared to other forms that might be appropriate for this project. In a three-story alternative, for example, the near-cube base building results in relatively low-cost exterior closure and foundations, yet demands a relatively higher cost for superstructure.

Preliminary Energy Needs Estimate and Assessment

The base building energy needs were estimated by the design team analyst in two ways. First, information was gathered from the local utility on the

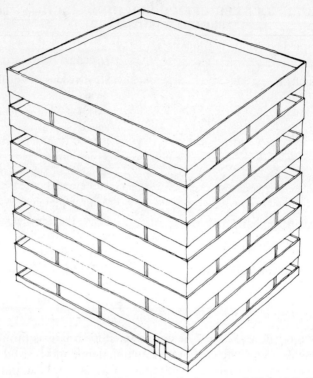

Figure 7.1. Denver base building, isometric. Courtesy of Michael E. Doyle.

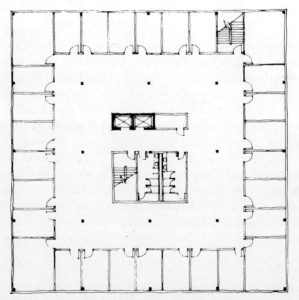

Figure 7.2. Denver base building, plan. Courtesy of Michael E. Doyle.

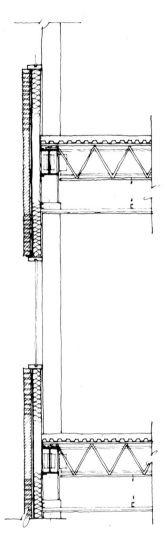

Figure 7.3. Denver base building, partial wall section. Courtesy of Michael E. Doyle.

annual energy needs of comparable new buildings in the region. From this information, the energy analyst found that $1.50/ft^2 per year is average, $1.20/ft^2 is good, and $1.00/ft^2 is very good and representative of buildings promoted as being energy efficient.

In order to divide this cost into specific uses and needs, the analyst performed a base building energy study using DOE 2.1A and following the techniques outlined in Chapter Nine. As shown in Table 7.4, the first-year, energy-related, operating costs were found to be $1.21/ft^2. Since the calculated estimate closely approximated the utility costs of actual buildings

TABLE 7.2.   DENVER BASE BUILDING SUMMARY

Location	Denver, flat urban site, no shading
Overall character	Slab-on-grade Steel construction, brick infill $100 \times 100 \times 81$ ft 10 ft floor/ceiling 13 ft 6 in. floor/floor Hung ceiling and carpeting Glass area = 50% of 10 ft floor/ceiling height
Opaque closure	R-14 walls R-25 roof R-4 perimeter slab
Glazing	U value = 0.58 Shading coefficient = 0.62
HVAC system	VAV system with perimeter baseboard heating. Gas-fired boiler that provides service hot water. Centrifugal chillers, in parallel with economizer cycle and enthalpy controls
Electrical	2.5 W/ft² lighting load, applying room factors 5.0 W/ft² perimeter offices 3.2 W/ft² interior offices and support spaces 0.2 W/ft² night (emergency lighting) 0.33 W/ft² equipment
Ventilation	7.5 cfm/person in office areas 15 cfm/person in conference rooms
Thermal control strategy	68°F heating/78°F cooling, occupied 55°F heating/90°F cooling, unoccupied
Service hot water	0.4 gal/person/day 50°F in/120°F out
Fuel costs	Gas = 2.80/MBtu Electricity = 0.0184/kWh 10.75/kW (demand)
Fuel costs escalation rate	15%/yr for first 2 yrs 10%/yr thereafter

in the area, the team was confident that the analysis was a reasonable approximation of energy use for the base building.

To better convey the relative importance of individual base building energy needs, the analyst graphically displayed total first-year energy costs as shown in Figure 7.4. Lighting is the largest single energy user, directly representing about 67% of the total costs of energy for the building. Cooling

TABLE 7.3. DENVER BASE BUILDING, CONSTRUCTION COST ESTIMATES

Cost Factors	Total Cost ($)	Cost ($/ft²)	% of Total Cost
Foundations	53,244	0.88	1.74
Superstructure	482,527	8.04	15.78
Exterior closure	361,008	6.02	11.81
Interior construction	98,815	1.65	3.23
Vertical conveyance	124,236	2.07	4.06
Finishes	283,968	4.73	9.29
Plumbing	143,973	2.39	4.71
HVAC systems	399,330	6.66	13.06
Electrical and lighting	343,720	5.73	11.24
Site preparation	151,917	2.53	5.07
Subtotal	2,442,738		
General contractor markup	244,274	4.07	8.01
Contingencies	366,411	6.11	12.00
Total	3,053,423	50.88	100.00

is the next largest at about 20% of total costs. Combined, lighting and cooling constitute 87% of the total first-year energy costs.

Electrical demand charges represent the largest single annual cost. These charges are more significant to total annual cost than how much energy is used over a year's time. In total, 74% of the annual utility bill (89¢ out of $1.21) are demand charges. Of the total annual cost for cooling, 85% is for demand (28¢ out of 33¢). Lighting and cooling combine for 96% of the annual demand charges (85¢ out of 89¢).

To further define the energy needs of the base building, the design team energy analyst generated rainbow plots for the four average days of each season and for a peak winter and summer day. The key facts from these charts are summarized as follows:

The major period of space heating need is for warming up the building to occupancy temperature on winter mornings.

The building peak demand for electricity occurs at midafternoon in every month when outdoor temperatures are warmer than the economizer cycle cutoff temperature and skies are clear, resulting in high solar heat gains through glazing; and

The peak-demand charges for the building are a result of the coincident need for full lighting and the monthly peak need for cooling.

TABLE 7.4. DENVER BASE BUILDING, ANNUAL UTILITY COST ESTIMATES

End-Use	Consumption						Demand		Total Cost (Cons. + Dem.) ($/ft²)
	Elec. (kBtu/ft²)	Elec. ($/ft²)	Gas (kBtu/ft²)	Gas ($/ft²)	Total (kBtu/ft²)	Total ($/ft²)	Elec. (W/ft²)	Elec. ($/ft²)	
Equipment	2.554	0.0138	–	–	2.554	0.0138	3.953	0.0425	0.0563
Hot water	–	–	1.675	0.0047	1.675	0.0047	–	–	0.0047
Cooling	9.304	0.0501	–	–	9.304	0.0501	25.963	0.2791	0.3291
Lighting	44.047	0.2374	–	–	44.047	0.2374	53.098	0.5708	0.8082
Heating	0.039	0.0002	2.504	0.0070	2.543	0.0072	0.0000	0.0000	0.0072
Total	55.944	0.3015	4.179	0.0117	60.123	0.3132	83.014	0.8924	1.2055

Notes: Equipment at 0.33 W/ft².

      Lighting at 5.6 W/ft² (offices), 3.2 W/ft² (core).

Rates: Gas—$2.80/MBtu = $0.0028/kBtu. (consumption only).

      Electric—$0.0184/kWh (consumption) = $0.00539/kBtu.

      $10.75/kW (demand) = 1.075¢/W.

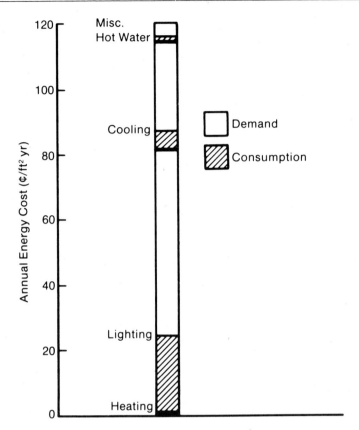

Figure 7.4. Denver base building, utility costs.

If the environmental-control systems are typical, the only base building assumption that appears as a major liability is the placement of 25% of the building's glazing on the west elevation. Instead of redoing the base building, the design team decided to continue the analysis while considering this possibility for future experimentation.

To clarify the actual interconnected causes of energy use for the base building, 100% elimination parametrics were generated as shown in Figure 7.5. The "w/o internal" loads bar is considerably smaller than the "w/o envelope" bar. The base building is internally load dominated.

The "w/o light" bar in Figure 7.5 shows the large impact of lighting on both heating and cooling. Eliminating lights from the building reduces cooling costs about 50% (33¢/ft² per year to 17¢/ft² per year). Heating costs, on the other hand, increase from 0.7–3.0¢/ft² per year, a 428% increase. Lighting is the controlling energy need of the building for both annual consumption and peak demand.

The envelope-related bars of Figure 7.5 demonstrate two very interesting

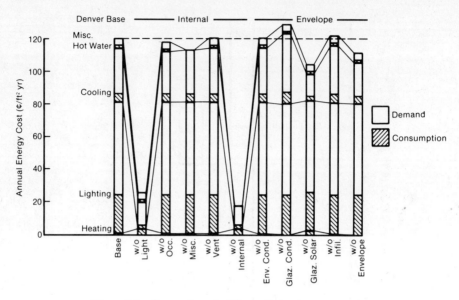

Figure 7.5.   Denver base building, elimination parametrics.

points. First, reducing glazing conduction to zero (all glass is assumed to be a perfect insulator) increases total annual energy costs. This indicates that the original double glazing of the base building actually aids in the beneficial loss of internal heat through the envelope during mild or cold weather. Heating costs do approach zero in the "w/o glazing conduction" bar, yet cooling costs jumped 8¢/ft^2 per year over the base-case bar.

The second interesting envelope-related elimination parametric is the "w/o glazing solar" bar. Both cooling consumption and demand are nearly halved by rejecting solar heat gains. Both the "w/o lights" bar and this bar suggest that the large majority of the peak cooling demand costs are directly attributable to lights and west-facade glass.

Preliminary Estimate of the Net Present Value of Energy-Related Improvements

To clarify the energy-related design challenge of the project, the team cost analyst combined the client economic criteria and the estimate of first-year utility cost using the step-by-step procedure presented in Chapter Eight. Figure 7.6, generated by this effort, shows how many additional dollars can be spent to reduce the annual utility cost of the building by a specific fraction and meet the minimum economic criteria of the client.

Assessing the Energy-Related Opportunities

Using the preceding energy and cost facts as a base, the design team focused on the annual consumption and peak demand of lighting and

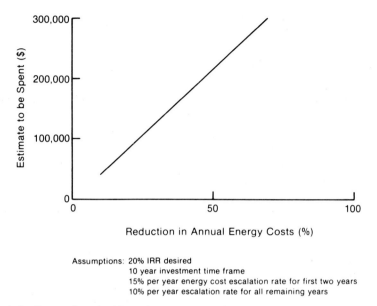

Figure 7.6.   Denver base building, the net present value of energy-related improvements.

cooling. They decided that the best possible solution is a building with very efficient lighting and cooling systems. These systems, if possible, should work best during the hot, clear afternoons associated with the peak-demand hours of each month. Likewise, the best possible architectural form for energy-related concerns is one that minimizes solar heat gains through glass from the afternoon sun. The cost of all these improvements must not exceed the benefit-to-cost limits suggested in Figure 7.6.

Schematic Design Experimentation

Proposed Alternatives

Addressing the controlling energy need of the building is fundamental to making a significant reduction in total building energy use. Therefore, the design team emphasized the selection of alternative lighting systems. The original base building lighting load, in watts per square foot, was determined from ASHRAE 90-75, which requires that the load be in accordance with the Illumination Engineering Society (IES) 1981 Handbook. The IES Handbook suggests a lighting load of 3.2 W/ft² for most office applications, and increases this value substantially as the size of a room decreases to represent the high light absorption of closely placed walls. Although 3.2 W/ft^2 satisfies the IES requirements, this value does not represent the current capability of many architects and engineers when emphasis is placed on the design of high-quality, energy-efficient lighting systems.

The design team believed that a properly designed electric lighting system using an energy-efficient, fluorescent, parabolic troffer luminaire could reduce the design lighting load to 2.0 W/ft^2 in all office spaces. This alternative would reduce the annual consumption and peak electrical requirements for both lighting and cooling and reduce the size of the cooling plant. The only liability of the lighting alternative would be a small increase in heating cost.

The design team also decided to try a daylighting alternative. Like a high-quality, energy-efficient, electric lighting system, daylighting would also address the controlling energy need of the building. One major advantage of daylighting in this project is that a large amount of natural light is available during the hours of building peak demand; that is, warm after-noons with clear skies and high solar heat gains. Although the daylighting alternative can substantially reduce the use of electricity on an annual basis, the design team was also excited about the potential of daylighting to greatly limit the use of electric lights during building electrical peak-demand periods. The major liability of the daylighting alternative is that the shape of the base building is too deep for adequate light penetration to the open-plan offices of the building's interior zone. The base building form must be changed, resulting in some loss of the construction cost advantages of the cubelike form of the base case.

The search for an energy-efficient cooling system that works best during periods of peak cooling demand led the design team to a direct/indirect evaporative cooling system. It was estimated that a direct/indirect evaporative cooling system could meet the peak-period cooling demand for the building with comparative COP of about 10. Although this system provided the team with exactly the performance criteria desired, its initial cost is considerably higher than conventional systems. How much the system reduces annual cost will indicate whether it is an acceptable alternative.

With these considerations as a base, the design team decided to evaluate two alternative buildings. The first design retained the original base building form and used a 2 W/ft^2 high-quality, energy-efficient electric lighting system and a direct/indirect evaporative cooling system. The second design had a narrower base building form with the long axis oriented east and west. This change permitted the team to study the cooling-load-reducing capabilities of a building with a very small western exposure and the daylighting potential of a narrow building oriented to the more favorable southern and northern skies. As in the first design, a direct/indirect evaporative cooling system was also assumed. In combination, the two experiments will indicate the comparative cost and energy differences between the two lighting systems, as well as the cost trade-offs between a narrow building with a smaller cooling plant and a less expensive, cubelike building with a larger cooling plant.

Evaluating the Alternatives

ALTERNATIVE DESIGN #1—ELECTRIC LIGHTS AND EVAPORATIVE COOLING.   As shown in Table 7.5, the high-quality, energy-efficient electric lighting system and direct/indirect evaporative cooling system proposed by the team added $228,738 to the estimated construction cost of the base building. Even with the overall reduction in the required cooling plant size due to the more efficient electric lights, the evaporative cooling system alone added about $2.60/ft^2 to the estimated project costs.

An analysis of the energy needs for the project produced Table 7.6 and Figure 7.7. Figure 7.8 shows the elimination parametrics for this design alternative. The total annual utility costs have been reduced by 57%. However, as shown by the total costs and elimination parametrics, even at 2.0 W/ft^2, lighting is still the controlling energy need and predominant annual energy cost for the building. Lighting and cooling combined represent 84% of total annual utility-related operating costs. Likewise, peak-

TABLE 7.5.   DENVER BUILDING ALTERNATIVE DESIGN #1, CONSTRUCTION COST ESTIMATES

Cost Factors	Total Cost ($)	Cost ($/ft^2)	% of Total Cost
Foundations	53,244	0.89	1.7
Superstructure	482,527	8.04	14.7
Exterior closure	361,008	6.02	11.0
Interior construction	98,815	1.65	3.0
Vertical conveyance	124,236	2.07	3.8
Finishes	283,963	4.73	8.6
Plumbing	143,973	2.40	4.4
Mechanical systems	551,689[a]	9.19	16.8
Electrical and lighting	374,117[b]	6.24	11.4
Site preparation	151,917	2.53	4.6
Subtotal	2,625,489		
Contractor markup	262,549	4.38	8.0
Contingencies	393,823	6.56	12.0
Total	3,281,861	54.70	100.0
Cost differential with base	228,738	3.81	7.0

[a]Reflects use of evaporative cooling and increased boiler size.

[b]Use of energy-efficient electric lighting system.

TABLE 7.6. DENVER BUILDING ALTERNATIVE DESIGN #1, ANNUAL UTILITY COST ESTIMATES

| | Consumption | | | | | | Demand | | Total Cost |
	Elec. (kBtu/ft²)	Elec. ($/ft²)	Gas (kBtu/ft²)	Gas ($/ft²)	Total (kBtu/ft²)	Total ($/ft²)	Elec. (W/ft²)	Elec. ($/ft²)	(Cons. + Dem.) ($/ft²)
End-Use									
Equipment	2.554	0.0138	—	—	2.554	0.0138	3.953	0.0425	0.0563
Hot water	—	—	1.675	0.0047	1.675	0.0047	—	—	0.0047
Cooling	2.234	0.0120	—	—	2.234	0.0120	5.795	0.0623	0.0743
Lighting	19.913	0.1073	—	—	19.913	0.1073	24.0	0.2580	0.3653
Heating	0.184	0.0010	7.048	0.0197	7.232	0.0207	0.0000	0.0000	0.0207
Total	24.885	0.1341	8.723	0.0244	33.608	0.1585	33.748	0.3628	0.5213

Notes: Equipment at 0.33 W/ft².
Lighting at 2.0 W/ft².

Rates: Gas—$2.80/MBtu = $0.0028/kBtu (consumption only).
Electric—$0.0184/kWh (consumption) = $0.00539/kBtu.
$10.75/kW (demand) = 1.075¢/W.

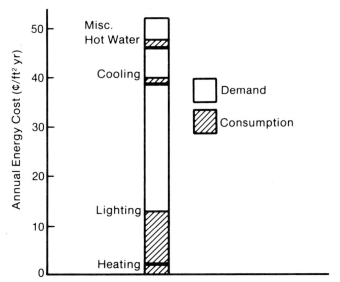

Figure 7.7.   Denver base building alternative #1, utility costs.

demand charges still represent the majority of annual cost. Although the total annual cost has dropped significantly, the basic nature of the energy needs of the building is similar to the original base building. This fact also applies to the west-facade glazing, even though the "w/o glazing solar" bar does not appear to show a significant decrease in total utility-related costs. As before, cooling costs are nearly halved by eliminating all solar heat gains through glass. However, since the cost of cooling has been substantially reduced via the evaporative cooling system, the increased need for heating nearly equals the decreased cost for cooling. The significance of west-facing glazing has indirectly been reduced by the cooling system change.

The $228,738 investment in energy efficiency of this alternative appears to meet the original cost-to-benefit economic criteria presented in Figure 7.6. To better define the financial benefits of this alternative, the team cost analyst generated the profitability and cash flow analysis presented in Table 7.7 according to the method described in Chapter Eight. Although the client specifically asked for a pretax rate of return, tax considerations were included in the analysis to show the effects of depreciation and the extent of the positive annual cash flow that the investment would generate. The 10-year investment would produce a 22.9% before-tax internal rate of return, and a 12.7% after-tax rate of return on cash flow. This after-tax return is based on the conservative assumptions of a simple 15-year, straight-line method of depreciation and a 46% corporate tax rate. For final analysis, the client would substitute actual tax-related variables. In this analysis it is

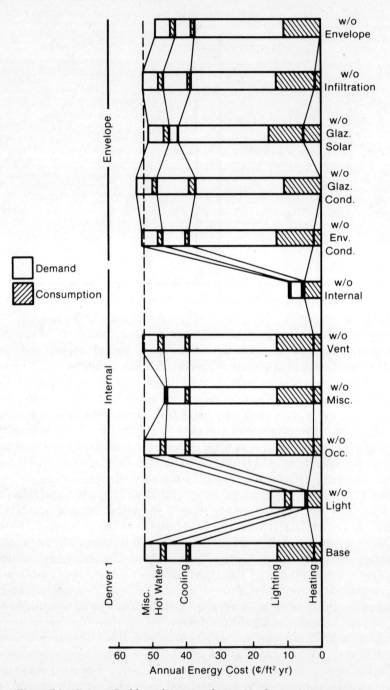

Figure 7.8. Denver Building alternative design #1, elimination parametrics.

232

TABLE 7.7. DENVER BUILDING ALTERNATIVE DESIGN #1, AFTER-TAX EARNINGS AND ANNUAL CASH FLOW DIFFERENTIALS

	Yr 1	Yr 2	Yr 3	Yr 4	Yr 5	Yr 6	Yr 7	Yr 8	Yr 9	Yr 10
Profitability Analysis										
Differential in energy-related operating costs	41,058	47,217	54,299	59,729	65,702	72,272	79,499	87,449	96,194	105,814
Differential in depreciation	(15,250)	(15,250)	(15,250)	(15,250)	(15,250)	(15,250)	(15,250)	(15,250)	(15,250)	(15,250)
Pretax earnings	25,808	31,967	39,049	44,479	50,452	57,022	64,249	72,199	80,944	90,564
Tax differential	(11,872)	(14,705)	(17,963)	(20,460)	(23,208)	(26,230)	(29,555)	(33,212)	(37,234)	(41,659)
Differential in after-tax earnings	13,939	17,262	21,087	24,019	27,244	30,792	34,695	38,988	43,710	48,904
Cash Flow Analysis										
Differential in energy-related operating costs	41,058	47,217	54,299	59,729	65,702	72,272	79,499	87,449	96,194	105,814
Tax differential	(11,872)	(14,705)	(17,963)	(20,460)	(23,208)	(26,230)	(29,555)	(33,212)	(37,234)	(41,659)
After-tax cash flow	29,186	32,512	36,337	39,269	42,494	46,042	49,945	54,238	58,900	64,154

Case assumptions: Client: Owner of owner-occupied building.
Financier and loan structure: Owner, internally financed.
Additional cost of energy-responsive building: $228,738.
Fuel escalation rate: 15%/yr for first 2 yrs, 10%/yr for next 8 yrs.

Note: Parentheses indicate negative cash flow.

assumed that 12.7% is the lowest after-tax rate of return that the investment could produce.

ALTERNATIVE DESIGN #2—DAYLIGHTING AND EVAPORATIVE COOLING. To study the advantages of daylighting, the design team reconfigured the base building so that all work stations were no further than 25 ft from a window. The new building plan is shown in Figure 7.9. The floor-to-floor height was increased to 15 ft and the floor-to-ceiling height to 12 ft to increase the penetration of daylight into this narrow building. The result is a building that is now 100-ft long, 50-ft wide, and 90-ft high.

Table 7.8 documents the construction cost impact of the new building form and systems. The greatest cost increase is for exterior closure. Foundations and superstructure have also increased in cost. One major advantage of the new form is that the size and cost of the evaporative cooling system is smaller since solar heat gains are better controlled and the proposed daylighting system is more efficient than the electric lighting system of Alternative #1 on both an annual- and peak-period basis. In total, Alternative #2 cost $303,588 more than the original base building and $74,850 more than Alternative #1.

Using the daylighting benefit estimation techniques presented in Chapter Ten, the team energy analyst found that approximately 0.5 W/ft^2 of electric lighting was required on an annual average to complement the daylighting strategy. The advantages of this daylighting strategy are evident in the annual energy-cost estimates for this alternative as shown in Table 7.9 and Figure 7.10. In total, Alternative #2 represents an 80% reduction in annual utility cost from the original base building and a 46% reduction in cost compared to Alternative #1.

Figure 7.11 shows the elimination parametrics for Alternative #2. The bars indicate that the design is no longer solely dominated by internal loads: the nature of the energy needs of the building has changed. Heating has now become a significant energy-related concern. Also, the rainbow plots indicate that the peak electrical use period of the building has shifted from

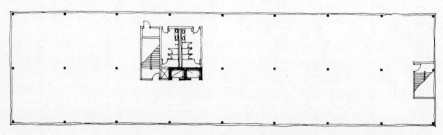

Figure 7.9.   Denver Building alternative #2, floor plan. Courtesy of Michael E. Doyle.

TABLE 7.8. DENVER BUILDING ALTERNATIVE #2, CONSTRUCTION COST ESTIMATES

Cost Factors	Total Cost ($)	Cost ($/ft²)	% of Total Cost
Foundations	57,794[a]	0.96	1.7
Superstructure	484,635[a]	8.08	14.4
Exterior closure	572,833[a]	9.55	17.1
Interior construction	56,013[a]	0.93	1.7
Vertical conveyance	124,236	2.07	3.7
Finishes	283,968	4.73	8.5
Plumbing	143,973	2.40	4.3
Mechanical systems	463,321[b]	7.72	13.8
Electrical and lighting	346,678[c]	5.78	10.3
Site preparation	151,917	2.53	4.5
Subtotal	2,685,368		
Contractor markup	268,537	4.53	8.0
Contingencies	402,805	6.79	12.0
Total	3,356,710	56.07	100.0
Cost differential			
with base	303,588	5.06	9.0
with first incremental change	74,850	1.25	2.2

[a]Costs reflect change in structural system because of change in form of building.

[b]Costs reflect the use of smaller evaporative cooling system and increased boiler size over first incremental change.

[c]Costs reflect the use of conventional electrical lighting system through building with automatic on/off control system.

the warm, clear-sky afternoon to a warm, cloudy-sky condition requiring backup electrical lights. This peak condition is not as great a liability since the peak cooling and lighting conditions are not reached at the same time. Further experimentation beyond Alternative Design #2 would require a reassessment of many of the energy-related needs and conditions suggested by the original base building.

The investment profitability and cash flow analysis of Alternative #2 is presented in Table 7.10. For a 10-year term, the pretax rate of return is 24.6%. The after-tax cash flow rate of return is conservatively estimated to be 13.9%.

TABLE 7.9. DENVER BUILDING ALTERNATIVE #2, ANNUAL UTILITY COST ESTIMATES

| End-Use | Consumption | | | | | | Demand | | Total |
	Elec. (kBtu/ft²)	Elec. ($/ft²)	Gas (kBtu/ft²)	Gas ($/ft²)	Total (kBtu/ft²)	Total ($/ft²)	Elec. (W/ft²)	Elec. ($/ft²)	(Cons. + Dem.) ($/ft²)
Equipment	2.554	0.0138	—	—	2.554	0.0138	3.953	0.0425	0.0563
Hot water	—	—	1.675	0.0047	1.675	0.0047	—	—	0.0047
Cooling	1.077	0.0058	—	—	1.077	0.0058	3.228	0.0347	0.0405
Lighting	4.978	0.0268	—	—	4.978	0.0268	6.009	0.0646	0.0914
Heating	0.549	0.0030	14.107	0.0395	14.656	0.0425	0.177	0.0019	0.0444
Total	9.158	0.0494	15.782	0.0442	24.940	0.0936	13.367	0.1437	0.2373

Notes: Equipment at 0.33 W/ft².
Lighting at 0.5 W/ft².

Rates: Gas—$2.80/MBtu = $0.0028/kBtu (consumption only).
Electric—$0.0184/kWh (consumption) = $0.00539/kBtu, $10.75/kW (demand) = 1.075¢/W.

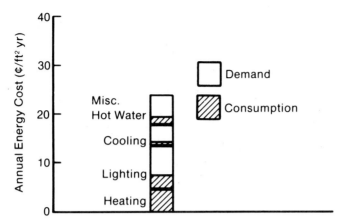

Figure 7.10. Denver Building alternative #2, utility costs.

Synthesis

The point at which a design team stops energy-related experimentation and incorporates the information into wider design requirements is a matter of choice. Experimentation can continue indefinitely. Alternative #2, for example, demonstrates the fluctuating nature of the building's energy needs: heating is becoming a significant energy-related concern while envelope assumes added importance beyond the concern for solar cooling loads. The team could continue to experiment with daylighting apertures that use the low winter morning sun to counteract the need for low-quality heat. Alternately, the team could stop experimentation at this time and use either alternative, or a combination of the two, as the basis for a final solution since the energy and economic objectives are well met by both (Fig. 7.12).

The aesthetic, functional, and employee comfort and productivity criteria of the client are typically better defined at this point of the design process than when the base building was initially generated. The cost and energy experiments of the two preceding alternatives can easily be integrated into wider design requirements and used as additional inputs to develop an appropriate final solution. Note that simple proportional analysis of the preceding facts can be used to estimate the energy needs of narrow buildings with electric lights, different building shapes with daylighting, or alternative cooling systems with different annual- and peak-period COPs. Whether the team's preference is a low-cost cube or a three-story atrium building that seeks to simultaneously improve energy use and occupant productivity, the preceding information still informs the design team of the most significant energy-related and cost issues for the project. The same tools and aids once again can be used to verify the comparative value and impact of the final schematic design proposed by the team.

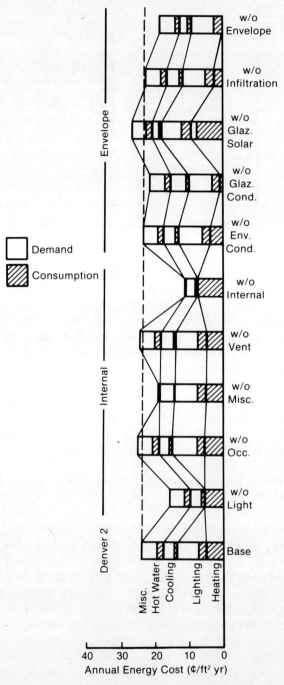

Figure 7.11. Denver Building alternative #2, elimination parametrics.

TABLE 7.10. DENVER BUILDING ALTERNATIVE #2, AFTER-TAX EARNINGS AND CASH FLOW DIFFERENTIALS

	Yr 1	Yr 2	Yr 3	Yr 4	Yr 5	Yr 6	Yr 7	Yr 8	Yr 9	Yr 10
Profitability Analysis										
Differential in energy-related operating costs	58,100	66,815	76,837	84,521	92,973	102,270	112,497	123,747	136,122	149,734
Differential in depreciation	(20,240)	(20,240)	(20,240)	(20,240)	(20,240)	(20,240)	(20,240)	(20,240)	(20,240)	(20,240)
Pretax earnings	37,860	46,575	56,597	64,281	72,733	82,030	92,257	103,507	115,882	129,494
Tax differential	(17,416)	(21,425)	(26,035)	(29,569)	(33,457)	(37,734)	(42,438)	(47,613)	(53,306)	(59,567)
Differential in after-tax earnings	20,444	25,151	30,593	34,712	39,276	44,296	49,819	55,894	62,576	69,927
Cash Flow Analysis										
Differential in energy-related operating costs	58,100	66,815	76,837	84,521	92,973	102,270	112,497	123,747	136,122	149,734
Tax differential	(17,416)	(21,425)	(26,035)	(29,569)	(33,457)	(37,734)	(42,438)	(47,613)	(53,306)	(59,567)
After-tax cash flow	40,684	45,391	50,803	54,952	59,516	64,536	70,059	76,134	82,816	90,167

Case assumptions: Client: Owner of owner-occupied building.
Financier and loan structure: Owner, internally financed.
Additional cost of energy-responsive building: $303,588.
Fuel escalation rate: 15%/yr for first 2 yrs. 10%/yr for next 8 yrs.

Note: Parentheses indicate negative cash flow.

Figure 7.12. Denver base building, possible schematic designs. Courtesy of Michael E. Doyle.

PITTSBURGH OFFICE BUILDING

Predesign Information

Project Facts and Criteria

The client for this project is a speculative developer. The client's major objective is to build, lease, and sell a building in Pittsburgh, Pennsylvania, in 3 years for the maximum possible profit. As stated in previous chapters, energy-related opportunities for any project are closely connected to the perceived financial advantages of the client. This example emphasizes the use of the recommended design approach when the goal is to generate large financial returns in short investment periods. To better focus on this specific factor, the Denver Office Building architectural program will be retained in this example.

It is generally assumed that a developer has no economic incentive to build an energy-responsive building since tenants bear the rising cost of energy. However, the reduction in operating costs for an energy-responsive building is money that the developer can use to his financial advantage. Whether the developer markets the low-energy-cost space to tenants at a higher rent or structures the leases to directly receive the savings in energy costs, more income can be realized from an energy-responsive building. The higher the income a building generates, the higher is its price to a buyer. Using classical real estate investment analysis methods such as the income theory of valuation or the tenant evaluation of costs theory, leased space is more valuable when operating costs are significantly below those of comparable projects. The difference between the actual energy-operating costs of a specific energy-responsive project and that of its competitors determines the amount of increase in resale value.

The developer of this project is interested in structuring the tenant leases so that an investment in energy-responsive design will generate a higher project annual income. As in the Princeton Professional Park case study of Chapter Four, the developer intends to lease the office space with a stop on energy-operating costs that is less than that of competitive structures, yet significantly above the estimated energy cost of an energy-responsive building.

The increase in annual income is the difference between the amount allocated to energy costs in the lease and the actual utility bills for the building. For example, if the stop on energy costs is at $1.00/\text{ft}^2$ and the actual energy costs for the building are $50\text{¢}/\text{ft}^2$ for the first year, the developer can make an extra $50\text{¢}/\text{ft}^2$ of leased space in the first year. The reliability of the estimated energy savings and the projected energy escalation costs are extremely important factors in this approach.

Developers in areas with extremely high energy costs are currently using this leasing strategy to both their own and their tenants' advantage. The

TABLE 7.11. DEVELOPERS' FINANCIAL ASSUMPTIONS AND CRITERIA

Client: Developer of speculative office building

Project objectives: Profit on sale of building after 3 yrs; highest positive flow during 3-yr construction and lease-up period

Financier: Commercial bank

Loan structure: 3-yr construction loan on 80% of project costs at 20%/yr interest only due annually

Average lease term: 3 yrs

Occupancy rate: 80% in first 6 months, 95% thereafter

Leasable space: 51,000 ft^2, or 85% of 60,000 ft^2 building

Fuel escalation rate: 30%/yr

Desired IRR: 20% of full cost of energy-related improvements

---

developer makes money on the differential between actual energy costs and the amount allocated to energy in the lease stop. The tenant in an energy-responsive building is protected from fuel-price escalation over the term of the lease, and the stop is typically lower than that used in comparable conventional buildings.

The construction loan for the project will be financed by a commercial bank for 3 years at 20%/annum, with interest only due annually. The loan is for 80% of the project costs and is due in full at the end of 3 years. All energy-related initial cost increases likewise will be 80% financed by the bank at 20% interest. To evaluate energy-related improvements, the client suggested that a 3-year term and a 20% rate of return be used. Since the client will borrow 80% of the added required cash, his actual return on equity will be much higher than 20%. Table 7.11 summarizes the financial assumptions of the client.

The Base Building

For simplicity, the base building is the same as the one used in the Denver Office Building example although different fuel costs and fuel escalation rates are assumed. The fuel costs are changed to reflect actual values for the Pittsburgh region. A very high fuel escalation rate of 30%/yr is assumed to make a conservative estimate of income to the developer. Since the utility cost stop is set when each 3-year lease is signed, all fuel cost increases during the term of the lease actually result in a loss of income to the developer over the short term.

Preliminary Construction Cost Estimate

Table 7.12 shows the base building estimated construction cost adjusted for the material and labor prices of Pittsburgh, Pennsylvania. Total estimated cost is slightly over $3,200,000 in this case.

TABLE 7.12. PITTSBURGH BASE BUILDING, CONSTRUCTION COST ESTIMATES

Cost Factors	Total Cost ($)	Cost ($/ft²)	% of Total Cost
Foundations	56,052	0.93	1.74
Superstructure	507,974	8.47	15.78
Exterior closure	380,056	6.33	11.81
Interior construction	104,026	1.73	3.23
Vertical conveyance	130,788	2.18	4.06
Finishes	298,944	4.98	9.29
Plumbing	151,566	2.53	4.71
HVAC systems	420,390	7.01	13.06
Electrical and lighting	361,847	6.03	11.24
Site preparation	163,043	2.72	5.07
Subtotal	2,574,686		
General contractor markup	257,687	4.29	8.01
Contingencies	386,203	6.44	12.00
Total	3,218,576	53.64	100.00

Preliminary Energy Needs Estimates and Assessment

As in the Denver example, the base building was used to generate estimates of annual utility costs. The annual costs are tabulated in Table 7.13, and graphically presented in Figure 7.13. The $1.12/ft² annual cost of the base building closely matches the actual utility bills of the last office building the developer constructed. A complete set of elimination parametrics is shown in Figure 7.14.

The Pittsburgh base building has an energy-use pattern very similar to the Denver base building, as shown by a comparison of Tables 7.4 and 7.13. Both base buildings are internally load dominated: climate has little influence on total annual energy cost. As in the Denver building, envelope-related elimination parametric bars indicate limited building sensitivity to climate-caused heat exchanges. The only substantial cost difference between the Denver and Pittsburgh examples is a result of the different utility rate structures and demand charges used in each city. Internally load-dominated buildings with conventional environmental-control systems typically show little sensitivity to climatic variations.

Preliminary Estimate of the Net Present Value of Energy-Related Improvements

When the financial value of energy-responsive design is based on income rather than on actual utility cost reductions, the net present value of energy-

TABLE 7.13. PITTSBURGH BASE BUILDING, ANNUAL UTILITY COST ESTIMATES

| End-Use | Consumption | | | | Demand | | Total (Cons. + Dem.) ($/ft²) |
	Elec. (kBtu/ft²)	Elec. ($/ft²)	Gas (kBtu/ft²)	Gas ($/ft²)	Elec. (W/ft²)	Elec. ($/ft²)	
Equipment	2.554	0.0224	—	—	3.953[a]	0.0288	0.0512
Hot water	—	—	1.675	0.0058	—	—	0.0058
Cooling[b]	9.792	0.0861	—	—	26.744	0.1947	0.2808
Lighting	44.047	0.3872	—	—	53.090[c]	0.3865	0.7737
Heating	0.058	0.0005	2.822	0.0097	—	—	0.0102
Total	56.451	0.4962	4.497	0.0155	83.787	0.6100	1.1217

[a]Equipment demand based on 0.33 W/ft²

[b]Includes HVAUX.

[c]Lighting demand based on 3.20 W/ft² (core), 5.60 W/ft² (perimeter).

Rates: Gas—$3.45/MBtu (no demand charge).
Elec.—$0.03/kWh (consumption) $9.70/MBtu, $7.28/kW (demand) ($2133/MBtu).

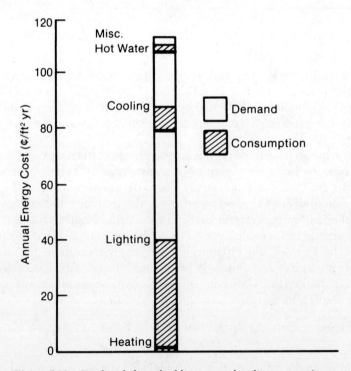

Figure 7.13. Pittsburgh base building, annual utility cost estimates.

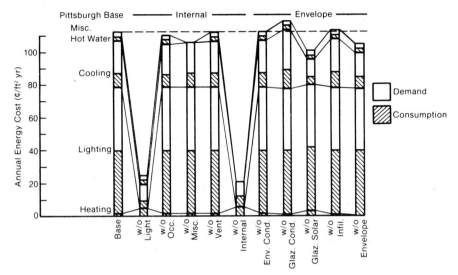

Figure 7.14. Pittsburgh base building, elimination parametrics.

related improvements should be calculated according to a range of possible incomes. As shown in Figure 7.15, the dollars that can be spent to improve energy efficiency vary according to the difference between the utility stop of the lease and the actual energy cost that the developer will pay on a square-foot basis. Figure 7.15 was generated according to the steps outlined in Chapter Eight.

Although this approximation of financial value does not consider

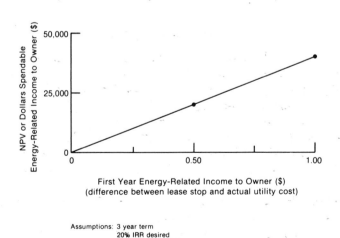

Figure 7.15. Pittsburgh six-story building, the net present value of energy-related improvements.

financing, depreciation, taxes, or resale value, the net present value of the income alone is an adequate estimate at this stage of design. Figure 7.15 summarizes well the economic constraints of the project. As a comparison of Figures 7.6 and 7.15 shows, far less money can be spent on energy-related improvements in the Pittsburgh Building as compared to the Denver Building.

Assessing Energy-Related Opportunities

Because few dollars are available to make energy-related improvements to the project, the design team must concentrate on the controlling energy need of lighting to achieve a significant annual cost reduction. The lights directly represent the largest single cost in both the consumption and demand categories and indirectly represent about half of the annual cooling consumption and demand charges. In addition, the heat of lights influences the size and cost of the cooling plant.

With these economic limits and energy relationships in mind, the design team focused on energy-efficient lighting systems that could partially pay for themselves by a reduction in cooling plant cost. Also, based on the successful experience gained in the Denver Building, this lighting system should break the simultaneous peak demands of lighting and cooling to lower the building's annual demand costs. The design team believed that realizing these goals was required to achieve a significant income differential for the developer within the initial cost constraints of Figure 7.15.

Schematic Design Experimentation

The Proposed Alternative

From its work on the Denver Building, the design team understood the advantages of both high-quality, energy-efficient electric lighting systems and daylighting systems. Improved electric lighting systems reduce the annual cost of lighting for both consumption and demand, reduce the annual cost for cooling in both categories, and reduce the size and initial cost of the cooling plant. The only disadvantage is that improved electric lighting systems will not break the coincidence of peak cooling needs and peak lighting needs that results in the building's monthly peak-demand charge.

Daylighting likewise can reduce the annual lighting consumption and demand charges as well as the annual cost for cooling in both the consumption and demand categories. Unlike improved electric light, daylighting has the potential to separate peak cooling and lighting needs to different design days. The major disadvantage of daylighting is the cost liability associated with a very narrow building form.

Since neither lighting system alone ensured the total end result desired by the design team, it was decided to experiment with both. To save time, the team studied one alternative design that combined the use of both systems. Where possible, the initial costs, annual cost savings, and the advantages and disadvantages of the two systems would be kept separate to permit a final lighting system decision to be made after the completion of experimentation.

The economic constraints for the project suggested that major building reconfigurations probably would not be beneficial in this case. Therefore, it was decided to keep the original base building form and plan. The perimeter offices would be daylit, and the interior offices would use high-efficiency electric lights.

For the internal zones, the 2.0-W/ft^2 fluorescent parabolic troffers of the Denver Building would again be used. At the perimeter, the original inexpensive and less-efficient luminaires of the base case were used as a backup system to daylighting. Automatic on/off controls were added so that the overhead lights of the perimeter offices are off when conditions permit. No override switch was provided. Each office worker could use a desk lamp whenever the overhead lights automatically darkened. This switching strategy ensures a majority of the daylighting annual cost savings potential, yet was seen by the design team as a comparative disadvantage since it required the owner to commit to a highly unconventional light-switching strategy.

Evaluating the Alternative

As shown in Table 7.14, the design alternative added $23,250 to the initial cost of the Pittsburgh Building. On the positive side, HVAC costs were decreased by $10,500. This savings represents a reduction in the cooling plant size from 200 to 130 tons, and an increase in the boiler size from 170 to 220 kBtu.

Electrical and lighting costs increased $29,312, or about 50¢/ft^2. On a square-foot basis, the high-quality electric lighting system added about 56¢ to the construction cost, and the daylighting controls added about 47¢.

Using the daylight benefit estimating technique of Chapter Ten, the design team found that over the year's time, an average of about 0.5 W/ft^2 of electric lighting was required in the perimeter offices. This annual average represents a quarter of the 2.0 W/ft^2 required in the internal offices. In addition, the daylighting system worked particularly well during the warm, clear afternoons associated with the original peak cooling period.

The new energy needs for the project are shown in Table 7.15 and Figure 7.16. This design alternative reduces annual energy costs by 68¢/ft^2 or 60% compared to the base case. Figure 7.17 shows the elimination parametrics for the proposed alternative design. Note that the bars indicate that the building is still dominated by internal loads.

TABLE 7.14. PITTSBURGH BUILDING ALTERNATIVE DESIGN, CONSTRUCTION COST ESTIMATES

Cost Factors	Total Cost ($)	Cost ($/ft²)	% of Total Cost
Foundations	56,052	0.93	1.7
Superstructure	507,974	8.47	15.7
Exterior closure	380,056	6.33	11.7
Interior construction	104,026	1.73	3.2
Vertical conveyance	130,788	2.18	4.0
Finishes	298,944	4.98	9.2
Plumbing	151,566	2.58	4.7
Mechanical systems	409,854[a]	6.83	12.6
Electrical and lighting	391,159[b]	6.52	12.1
Site preparation	163,043	2.72	5.0
Subtotal	2,593,462		
Contractor markup	259,347	4.32	8.0
Contingencies	389,019	6.48	12.1
Total	3,241,828	54.07	100.0
Incremental cost differential with base building	23,250	0.39	0.7

[a]Reflects reduced cooling plant size and increased boiler size.

[b]Use of energy-efficient electric lighting system in core, and perimeter daylighting with conventional electric lighting system.

TABLE 7.15. PITTSBURGH BUILDING ALTERNATIVE DESIGN, ANNUAL UTILITY COST ESTIMATE

End-Use	Consumption				Demand		Total (Cons. + Dem.) ($/ft²)
	Elec. (kBtu/ft²)	Elec. ($/ft²)	Gas (kBtu/ft²)	Gas ($/ft²)	Elec. (W/ft²)	Elec. ($/ft²)	
Equipment	2.554	0.0224	—	—	3.953	0.0288	0.0512
Hot water	—	—	1.675	0.0058	—	—	0.0058
Cooling	5.767	0.0507	—	—	10.866	0.0791	0.1298
Lighting	12.296	0.1081	—	—	14.821	0.1079	0.2160
Heating	0.379	0.0033	11.226	0.0387	0.055	0.0004	0.0424
Total	20.996	0.1845	12.901	0.0445	29.695	0.2162	0.4452

Rates: Gas—$3.45/MBtu = $0.00345/kBtu.
Electric—$0.03/kWh (consumption) = $0.00879/kBtu, $7.28/kW (demand).

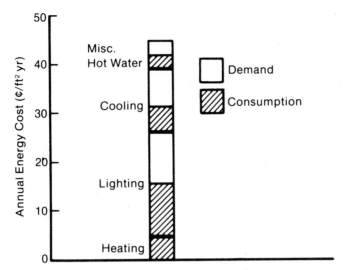

Figure 7.16. Pittsburgh design alternative, annual utility cost estimate.

The rainbow plots for this design suggest that the monthly peak electrical need for the project occurs on cloudy days in cool or mild months when all the perimeter electrical lights are used, and on clear, sunny days during the hottest months of summer when only the interior office lights are on in full. However, the building's summer electrical peaks are still reduced by the absence of full perimeter electrical illumination. A complete split in the lighting and cooling peaks has definitely been achieved, even if the building electrical demand summer peak still occurs on the hot, clear-sky day.

A simple proportional evaluation of the two lighting systems allows the design team to compare the cost savings attributable to each system. Assuming the total building area served by each lighting system is about equal, the consumption and peak-demand limiting potential of each can be directly compared. In the interior offices, the lighting load has been reduced from 3.2 to 2.0 W/ft^2 for a savings of 1.2 W/ft^2 for half of the building. The perimeter office lighting load has dropped from 5.0 to 0.5 W/ft^2 on an annual average basis for a savings of 4.5 W/ft^2 for half the building. Therefore, about 80% of the cost savings of this alternative design is directly attributable to daylighting. Note that this result has as much to do with the higher lighting energy needs of the small perimeter offices as it does with the comparative abilities of the two lighting alternatives.

Since this design alternative produces an estimated annual energy cost reduction of 68¢/ft^2, the design team decided to test the investment benefit of the $23,250 expenditure based on a 50¢/ft^2 annual income to the developer. As shown in Table 7.16, the first step in this task was to project the differential in income over the 3-year period. The phasing of occupancy and the energy cost escalation rate makes these income projections considerably less than 50¢ times 60,000 ft^2 times 3 years.

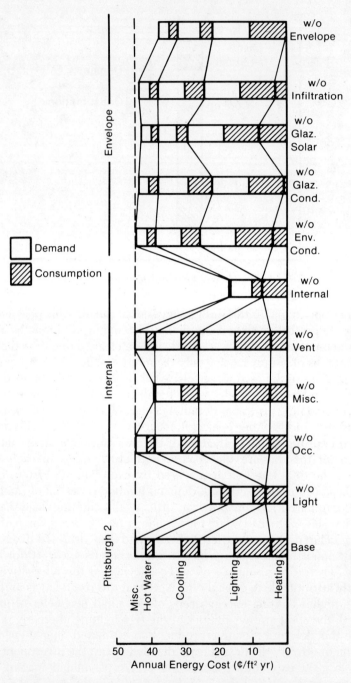

Figure 7.17. Pittsburgh design alternative, elimination parametrics.

TABLE 7.16. PITTSBURGH BUILDING ALTERNATIVE DESIGN,
INCOME DIFFERENTIAL USING LEASING STRATEGY

Yr	Income to Developer ($)	Assumptions
1	0	Building is not completed until 18th month.
2	10,200	Energy operating costs are 50¢/ft² less than stop in lease. Occupancy of the 51,000 leasable ft² is 80% for last 6 months of second year.
3	16,958	Energy costs have risen 30%, reducing difference between operating costs and stop to 35¢/ft². Occupancy is 95% for year.

In Table 7.17, the income projections are added to the initial expenditure and annual interest payments to produce a before-tax cash flow analysis. The cash flow analysis shows that although the developer must absorb a negative cash flow of $6513 while the project is under construction, the $6480 net income from the investment in energy improvements during the first year of operation alone almost pays back the required cash outlay. The $13,238 net income from the second year of operation, or the third year of the loan, makes the investment very profitable. This investment, as structured, represents a return on equity of 99% for 3 years (return on equity is the interest equivalent earned on the initial cash outlay and includes financing cost). The design team did not study depreciation, income tax, or resale value effects since the strategy is clearly a successful investment.

Synthesis

The preceding experimentation is adequate to inform the design team of significant energy-related concerns that can influence the generation of the final schematic design. Once again, the final solution could be three, six, or nine stories. It could be a specific combination of daylighting and electric lighting, or high-efficiency electric lights only. The area and benefit proportions previously discussed can be used to assess many lighting alternatives without returning to a full-building energy analysis. Experimentation allows the basic relationships between income, cost, and the ability of lighting system alternatives to become apparent. After the schematic design is generated, final cost, energy, and investment analysis can be performed for the client's review and approval.

This example is significant because it counters a prevailing myth that an additional investment in an energy-responsive building is not economically

TABLE 7.17. PITTSBURGH BUILDING ALTERNATIVE DESIGN,
CASH FLOW ANALYSIS

	Yr 1	Yr 2	Yr 3
Additional cash for higher initial cost[a] ($23,250 × 20%)	(4,650)		
Additional interest on project loan[b] [($23,250 × 80%) × 20%]	(1,860)[d]	(3,720)	(3,720)
Additional income from difference between stop and actual energy costs of 50¢/ft² in year 2, 35¢/ft² in year 3[c]	0	10,200	16,958
Cash flow attributable to investment in energy-responsive building	(6,510)	6,480	13,238

[a]Initial cost differential is $23,250. 20% of this total is paid directly by the developer, the remainder is financed.

[b]80% of initial cost differential is financed on a 3-yr construction loan at 20%/yr; interest only due annually.

[c]Occupancy begins at 18th month. Second year occupancy assumed as 80% of last 6 months. Third year occupancy assumed as 95%. Income varies between year 2 and 3 because fuel escalation rate is assumed to be 30% in this case (intentionally set high to generate a conservative estimate of financial value). Total reasonable area for the building is 51,000 ft².

[d]Construction loan interest at one-half on partially constructed project.

feasible for short-term investors of speculative office buildings. The task may be harder for the design team, but not impossible. Identifying advantages for the client is again the key to finding appropriate energy-related alternatives. The standard steps of the recommended approach of this book allows a great many motives and perceived advantages to be clarified and converted into design decision-making guidelines and indicators.

CHATTANOOGA SECONDARY SCHOOL

The final example of this chapter, a secondary school classroom wing addition, shows several variations of the recommended approach. Commercial building types other than office buildings can pose different energy-related design challenges. The recommended design approach presented in this book is equally useful and informative to these challenges.

  The site for this example was selected to illustrate how unique utility rate structures can influence the search for appropriate energy-related alternatives. Chattanooga is in the Tennessee Valley Authority (TVA) utility network. TVA is one of a number of utility companies that permits a base peak-demand usage without a charge to the customer. In this case, the first 50 kW of monthly electrical demand are free.

A secondary school provides an example of a nontaxed, government client. With such clients, the financial criteria, term of investment, and the lack of taxation on energy-related cost reductions can also be favorable to the adoption of energy-related improvements. Disadvantages of these clients include a preset construction budget and the loss of the paper expense of depreciation.

Predesign Information

Project Facts and Criteria

Ten classrooms are to be added to an existing secondary school. A $420,000, 20-year, 8% bond issue with a sinking fund provision was approved to construct the proposed 11,000–12,000 gross ft² addition. The school board asked that the new addition be energy efficient to serve as an example for the community and to lower annual operating costs. The board specifically requested that the energy-related improvements be visually obvious to serve as an informative example to students and the public. No additional funds were available beyond the existing bond issue for energy-related improvements. If any additional dollars beyond conventional costs would be required for energy-related alternatives, these dollars must be found by reducing cost elsewhere on the project. This cost-balancing exercise for a government client is similar to the Bateson Building case study presented in Chapter Four.

The board also stipulated that any monies beyond conventional costs for energy-related improvements must return an annual cost savings greater than the bond financing costs and any additional costs for maintenance and replacement. For simplicity, the board determined this rate of return to be 12%. This criterion guarantees that all energy-related investments provide a positive cash flow to the school district from the first year.

While the life of the building is presumably 40 years, the board did not believe that accurate cost projections could be made that far into the future. The board was most interested in a 10-year investment, and stated that all energy-related expenditures beyond conventional cost for those items must return the 12% rate in that period. However, the board also requested that the projected annual energy cost savings be assessed for the 20-year term of the bond to approximate benefit to the total cost of financing the improvements.

The Base Building

Since the energy challenge of this project is inseparable from cost issues, the design team used the base building exercise to test the cost implications of

TABLE 7.18.   CHATTANOOGA SCHOOL BASE BUILDING,
ARCHITECTURAL PROGRAM SUMMARY

Chattanooga Board of Education; government client	
Area breakdowns	10 classrooms: 7500 ft^2
	circulation space: 3050 ft^2
	support space: 550 ft^2
Total building area	11,100 gross ft^2
Building configuration	single-story
Occupancy patterns	year-round use; 07.00–17.00 hr (includes start-up and cleaning)

alternate floor plans and construction techniques. In this approach, the base building becomes a mean to explore several different design issues beyond the design team's experience.

A careful assessment of the programmatic needs of the client led the team to a variety of possible floor plans. The team selected the floor plan of Figure 7.19 as a starting point since it efficiently met the needs of the client in 11,100 gross ft^2 and was amenable to low-cost construction techniques. Since the original bond issue assumed a 12,000 ft^2 building at \$35/ft^2, additional money was available for energy-related improvements. The architectural program based on the 11,100 ft^2 plan is summarized in Table 7.18.

Coincident with developing the programmatic and floor plan studies, the team investigated alternative construction techniques and materials. For reasons of simplicity and cost, the selection was a single-story, slab-on-grade building with open web joints, a metal deck, and brick wall panels. This construction approach appeared to be the least expensive alternative that would meet the client's maintenance and life expectancy criteria.

The final base building is illustrated in Figures 7.18–7.20. Additional assumptions about the base case are presented in Table 7.19.

Preliminary Construction Cost Estimate

Total base building construction costs were estimated to be \$380,927. This figure is \$39,000 below the preliminary construction estimate and bond issue total. As shown in the breakdown in Table 7.20, the cost is \$34.32 ft^2. This value is only 68¢/ft^2 below the original cost estimate. The efficient floor plan rather than the low-cost construction techniques resulted in the availability of extra money at this point in the study.

Preliminary Energy Assessments

As shown in Table 7.21 and Figure 7.21, the base building has an estimated annual utility cost of 74¢/ft^2. The school board verified the similarity of this

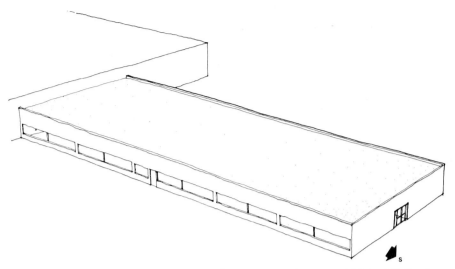

Figure 7.18. Chattanooga School base building, isometric. Courtesy of Michael E. Doyle.

estimate to newer existing schools in the region. Therefore, the design team presumed the estimate was a good approximation of the annual energy needs for the base building.

Unlike the previous examples in this chapter, the school addition is not dominated by demand costs. This is a result of the local utility rate structure rather than an indication that demand charges are not a major concern in school buildings. Since there is no charge for the first 50 kW of demand, over 60% of the building's peak electrical demand is free in this utility district. In total, demand charges only represent 25% of annual utility cost (17.7¢ out of 73.7¢).

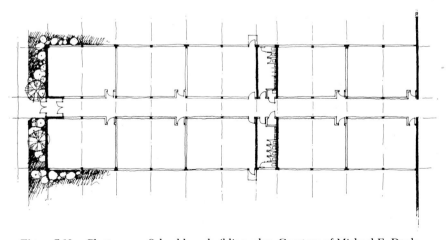

Figure 7.19. Chattanooga School base building, plan. Courtesy of Michael E. Doyle.

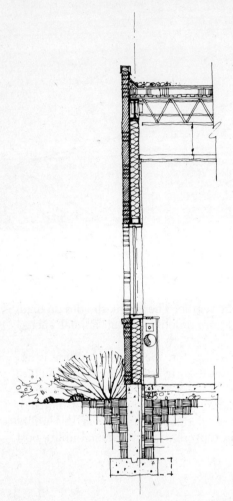

Figure 7.20. Chattanooga School base building, typical wall section. Courtesy of Michael E. Doyle.

The largest direct energy need for the project is cooling. Cooling costs represent 50% of the annual total for the building. Lighting is a close second major energy need at 46% of the annual total. The remaining 4% is split between space heating and service hot water.

The elimination parametrics of Figure 7.22 tell a different story of the major energy needs of the base building. As in all preceding examples, the parametrics indicate that the building is internally load dominated and that lights are the controlling energy need. When the cooling requirements of the lights are considered, lighting once again becomes the major energy need of the building.

Like the Denver and Pittsburgh examples, the elimination parametrics of the Chattanooga School indicate that the heat gains through the envelope create a substantial portion of the annual need for cooling. This is apparent

TABLE 7.19. CHATTANOOGA BASE BUILDING, SUMMARY

Location	Chattanooga, TN, flat urban site, no shading
Overall character	slab-on-grade
	light steel construction, brick infill panels
	60 × 185 × 14 ft
	10 ft floor/ceiling
	glass area = 40% of floor/ceiling height
Opaque closure	R-19 walls
	R-24 ceiling
	R-4 perimeter
Glazing	U = 0.58
	SC = 0.56
HVAC system	package multizone unit, with economizer enthalpy control
Electrical	2.5 W/ft² lighting
	0.2 W/ft² night, emergency lighting
Ventilation	7.5 cfm/person
Thermal control strategy	68°F heating/78°F cooling, occupied
	55°F heating/90°F cooling, unoccupied
Service hot water	1.0 gal/person/day
	50°F in/120°F out
Fuel costs	gas = $3.80/MBtu
	electricity = $0.049/kWh
	0-50 kW = 0
	50 + kW = $6.07/kW
	New meter and panel for addition; utility cost to be billed separate from existing structure
Fuel escalation rate	10%/yr

by comparing the size of the cooling cost in the "w/o internal" and "w/o envelope" bars. In particular, solar heat gains through glazing appear to have the most influence on the comparatively high annual cooling consumption and demand cost. A quick review of the base building's rainbow plots confirms this fact. Because the building is oriented with the long axis running north and south, one-half of the total glazing faces west. Since the board specifically suggested this orientation and how the new addition should attach to the existing school, the base building would not be changed and solar gains would be assessed in greater detail through experimentation.

Preliminary Estimate of the Net Present Value of Energy-Related Improvements

Before improvements could be proposed, the relationship between annual energy-cost reductions and spendable construction dollars had to be

TABLE 7.20. CHATTANOOGA SCHOOL BASE BUILDING, COST ESTIMATES

Cost Factors	Total Cost ($)	Cost ($/ft²)	% of Total Cost
Foundations	27,993	2.52	7.3
Superstructure	18,985	1.71	5.0
Exterior closure	91,655	8.26	24.1
Interior construction	43,494	3.92	11.4
Finishes	12,032	1.08	3.2
Plumbing	21,892	1.97	5.8
Mechanical	45,801[a]	4.13	12.0
Electrical	41,918	3.78	11.0
Site work	13,669	1.23	3.6
Subtotal	317,439		
Contractor add on	31,744	2.86	8.3
Contingencies	31,744	2.86	8.3
Total	380,927	34.32	100.0

[a]Includes both heating and cooling plant: school open year-round.

TABLE 7.21. CHATTANOOGA SCHOOL BASE BUILDING, ANNUAL UTILITY COST ESTIMATES

	Consumption				Demand[b,c]		Total (Cons. + Dem.)
End-Use	Elec. (kBtu/ft²)	Elec. ($/ft²)	Gas (kBtu/ft²)	Gas ($/ft²)	Elec. (W/ft²)	Elec. ($/ft²)	($/ft²)
Fans	—	—	—	—	—	—	—
Hot water	—	—	2.03	0.008	—	—	0.005
Cooling[a]	18.76	0.263	—	—	17.462	0.106	0.369
Lighting	18.92	0.265	—	—	11.697	0.071	0.336
Heating	—	—	6.43	0.024	—	—	0.024
Total	37.68	0.528	8.46	0.032	29.159	0.177	0.734

[a]Includes HVAC auxiliary.

[b]Sum of monthly demand.

[c]"Free" kW deducted on a proportional basis.

Rates: Gas—$3.80/MBtu (no demand) [$0.0038/kBtu].
Electric—$0.049/kWh (consumption) [$0.014/kBtu], $6.07/kW over 50 kW [$1.778/kBtu].

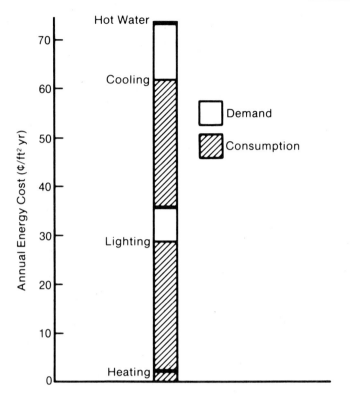

Figure 7.21.   Chattanooga School base building, annual utility cost estimates.

determined. The differential between the base building construction cost estimate and the bond issue total suggested an upper limit of $39,000 for energy-related cost increases. Figure 7.23 was generated to project the annual cost savings required to meet the client's economic criteria for this maximum value as well as lower cost energy-related investments. To spend $39,000 and meet a 12% rate of return in a 10-year period, the annual first-year energy cost must be reduced by 57%.

Assessing Energy-Related Opportunities

Once again, the base building facts clearly indicate that lighting and cooling are the most significant energy needs for this project. Based on the learning experiences gained in the previous two buildings, the team understood that annual operating costs could be easily halved by reducing the annual energy consumption of lighting and cooling and breaking the coincidence of peak need for these two end uses. In this case, annual consumption is more important than peak demand, yet the design team decided that demand

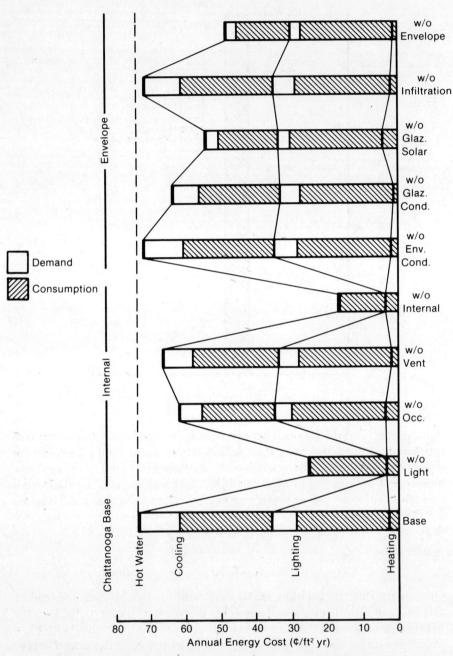

Figure 7.22. Chattanooga School base building, elimination parametrics.

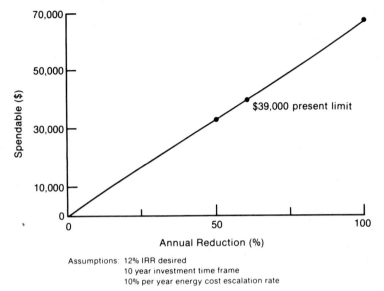

Figure 7.23. Chattanooga School base building, the net present value of energy-related improvements.

should be reduced to the 50-kW allowance to eliminate this charge altogether.

Schematic Design Experimentation

Proposed Alternative

Rather than experimenting with lighting alternatives, the team began with the assumption that a daylighting scheme was well-suited to this project. This decision resulted from the design team's appraisal of the appropriateness of the strategy for a building with this type of energy need, and the client's desire for a highly visible energy-related improvement.

With daylighting already assumed, experimentation could center around the best means to use daylighting to reduce the annual energy costs of cooling and heating. Based on past experience, the team anticipated that a daylit school wing would significantly increase heating. The team decided to change the nature of the building's energy needs and anticipated the next level of energy-related concerns for the project. This level of experimentation is notably different than that of the preceding examples: it assumes a higher level of understanding of the energy needs of buildings and the potential savings and impact of specific alternatives.

Since annual energy consumption costs are three times greater than peak-demand costs for the project, the team decided to experiment with a daylighting design that could light classrooms on both cloudy and clear-sky days. For such a design, the area of window aperture would need to be increased. The purpose of this schematic design experimentation was to determine how this modification would impact the annual cost of heating and cooling, and how the scheme could be altered to offset these liabilities.

To initiate cost- and energy-related experimentation, the design team assessed the daylighting potential of the base building. In general, the team found that the overall area of glazing would need to be doubled to allow sufficient illumination on cloudy days. Also, this added aperture would need to be placed over the corridor and classroom areas farthest away from the existing windows. In anticipation of the increased need for heating and cooling caused by the added glass area, the team decided to use vertical, south-facing glass in roof monitors over the corridors and classroom areas farthest from the windows.

A major liability of the base building was the orientation of all windows to the east and west. The low morning and afternoon sun angles would be detrimental to visual comfort. This problem could be offset on clear days with inverted blinds that could bounce daylight to the classroom ceiling. However, the amount of excess solar heat admitted to the western classrooms during the building's peak electrical period would make this alternative a trade-off of limited advantage.

For either daylighting or the control of peak-period cooling loads, the long north/south axis of the building was a major liability. Extensive permanent solar shading of west-facing windows would reduce the summer afternoon peak cooling loads, yet eliminate useful daylight on cloudy days along these windows. The team had two choices. First, if the addition could be connected to an existing exit on the west side of the main building, the windows would then face south and north. If the client was not amenable to such a change, either a T-shaped addition could be used or investments could be made in movable solar control devices that would balance the need for light and the rejection of heat.

In a conference with the school principal, approval was given to placing the addition on the west side of the main building. The logic of the energy-related advantages of orienting the addition to the north and south superseded the original intent to place the addition a few steps closer to the principal's office.

The new classroom wing orientation also permitted a less expensive means to penetrate the roof to gain access to natural light. Rather than using numerous roof monitors, the team decided that a series of three continuous sawtooths in the roof would be less expensive. As shown in Figures 7.24 and 7.25, these apertures provide adequate daylighting to the remainder of the classrooms, the restrooms, and the interior double-loaded corridor.

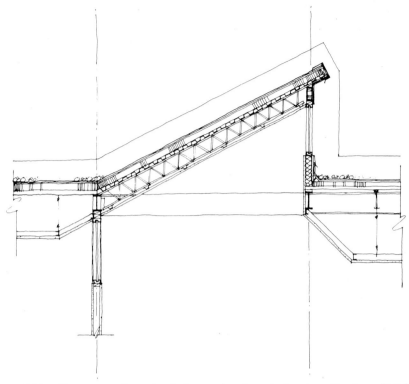

Figure 7.24. Chattanooga alternative design, section through clerestory. Courtesy of Michael E. Doyle.

Evaluation

Table 7.22 presents the construction costs for the daylit alternative. In total, construction costs have increased by $30,869 over the original base-case building. The large majority of this increase is in exterior closure. The slight decrease in electrical cost is the result of the selection of very inexpensive luminaires for backup lighting. Since the structure will be daylit on both clear and cloudy days, a minimal investment in electric lights makes the most sense. In this case, bare-bulb fluorescent tubes are assumed that indirectly bounce light from the ceiling to the classroom. Automated lighting controls are also provided.

The energy needs of the daylit building are presented in Table 7.23. Total costs are illustrated in Figure 7.26 and the elimination parameters are in Figure 7.27. Total annual costs have been reduced by about 52%. The goal to eliminate demand charges has almost been reached, with a reduction of 99% of these costs. Although the total cooling cost has dropped 32%, the

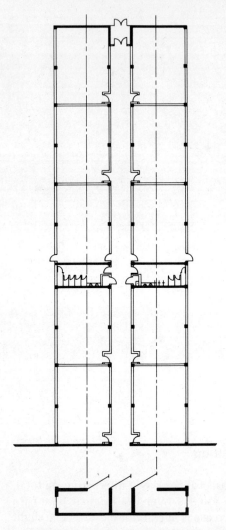

Figure 7.25. Chattanooga alternative design, plan and section.

majority of these savings is in reduced demand costs rather than savings in actual consumption costs. Annual cooling consumption costs have not significantly dropped since the glass area has been doubled. However, this large amount of glass still requires less total cooling for both annual and peak periods because of its more favorable orientation.

The 52% annual utility cost reduction for an investment of $30,869 fits the original economic target shown in Figure 7.23. Table 7.24 was generated to compare the 20-year annual savings to the bond financing cost dedicated to the energy-related improvements. Using a financial calculator and the cash flow results of the first 10 years of Table 7.24, the rate of return of this energy-related improvement is 14.9% before financing costs are included, and 3.2% on net cash flow after financing. Over the 20-year period of the

TABLE 7.22. CHATTANOOGA SCHOOL ALTERNATE DESIGN,
CONSTRUCTION COST ESTIMATES

Cost Factors	Total Cost ($)	Cost ($/ft²)	% of Total Cost
Foundations	27,993	2.52	6.8
Superstructure	19,609[a]	1.77	4.8
Exterior closure	118,615[c]	10.69	28.8
Interior construction	44,739[b]	4.03	10.9
Finishes	12,032	1.08	2.9
Plumbing	22,969	2.07	5.6
Mechanical	45,801	4.13	11.1
Electrical	37,736[d]	3.40	9.2
Site work	13,669	1.23	3.3
Subtotal	343,163		
Contractor add on	34,316	3.09	8.3
Contingencies	34,316	3.09	8.3
Total	411,795	37.10	100.0
Incremental construction costs increase over base or first incremental change	+30,869	+2.81	+7.6

[a]Reflects change in structural system to allow for sawteeth.

[b]Reflects costs for interior finishes around sawteeth.

[c]Reflects added cost for additional roof drain, curbing, and glazing.

[d]Reflects use of inexpensive luminaires and continuous dimming system used in daylit building.

bond, these same rates of return would be 22.2% and 15.3% respectively. In the end, the school board would need to add the annual expected differentials in glass cleaning and replacement to see if this specific alternative adequately meets the original investment criteria for energy-related improvements.

In situations like this where the client is only interested in breaking even on energy-related improvements, it is often advantageous to convert the consumption and demand savings for a proposed design into an equivalent primary energy-use reduction. For instance, using the embodied energy references introduced in Chapters Three and Five, the Chattanooga School alternate design saves 66,000 gal of refined oil in a 10-year period. These savings are about equally divided between the embodied energy savings of a lowered peak demand and the 10-year annual primary energy savings for consumption.

TABLE 7.23.   CHATTANOOGA SCHOOL ALTERNATE DESIGN, ANNUAL UTILITY COST ESTIMATES

	Consumption				Demand[b,c]		Total
End-Use	Elec. (kBtu/ft²)	Elec. ($/ft²)	Gas (kBtu/ft²)	Gas ($/ft²)	Elec. (W/ft²)	Elec. ($/ft²)	(Cons. + Dem.) ($/ft²)
Hot water	—	—	2.030	0.0077	—	—	0.0077
Cooling	16.720	0.2341	—	—	2.603	0.0158	0.2499
Lighting	3.435	0.0481	—	—	0.280	0.0017[b]	0.0498
Heating	—	—	12.257	0.0466	—	—	0.0466
Total	20.155	0.2822	14.287	0.0543	2.883	0.0175	0.3540

[a]Includes HVAC average.

[b]Sum of monthly demand (lighting at 0.5 W/ft²).

[c]"Free" kW deducted.

Rates: Gas—$3.80/MBtu (no demand) [$0.35/kBtu].
Electric—$0.049/kWh (consumption) [$0.14/kBtu], $6.07/kW over 50 kW [$1.775/kBtu].

Synthesis

The original experiment proved to the design team that a significant increase in window area could result in an effective clear- and cloudy-day daylighting scheme that also reduces annual- and peak-period cooling costs. If this basic scheme is acceptable to the school board and the design team, the experiment could be used as the basis for the final schematic design (Fig. 7.28). Alternately, experimentation could continue to further balance the

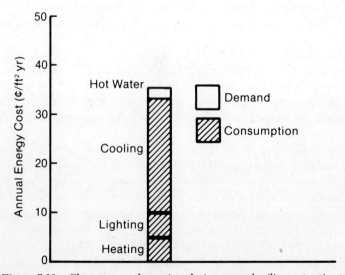

Figure 7.26.   Chattanooga alternative design, annual utility cost estimates.

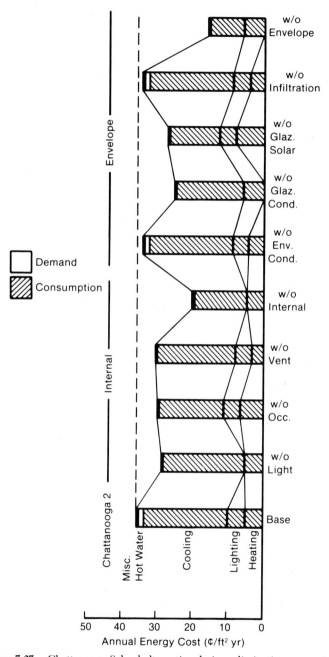

Figure 7.27. Chattanooga School alternative design, elimination parametrics.

TABLE 7.24. CHATTANOOGA SCHOOL ALTERNATIVE DESIGN, CASH FLOW ANALYSIS

	Yr 0	Yr 1	Yr 2	Yr 3	Yr 4	Yr 5	Yr 6	Yr 7	Yr 8	Yr 9	Yr 10
Initial cash outlays	0										
Expected reduction in energy-related operating costs		4,290	4,719	5,191	5,710	6,281	6,909	7,600	8,360	9,196	10,116
Financing costs: bond interest and sinking fund payments		(3,010)	(3,010)	(3,010)	(3,010)	(3,010)	(3,010)	(3,010)	(3,010)	(3,010)	(3,010)
Cash position after financing costs and reduction in energy-related operating costs		1,280	1,709	2,180	2,700	3,271	3,900	4,590	5,350	6,186	7,106

	Yr 11	Yr 12	Yr 13	Yr 14	Yr 15	Yr 16	Yr 17	Yr 18	Yr 19	Yr 20
Expected reduction in energy-related operating costs	11,127	12,240	13,464	14,810	16,291	17,920	19,712	21,684	23,852	26,237
Financing costs: bond interest and sinking fund payment	(3,010)	(3,010)	(3,010)	(3,010)	(3,010)	(3,010)	(3,010)	(3,010)	(3,010)	(3,010)
Cash position after financing costs and reduction in energy-related operating costs	8,117	9,230	10,454	11,800	13,280	14,910	16,702	18,674	20,842	23,227

Assumptions: Average annual energy cost escalation rate—10%. Interest on 8%, 20-yr bond—$2,470. Sinking fund payments (10%, 20 yrs)—$540. Additional construction costs—$30,869.

268

Figure 7.28. Possible schematic design for Chattanooga School. Courtesy of Michael E. Doyle.

heating, cooling, and lighting abilities of the daylighting apertures. Since the "w/o envelope" parametric bar is smaller than the "w/o internal load" bar, it appears that additional energy-cost reductions are possible by optimizing the size and orientation of the glass. In effect, the design team now has a new base building to study. The new nature of the energy needs of this structure is evident in the elimination parametrics and the rainbow plots. From these energy-need design indicators, a final schematic design can be proposed and once again evaluated to determine the final estimate of energy-effectiveness and financial value.

Conclusion to the Recommended Design Approach

As the preceding examples show, the recommended approach is a means to organize and present energy-related information on a whole-building level. The purpose of this approach is to inform and guide the design team toward the most significant energy-related building needs and opportunities. This approach clarifies rather than directly solves the problem. Alone, the recommended approach does not replace energy-related information on a component level. Rather, it is an attempt to use the great wealth of information on the component or single-concept level in the context of the energy-related needs and opportunities of the whole building.

The three preceding case studies were intentionally selected to indicate the large difference between a substitute component approach and the study of the interconnected needs and opportunities of commercial buildings. For instance, daylighting was used in the Denver Building example as an alternative to electric lighting. Studying the interconnected energy needs of the whole building, the design team realized that daylighting's greatest value was not as a substitute for electric lighting, but as an option that clearly has qualities and benefits beyond electric lighting in controlling the peak-energy needs of the building. By the end of the three examples, the design team readily assumed that breaking the coincident peak demand for cooling and lighting was an achievable goal. The study of the energy-related needs and opportunities of buildings reveals important insights that can be easily missed by appraising the problem as substitute components or systems.

The three examples of this chapter also demonstrate that the design of energy-responsive commercial buildings is not a one-shot leap to the best possible solution. It is a combination of education and exploration that becomes easier and less time-consuming as knowledge and insight are gained. In the preceding three examples, the design team required detailed information on the interconnected energy needs and opportunities of conventional buildings. However, as experience is acquired, many of the basic energy-need tasks can become intuitive and not require detailed appraisal. For instance, it is not necessary to generate a conventional base building cost and energy analysis for every future project. For a particular building type and climate, three or four such studies will make the information gained a matter of intuition. At this point, base building cost and energy needs can be assumed from previous projects, and energy-related design tasks can center on the reinvention of form, envelope, and equipment to suit new purposes.

We encourage readers to change the techniques presented in this book to match the specific educational needs of the design team. Since designers have many different levels of skill and experience in the design of energy-responsive commercial buildings, no one technique or approach can ever meet everyone's needs. However, we strongly recommend that energy issues always be assessed at the whole-building level. Clearly, the expansion of energy-related issues to the whole-building level is the next step in our collective experience toward the ultimate resolution of this design challenge.

At this point, the emphasis of Part Two breaks from the presentation of the overall recommended design approach to the discussion of core elements of the process. In the next chapter, building financial analysis is discussed in greater detail. Chapter Nine addresses the means and techniques of performing building energy analysis. Chapter Ten then focuses on a technique to appraise the benefits of new strategies, such as daylighting, that are at present beyond the abilities of most building energy calculation techniques.

chapter eight

THE FINANCIAL VALUE OF ENERGY-RESPONSIVE DESIGN

The main business of an enlightening minority is not fighting the majority but showing them how.

John Platt*

This chapter reviews the fundamentals of applying classical investment analysis methods to the design of energy-responsive commercial buildings. The objective is to teach the reader how to construct the net present value (NPV) of energy-responsive design graph (Fig. 8.1) and the net cash flow chart (Table 8.1) that were introduced in the two previous chapters.

As described in the recommended design approach of Chapter Six, and exemplified in the designs of Chapter Seven, investment analysis methods clarify the financial value of limiting nonrenewable energy use for both building owners and designers. Clarifying financial value has four very important advantages. First, building owners may become more disposed to initiate energy-related improvements if they can see how these alternatives support the major financial objectives of the entire project. Second, achievable energy-related goals can be negotiated between the owner and design team before the solutions are proposed. Third, clarifying the financial value of energy-responsive design informs the design team of the

---

*John Platt, *Step to Man*, 1967.

271

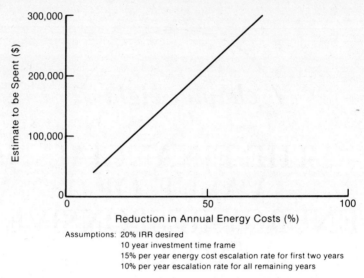

Assumptions: 20% IRR desired
10 year investment time frame
15% per year energy cost escalation rate for first two years
10% per year escalation rate for all remaining years

Figure 8.1.   Net present value of energy-responsive design—Denver Building.

range of initial cost dollars that can be spent to derive specific levels of
energy-effectiveness. Fourth, the actual financial value of any proposed
solution can be easily evaluated according to the established economic
criteria for the project.

The major purpose of using financial value techniques is to jointly
consider energy-related and profit concerns in an attempt to reduce the use
of nonrenewable energy in the built environment. As shown in the examples
of Chapter Seven and many of the case studies of Part One, substantial
energy-related savings are achievable by design through the incorporation
of different motives and the development of new perceived advantages in
innovative solutions. Many of the solutions used in examples in this book
would not have been found without the integration of energy issues into the
whole of building design and ownership. Investment analysis is used here to
stimulate innovation and reinvention, rather than as an after-the-fact assessment for a final solution.

The key to applying investment analysis to the design of energy-
responsive buildings is to match the methods used by the client to assess
financial value for the entire project. The investment analysis methods
presented here reflect the techniques most commonly used by real estate
decision makers. Specifically, the emphasis is on net present value of the
reduction of future utility bills for initial goal setting and cash flow and
internal rate of return for the evaluation of solutions. The following sections
cover the general fundamentals and principles of investment analysis
methods, the calculation of the financial value products shown in Figure 8.1
and Table 8.1, and additional real estate considerations that can affect value
and profit for some building owners.

TABLE 8.1. DENVER BUILDING ALTERNATIVE DESIGN #1, AFTER-TAX EARNINGS AND ANNUAL CASH FLOW DIFFERENTIALS

	Yr 1	Yr 2	Yr 3	Yr 4	Yr 5	Yr 6	Yr 7	Yr 8	Yr 9	Yr 10
Profitability Analysis										
Differential in energy-related operating costs	41,058	47,217	54,299	59,729	65,702	72,272	79,499	87,449	96,194	105,814
Differential in depreciation	(15,250)	(15,250)	(15,250)	(15,250)	(15,250)	(15,250)	(15,250)	(15,250)	(15,250)	(15,250)
Pretax earnings	25,808	31,967	39,049	44,479	50,452	57,022	64,249	72,199	80,944	90,564
Tax differential	(11,872)	(14,705)	(17,963)	(20,460)	(23,208)	(26,230)	(29,555)	(33,212)	(37,234)	(41,659)
Differential in after-tax earnings	13,939	17,262	21,087	24,019	27,244	30,792	34,695	38,988	43,710	48,904
Cash Flow Analysis										
Differential in energy-related operating costs	41,058	47,217	54,299	59,729	65,702	72,272	79,499	87,449	96,194	105,814
Tax differential	(11,872)	(14,705)	(17,963)	(20,460)	(23,208)	(26,230)	(29,555)	(33,212)	(37,234)	(41,659)
After-tax cash flow	29,186	32,512	36,337	39,269	42,494	46,042	49,945	54,238	58,900	64,154

Case assumptions: Client: Owner of owner-occupied building.
Financier and loan structure: Owner, internally financed.
Additional cost of energy-responsive building: $228,738.
Fuel escalation rate: 15%/yr for first 2 yrs, 10%/yr for next 8 yrs.

Note: Parentheses indicate negative cash flow.

FUNDAMENTALS AND PRINCIPLES

The benefits of energy-responsive design can be financial, nonfinancial, or a combination of both. Since many clients view energy-related alternatives as investments, a design team needs to view these strategies from an investment perspective. This section reviews the basic principles and fundamentals of investment analysis that a design team should understand to effectively address this perspective.

The value of energy-related investments is largely dictated by a client's desires. A particular energy-responsive design may be very beneficial and profitable to one client yet completely unacceptable to another depending on financial motives and economic perspectives and circumstances. To some clients, the financial value of energy-responsive design stems from moderating the impact of future energy-operating costs. To others, such as the speculative developer example in Chapter Seven, value is based on added income over a short period of time and the effect this documented income may have on resale value. Each client places different weight on factors such as extra initial cost, income, operating cost, resale value, tax implications, and cash flow. Understanding the client's economic perspective is necessary to find the leverage and motives required to suggest added project cost for energy-related alternatives. Four principles should be considered in this process of evaluating a client's financial situation: the time value of money, opportunity costs, the equivalency of income and reduced expenses, and differential analysis.

1. *The Time Value of Money.* Interest rates give money its time value. Assuming money is not held in cash, the value of $1 varies with the amount of time and the interest rate at which it has been or can be invested. Net present value expresses the value in today's dollars of income received and expenses incurred in the future, based on a specified interest rate. The interest rate is often called the discount rate. The net present value of $1 to be received 5 years from now is 62¢, assuming a discount rate of 10%. The future value of $1 invested today compounded at 10% annually for 10 years is $2.59. A net present value of energy-responsive design chart reflects the time value of money. This chart assesses the net present value of utility cost reductions over a specific time frame and for an interest rate the client expects to receive on money invested in reducing annual utility-related expenses.

2. *Opportunity Costs.* Opportunity costs are the other options available for using money, options that are foregone when a particular investment choice is made. If the investment options are A, B, C, and X, and investment X is selected, the opportunity costs of investment X are options A, B, and C. Another example: a real estate investor who can buy only one project this year has to select a hotel, an apartment house, or an office

TABLE 8.2. THE EQUIVALENCY OF INCOME AND REDUCED EXPENSES

Factors	Base Case ($)	Revenues Increased $100 ($)	Costs Reduced $100 ($)
Revenues	1,000	1,100	1,000
Costs	900	900	800
Pretax profit	100	200	200

building. The opportunity costs of buying the office building are the hotel and the apartment house that are not bought.

Opportunity costs are not conclusively reflected in the investment analysis techniques of this book, but a bottom-line rate of return that can be compared to other investment opportunities is always calculated and benefit is always compared to a conventional building. Since investors constantly compare the risks and benefits of alternative investments, standardized means and forms have evolved for this purpose. The cash flow analysis chart reflects these standardized outputs, and permits the client to evaluate energy-responsive design in a format compatible with the analysis of other investment opportunities.

3. *The Equivalency of Income and Reduced Expenses.* Mathematically, reducing expenses or costs by $1 is the same as increasing income by $1. Without considering tax implications, "a penny saved is a penny earned." Reduced operating expenses through an investment in energy-responsive design has the same impact on pretax profits as do higher revenues.

Investments in energy-responsive design can either reduce cost or increase revenue, yet the end result is a taxable profit. Short-term investments in energy-responsive design generally attempt to find advantages through increasing revenue. Longer-term investments generally seek a profitable reduction of costs. In either case, however, savings equals income and both produce a profit that can be calculated with the same basic mathematical formulas.

4. *Differential Analysis.* In investment analysis, those factors are isolated that would be affected by the investment decision. The focus of the analysis is on the differences that an investment would make on those isolated factors. Differential analysis is also called marginal analysis or incremental analysis (Table 8.3).

The numbers in the column on the far right in Table 8.3 represent the cost differences between an energy-responsive building and a conventional building. Throughout this book, the financial analysis focuses on the monetary differences created by an investment in energy-related improve-

TABLE 8.3.   DIFFERENTIAL   ANALYSIS

Cash Flow ($)	A Conventional Building ($)	B Energy-Responsive Building ($)	A Less B Differential ($)
Initial costs	2,000,000	2,050,000	50,000
Energy costs (first year)	60,000	30,000	30,000
Maintenance costs (first year)	2,000	2,000	0
Depreciation (first year)	133,333	136,667	3,334

ments. These differences are calculated by using the base building technique presented in Chapter Six.

The financial benefit of energy-responsive design for a particular client depends on whether the building will be leased or owner-occupied, the period of time the client expects to own the project, how the project is financed, what rate of return the client expects on the investment, the client's tax status, and the expected escalation rate for energy costs by the servicing utility. The impact of many of these factors varies greatly with different types of clients.

In general, clients fall into the following categories:

Developers who initially intend to lease the building, but sell the project in the short term.

Investors who plan to lease a building and hold it for a long-term investment.

Businesses that plan to use the building for housing their own operations, and often lease part of it.

Government entities who will use the building for government functions or public use.

Nonprofit organizations who plan to occupy, lease, or sell the building.

Clients may be corporations, partnerships, or individuals; the tax effects of building ownership and sale will vary with their status. Normal concerns and financial criteria of each client type are summarized below. The weight of these factors varies with the individual client.

The financial goal of a short-term speculative developer is to maximize profit in a short period of time. The primary source of profit is from selling the building quickly at a high price. Price is generally established by assessing the income-generating capability of the project. Therefore, developers want space that leases quickly for the highest possible rate and that costs little to operate. Maximizing income allows high short-term appreciation of the building and makes it attractive to long-term investors.

Long-term investors of leased space seek profits through the advantages of real estate ownership and capital gains on the building's appreciation at resale. The long-term perspective of this investor makes depreciation and other real estate ownership tax advantages very important. Long-term investors desire high occupancy rates, low operating costs, and reliability of building performance.

A building occupied by the owner will generally have long-term financial objectives that include increased productivity and reduced operating cost. In such cases, reduced operating cost directly impacts net earnings. Tax advantages such as depreciation are also important to this type of client.

Government entities typically use a long-term perspective and likewise seek increased productivity and the reduction of operating cost. As in the case of the Bateson Building presented in Chapter Four, it is often much less costly in the long term for the government to build than to lease. Reductions in utility-related operating expenses flow directly to the government entity that owns the building, without tax implications.

The economic concerns of a nonprofit organization are a blend of the owner-occupied and governmental clients. Nonprofit organizations must generate funds to support their activities and often have tight budgets. Once again, a reduction in operating cost is equivalent to income. A penny saved is a penny collected in this case. Tax considerations are not applicable.

In most cases, cash flow and internal rate of return are the key measures that all these client types use for final real estate decision making. A cash flow analysis is a projection for each year of the outflow of cash for increased initial costs, expenses, and taxes, and the inflow of cash from income and reduced operating expenses and taxes. The difference in yearly cash outflows and inflows is the annual net cash flow. A cash flow analysis based on the differential cost attributable to an investment charts how much actual cash the client will save or spend each year because of that investment.

In addition to having a keen interest in cash flow, real estate clients are also concerned about internal rate of return. IRR shows the actual rate of return on an investment, based on cash flow and not including financing costs. Internal rate of return allows the client to compare an investment in energy-responsive design with either the cost of financing energy-related initial costs or with alternative uses of investment money.

Net present value, cash flow, and internal rate of return analysis all use the same financial principles and mathematical formulas. They are all investment analysis tools that evaluate the comparative costs and benefits of investment options. The major difference among them is the output produced. The selection of one over the others depends on what the user wants to know. The specific outputs that are most helpful at different stages of the design process are described in the following section.

TARGETING THE NET PRESENT VALUE OF ENERGY-RESPONSIVE DESIGN

Starting each project with a base building permits differential analysis. To clarify financial design goals before solutions are proposed, the base-case utility cost can be appraised to set the approximate monies that may be spent initially to reduce the annual utility cost by different proportions while achieving a specific rate of return for the owner. The importance of this appraisal is that it allows the owner and design team to negotiate and set specific energy-related financial design goals and it informs the design team of the range of dollars that may be spent to achieve specific end results.

The first piece of information required to start this process is a commitment from the client that additional funds are available for profitable energy-related design alternatives. If funds are not available, the design team must use cost-balancing techniques as explained in Chapter Six. If additional capital is available, the upper limit should be determined.

The second important set of facts to collect is the estimated annual operating cost of the base building. The energy analysis techniques described in Chapter Six and explained in detail in Chapter Nine can be used for this purpose. The annual dollar total should be checked against utility company information for similar buildings of comparable size and use in the locale of the proposed project. As with most steps of the recommended design approach of Chapter Six, the determination of base utility cost is a simple task for retrofit projects. In such cases, real utility bills for the existing structure can be normalized.

The third piece of information needed is the expected escalation rate for energy costs. Escalation rates are highly utility-specific and must be based on expectations for the area in which the building is located. Using the accepted overall escalation rate is more productive than attempting to define a precise rate for each year.

Selecting an energy cost escalation rate is extremely complicated if a high degree of precision is sought. Projections are often expressed in percent increases over inflation, involving the selection of two estimates of future cost increases. Utility rate forecasts are extremely complex and depend on several other forecasted factors. Small variances in the escalation rate used do not significantly affect the relative profitability of a project. In selecting an energy cost escalation rate, the most sensible approach is to find out the rate used by the business economists of the area. For use in these investment analysis techniques, this rate should include inflation. Escalation rates for different fuel types can be applied in a more complex analysis; this degree of precision is rarely warranted at this stage of design.

The fourth and fifth pieces of information essential to this process are the client's expected rate of return on investments and the client's investment time frame. These values are critical to the client's definition of a profitable investment in energy-responsive design and will greatly affect the design team's challenge to derive a solution within the set financial constraints.

Although clients are aware that energy-related operating costs will decrease over the years and that the investment is good for the life of the building, many of them are concerned only with the short- and mid-term costs and benefits. Projections of costs and benefits too far into the future have an unreal character, even though they may be based on the best available inflation and escalation figures.

Knowledge of each client's desired rate of return for an investment in energy-responsive design and his or her investment time frame (the number of years over which a client will consider the investment feasible) is necessary to compare energy-responsive design with other investment options. Some clients and designers may not feel as comfortable discussing the financial criteria of a project as they do discussing its nonfinancial objectives. In such cases, client's criteria can be approximated with data from a similar client, financial institutions, real estate development consultants, or professional associations.

Assumptions about the client's financial criteria and conditions must be conservative at all levels of investment analysis. Overstating profit advantages only results in an eventual lack of credibility. For this reason, the client should be included in the determination of the five sets of facts just described. If agreement is lacking between the owner and design team on this approach or the assumptions it uses, the results may not be considered valid by the owner.

Two examples illustrate how the five inputs are used to produce net present value targets for energy-responsive design. The first example, the one-story Pittsburgh Building from Chapter Six, shows how net present value targets are generated for a project that derives value from future reductions in utility-related operating expenses. The second example, the six-story Pittsburgh Building from Chapter Seven, explains how net present value cost targets are determined where profit is generated by increasing the future income of the building owner.

In the one-story Pittsburgh example, the client desires an energy-responsive building and has committed to spend additional dollars over the base building construction cost if each additional dollar produces at least a 20% rate of return over a 10-year period. The energy cost escalation rate is conservatively set at 10%/yr for each of the 10 years analyzed. The total first-year energy cost for the base case is approximately $6095.

The first step in generating a net present value of energy-responsive design graph is to select three or more assumed levels of energy-use reduction and project these annual energy cost savings over the investment term. Table 8.4 shows the annual energy cost savings for buildings that

**TABLE 8.4.   ENERGY   COST   SAVINGS   PROJECTED   OVER   10   YEARS
FOR   ASSUMED   LEVELS   OF   IMPROVEMENT
OVER   THE   BASE   CASE**

% Reduction	Yearly Savings ($)									
from Base Case	Yr 1	Yr 2	Yr 3	Yr 4	Yr 5	Yr 6	Yr 7	Yr 8	Yr 9	Yr 10
25	1524	1676	1844	2028	2231	2454	2699	2969	3266	3593
50	3048	3352	3687	4056	4462	4908	5399	5939	6533	7186
75	4571	5028	5531	6084	6693	7362	8098	8908	9799	10,779

Assumptions: 10% annual energy cost escalation rate.
                     Base-building energy use = $6095 for first year.
NPVs: NPV of 25% reduction = $9085
              (based on 10-yr term and 20% expected rate of return).
              NPV of 50% reduction = $12,042
              (based on 10-yr term and 20% expected rate of return).
              NPV of 75% reduction = $18,978
              (based on 10-yr term and 20% expected rate of return).

achieve a 25%, 50%, and 75% reduction in total annual energy cost over the
base building. A building that reduces annual energy cost by 50% has a first-
year savings of $3047.50 over the base case. Due to the energy cost
escalation rate, the second-year savings is $3047.50 × 1.1 = $3352.25. All
three lines of this chart begin with an assumed first-year energy cost
differential, and are projected to the end of the 10-year term by multiplying
each preceding year by one plus the energy cost escalation rate. The
escalation rate is numerically expressed as a fraction of one.

Once the 10-year, energy-related cost savings have been generated, each
string of numbers is entered into a financial calculator (or the formula for
NPV at the end of the next section may be used) to determine the net
present value for each of the three energy-use reduction scenarios. In each
of these three cases the value of the energy savings over the client's time
frame is discounted by the client's required rate of return to express the
amount, in today's dollars, by which building costs can be increased to
achieve that reduction in operating costs. This amount, or the net present
value to the client, represents an economically feasible investment, by the
client's criteria, competitive with other investment options.

Using the three net present values generated from the cash flows of Table
8.4, a net present value of energy-responsive design graph can be generated
as in Figure 8.2. This graph can be used as the basis for an agreement
between the client and design team that expresses the value of reducing
annual energy costs over a set period of years. We feel it is the best method
for energy-related goal setting for situations where the client is prepared to
pay more now to avoid future utility-related costs.

Short-term investors often will not retain a building long enough to

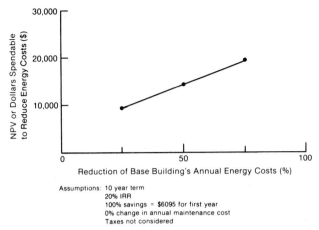

Figure 8.2.   Net present value of energy-responsive design—Pittsburgh one-story example.

warrant energy-related investments that base profit on a long-term reduction in energy-operating expenses. For this type of client, the design team needs to find a means to generate additional income from energy-related alternatives. Such means range from options like on-site power generation to, as shown in the six-story Pittsburgh example of Chapter Eight, profit-generating, utility-related leasing strategies. A net present value of energy-responsive design chart for income-related profit scenarios is generated as in the above example, except that operating energy cost reductions are replaced by assumed levels of income generated by the energy-related design alternatives. For example, the net present value of energy-responsive design graph for the Pittsburgh speculative developer case study is generated as shown in Table 8.5 and Figure 8.3.

Both of the preceding examples equate the value of energy-responsive design to the economic criteria of the client. From our experience, the client's economic criteria appears to largely determine what can be done to limit the use of nonrenewable energy for a proposed project. What is profitable for a specific project varies greatly with the required rate of return, investment time frame, and utility cost escalation rates. Tables 8.6 and 8.7 exemplify the impact of the net present value of energy-responsive design when the investment time frame or the client's desired rate of return are changed while all other factors are held constant.

Awareness of the impact of these factors is valuable in developing acceptable design alternatives and determining economic value. Solutions are more cost-effective as the desired rate of return decreases, investment time frame lengthens, or projected cost of energy increases. Conversely, solutions are less cost-effective as the desired rates of return increase, the investment time frame shortens, or the projected cost of energy decreases. A design strategy that is not profitable for one client may be well-suited for

TABLE 8.5. PROJECTING INCOME AND NET PRESENT
VALUE FOR TWO LEVELS OF IMPROVEMENT,
THE SIX-STORY PITTSBURGH EXAMPLE

Assumed First-Year Income ($/ft²)	Yr 1[a]	Yr 2[b]	Yr 3[c]
0.50	0	10,200	17,000
1.00	0	20,400	34,000

[a]Yr 1 income = 0 since building is not completed until 18th month.

[b]Yr 2 income based on 80% occupancy for last 6 months of second year.

[c]Yr 3 income based on 95% occupancy for year. Energy costs are assumed to have risen
by 30%, reducing the difference between operating costs and stop to 70% of initial
year per square-foot savings.

Assumptions: 30% annual utility cost escalation rate (a high estimate here is conservative
and actually reduces NPV).
3-yr investment term; 20% rate of return expected by client.

NPVs (calculated on the additional income in years 2 and 3 only):
NPV of $0.50/ft² first-year income = $20,500.
NPV of $1.00/ft² first-year income = $41,000.

another with a lower expected rate of return or longer investment time
frame. Similarly, the value of a specific design strategy changes for any
given solution if the client substantially modifies the investment time frame
or desired rate of return during the design process.

This simple method of targeting profitable investments in energy-
responsive design does not consider factors that affect the profitability of
some final design solutions. In particular, the impact for tax-paying clients is
not yet included in the investment analysis. However, this simple approach

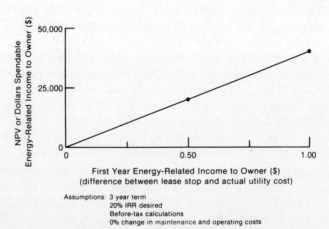

Assumptions: 3 year term
20% IRR desired
Before-tax calculations
0% change in maintenance and operating costs

Figure 8.3. Net present value of energy-responsive design—Pittsburgh six-story example.

TABLE 8.6. IMPACT ON NET PRESENT VALUE
OF CHANGING THE INVESTMENT TIME FRAME

Investment Time Frame (Yr)	Desired Internal Rate of Return (%)	NPV of Investment ($)
5	20	115,676
10	20	197,976
15	20	251,244

Assumptions: $30,175 energy operating cost reduction, 10% energy cost escalation rate.

TABLE 8.7. IMPACT ON NET PRESENT VALUE
OF CHANGING THE CLIENT'S DESIRED RATE
OF RETURN

Investment Time Frame (Yr)	Desired Internal Rate of Return (%)	NPV of Investment ($)
20	8	48,510
20	10	39,661
20	12	32,890
20	15	25,469

Assumptions: $1865 energy operating cost reduction, 20-yr investment time frame, 15% energy cost escalation rate for first 5 yrs and 10% thereafter.

is generally adequate for initial cost targets that are to be used at the earliest design stages. The primary value of the method is that it provides a balance between accuracy and ease for an early ball-park determination of allowable investments in energy-responsive design. If desired, all the additional real estate investment considerations presented in the remainder of this chapter may be included in assessing net present value before design begins. However, we recommend that the reader begin with the simplest application of this method before proceeding to more complicated versions.

Targeting the net present value of energy-responsive design is a simple process. The facts that must be collected to generate this material are essential to clarifying the energy-related goals of a project. With an inexpensive financial calculator, a variety of net present values can be computed in only a matter of minutes. The effort of this additional step in the design of energy-responsive commercial buildings is well worth the information derived.

ANALYZING NET CASH FLOW AND INTERNAL RATE OF RETURN FOR SPECIFIC SOLUTIONS

In this section the focus of investment analysis shifts from working with cost reduction targets to evaluating the financial merits of alternative or final design solutions. As in the last section, financial value is based on the differential between a base building and an energy-responsive design. The major difference here is that one can use initial cost and annual energy cost differentials that reflect a specific proposed solution. Since more specifics are known at this level, a greater degree of detail is appropriate to assess the investment advantages of the proposed solution(s).

We begin by outlining how a simple net cash flow analysis is generated. Four examples from the preceding two chapters show the construction of the type of cash flow analysis that is required for different types of clients. The section concludes with how a completed net cash flow analysis is used to derive the approximate internal rate of return that the client can expect from the proposed solution.

The facts needed to perform a cash flow analysis for a specific client vary substantially according to the type of client. To begin, we discuss the core facts essential to investment analysis at this level for all types of clients and projects. By example, we then widen our concerns to additional considerations that are more appropriate for specific client types. These core factors that are essential to generating a net cash flow and internal rate of return analysis for a specific solution are as follows:

Energy-operating costs of the base building for the first year.

Energy-operating costs of the energy-responsive building for the first year.

Energy cost escalation rate for the locale.

Differential in maintenance and repair expenses and replacement costs, if any.

Initial construction cost of the base building.

Initial construction cost of the energy-responsive building.

Client's desired rate of return on an energy-related investment.

Client's time frame for considering an investment cost-effective.

Most of these factors have already been determined and discussed in the preceding section. The new facts that must be determined relate directly to the actual cost differentials of the proposed solution. This new information sets the first-year energy-operating cost and initial construction cost difference between the base building and the proposed solution. As before, the first-year operating cost differential is multiplied by the utility cost escalation rate to establish the annual benefit of the energy-responsive design through the investment term established by the client.

A major core factor not discussed in the previous section is additional cost differences that can be attributed to the proposed energy-responsive design (the fourth factor listed). Significant differences in maintenance, cleaning, and replacement costs should be recorded and presented on the cash flow sheet just as energy cost differences are projected. These new differences may be positive or negative, or assumed to be zero when appropriate. For example, if glass area is increased by 400% to achieve a high degree of daylighting, the increases in window cleaning and estimated expenditures for increased glass replacement should be evaluated and presented in the cash flow analysis. All such future cost differences should be projected at the expected inflation rate. The client will appreciate the consideration of the consequences of these additional cost differences. Also, these factors are often seeds for innovation and reinvention. Combining energy-related cost differences with other positive maintenance and replacement cost differences is a good way to find superior energy-responsive solutions that would not be obvious by focusing on energy issues alone.

We caution the reader not to use construction cost differentials that are only analyzed or calculated at the single component level. The interdependency of building systems causes changes in one part of a building to affect others. For example, reductions in lighting loads can affect the size of the cooling system. Innovative structural systems can reduce initial cost and permit additional expenditures in other areas. For these reasons, it is recommended that only whole-building construction cost differentials between the base and proposed cases be used.

The simplest cash flow analysis that can be generated is one that only compares the initial construction cost differential to the annual operating cost differential over the term of the investment period. Such an example, the Chattanooga School from Chapter Seven, is presented in Table 8.8.

The first step to construct such a chart is to determine the initial construction cost differential. In this case, this differential is $30,869 and is placed on the first line under year zero. Parentheses indicate a cash outflow. This initial dollar outflow is the base against which the value of all future net benefits from the investment will be evaluated. For projects requiring construction times greater than 1 year, the initial costs might be spread over 2 or more years. The possible applicability of energy-related tax credits is another example of a variation in the initial cost differential. In such cases, initial costs are reduced directly by the amount that is refunded in the initial year.

A second step required to construct Table 8.8 is to project the reduction in operating costs attributed to the energy-responsive design investment for each year of the client's time frame. Once again, any significant positive or negative replacements or maintenance cost differentials should be calculated and entered under the appropriate year. These considerations add credibility to the analysis. In the simple example in Table 8.8, these differences were assumed to total zero.

TABLE 8.8. A SIMPLE CASH FLOW ANALYSIS OF CORE FACTORS

Cash Flow Factors ($)	Yr 0	Yr 1	Yr 2	Yr 3	Yr 4	Yr 5	Yr 6	Yr 7	Yr 8	Yr 9	Yr 10
Expected differential in initial project costs	(30,869)										
Expected differential in energy operating costs (assuming differential maintenance and repair = 0)		4290	4719	5191	5710	6281	6909	7600	8360	9196	10,116
Expected annual net cash flow		4290	4719	5191	5710	6281	6909	7600	8360	9196	10,116

This example is from the Chattanooga School case.
IRR = 12.1% and fuel escalation rate = 10%/yr.
Note: Parentheses indicate negative cash flow.

Projection of the differential in the initial project costs, any replacement costs, and the differential in future operating expenses form the core of the cash flow analysis for all types of clients. These numbers for the same project would not vary with the criteria or objectives of different client types, as they represent the inflows and outflows of cash attributable solely to construction costs, replacement costs, utility bills, and maintenance costs. However, most clients also require that some additional factors be assessed to reflect their special economic circumstances. The following three examples illustrate cash flow variations that go beyond the core factors to meet the needs of a specific client.

The first example is a case in which the client wants to compare the cash flow and internal rate of return to the cost of financing. Financing costs are traditionally not included in cash flow analysis or in the calculation of internal rate of return from the cash flow spread sheet, in order to allow the investor to evaluate the rate of return on a project against the cost of capital (the composite interest rate that is paid to finance the project). However, for a project on which the financing costs can be easily calculated, a comparison of annual financing costs and net benefits can be very informative. Particularly effective is a comparison of the differential in fixed rate mortgages or bond interest payments and the net cash flow.

Such an example is presented in Table 8.9, the Chattanooga School building. This figure sets the initial cost differential to zero and projects the 20-year cost of financing the original $30,869 cost increase. The final net cash flow in this case represents the difference between energy-operating cost reductions and the financing cost of the investment. The advantage of such an analysis is that it shows that the benefits derived by the design are greater than the financing costs from year 1. Clients are generally very interested in whether an investment can produce a positive cash flow from the first year. If additional capital is available from a lender, showing how the benefits of energy-responsive design can be greater than the cost to finance the improvement is a powerful means to encourage building owners to invest in energy-responsive design.

Perhaps the most important variation in the cash flow methods already presented is the impact of taxes on clients who operate for profit. Tax implications vary with the client's tax status. Depending on the client-designer relationship, tax-related factors may or may not be available to the design team. Where specific factors are not available, the design team can approximate these values for typical clients. In such cases, the client can substitute his or her own tax variables for a final in-house appraisal.

Emphasis should be placed on showing the after-tax cash flow differential for tax-paying clients. Most important are the effects of depreciation and taxable income. A higher initial cost for an energy-responsive building will result in increased depreciation as well as lower overall operating costs. The money saved on energy-operating costs and the depreciation allowance are both equivalent to income and will be taxed.

TABLE 8.9. THE NET CASH FLOW DIFFERENCE BETWEEN ENERGY-OPERATING COST REDUCTIONS AND FINANCING COSTS

Cash Flow Factors ($)	Yr 0	Yr 1	Yr 2	Yr 3	Yr 4	Yr 5	Yr 6	Yr 7	Yr 8	Yr 9	Yr 10
Initial cash outlay	0										
Expected differential in operating costs		4290	4719	5191	5710	6281	6909	7600	8360	9196	10,116
Interest on 8%, 20-yr bond		(2470)	(2470)	(2470)	(2470)	(2470)	(2470)	(2470)	(2470)	(2470)	(2470)
Sinking fund, with 10% interest		(540)	(540)	(540)	(540)	(540)	(540)	(540)	(540)	(540)	(540)
Net cash difference between operating cost reduction and financing costs		1280	1709	2180	2700	3271	3900	4590	5350	6186	7106

Cash Flow Factors ($)	Yr 11	Yr 12	Yr 13	Yr 14	Yr 15	Yr 16	Yr 17	Yr 18	Yr 19	Yr 20
Initial cash outlay										
Expected differential in operating costs	11,127	12,240	13,464	14,810	16,291	17,920	19,712	21,684	23,852	26,237
Interest on 8%, 20-yr bond	(2,470)	(2,470)	(2,470)	(2,470)	(2,470)	(2,470)	(2,470)	(2,470)	(2,470)	(2,470)
Sinking fund, with 10% interest	(540)	(540)	(540)	(540)	(540)	(540)	(540)	(540)	(540)	(540)
Net cash difference between operating cost reduction and financing costs	8,117	9,230	10,454	11,800	13,280	14,910	16,702	18,674	20,842	23,227

This example is from the Chattanooga school case.

Note: Projections in energy cost differentials are made for 20 yrs in this chart to match the term of the bond and sinking fund. Parentheses indicate negative cash flow.

The reason for including depreciation and the income tax differential is to show the client that the additional depreciation will help offset the impact of taxation of the energy savings: half of what is saved is not paid out in income taxes. Going to this level of detail in a presentation on economic value serves the purpose of identifying and clarifying all the dollar-related impacts for the client. An after-tax cash flow analysis shows how much cash will be available to the client after taxation to spend or invest in other areas. Uses of this cash might include building up working capital, repayment of debt, corporate expansion, or investment.

The effect of depreciation is to reduce the income taxes paid by individuals, partnerships, or corporations. Depreciation is not a sum of money that a building owner receives but a "paper expense" that reduces income taxes and net profits. In generating a cash flow analysis, the amount that is saved on income taxes due to the additional depreciation expense should be added as a financial benefit. Under the Economic Recovery Act of 1981 several methods of depreciation are available for tax-paying clients. We present only one of these choices: the 15-year straight-line method of depreciation which we believe is the method most clients will elect.

An example of a cash flow analysis that includes depreciation and the tax on earnings is shown in Table 8.10. This figure is the daylit and evaporative-cooled Denver Building example of Chapter Seven. Note that this chart shows two types of analysis. The first is a profitability analysis. A profitability analysis results in a bottom line of the differential in after-tax earnings. A cash flow analysis ends with an after-tax cash flow value. These two end totals are different since one includes the paper expense of depreciation. Profitability analysis reflects how income is calculated for tax purposes. Cash flow analysis documents the real after-tax money received by the client. Presenting these two analysis methods together allows the client to see the benefit of the depreciation differential and indicates how the tax differential was calculated for inclusion in the cash flow analysis.

The first line of both the profitability and cash flow analyses (lines A and F) is the energy-cost differential projected over the term of the investment analysis. The first-year operating cost differential is derived and projected as in the earlier examples. Line B is the differential in depreciation. Assuming a 15-year straight-line method of depreciation, this value is calculated by dividing the initial project cost differential by 15. Line C, pretax earnings, is the operating cost differential minus the depreciation differential (line A minus line B for each year analyzed).

To calculate the tax differential (line D) that the energy-responsive design causes, a standard corporate federal tax rate of 46% was assumed. Again, this standard will not apply to all clients, yet represents a good conservative assumption to stimulate the client to think of energy-responsive design as an investment. In Table 8.10, the tax differential for each year is calculated by multiplying the pretax earnings (line C) by 0.46.

Subtracting the tax differential (line D) from the pretax earnings gives

TABLE 8.10. DENVER BUILDINGS, IMPACT OF REDUCED ENERGY-OPERATING COSTS ON EARNINGS AFTER TAXES AND ANNUAL CASH FLOW

Cash Flow Factor ($)	Yr 1	Yr 2	Yr 3	Yr 4	Yr 5	Yr 6	Yr 7	Yr 8	Yr 9	Yr 10
Profitability										
A. Differential in energy-related operating costs	58,100	66,815	76,837	84,521	92,973	102,270	112,497	123,747	136,122	149,734
B. Differential in depreciation	(20,240)	(20,240)	(20,240)	(20,240)	(20,240)	(20,240)	(20,240)	(20,240)	(20,240)	(20,240)
C. Pretax earnings	37,860	46,575	56,597	64,281	72,733	82,030	92,257	103,507	115,882	129,494
D. Tax differential	(17,416)	(21,425)	(26,035)	(29,569)	(33,457)	(37,734)	(42,438)	(47,613)	(53,306)	(59,567)
E. Differential in after-tax earnings	20,444	25,151	30,593	34,712	39,276	44,296	49,819	55,894	62,576	69,927
Cash Flow										
F. Differential in energy-related operating costs	58,100	66,815	76,837	84,521	92,973	102,270	112,497	123,747	136,122	149,734
G. Tax differential	(17,416)	(21,425)	(26,035)	(29,569)	(33,457)	(37,734)	(42,438)	(47,613)	(53,306)	(59,567)
H. After-tax cash flow	40,684	45,391	50,803	54,952	59,516	64,536	70,059	76,134	82,816	90,167

Case assumptions: Client: Owner of owner-occupied building.
Financier: Owner, internally financed.
Additional cost of energy-responsive building: $303,588.
Reduction in energy operating costs: $58,100 in first year.
Fuel escalation rate: 15% for first 2 yrs, 10% for each remaining year.

Note: Parentheses indicate negative cash flow.

line E, the differential in after-tax earnings. In total, this profitability analysis is only used outside the corporation for purposes such as income tax reporting.

The cash flow analysis (lines F, G, and H) results in a total that reflects the true cash received by the corporation. Lines F and G are equal to lines A and D, respectively. A major benefit of performing and documenting a profitability analysis is to isolate line G, the tax differential. Line H, the after-tax cash flow, is the value most investors want to know, and is found by subtracting line G from line F. The after-tax cash flow is the same as the after-tax earnings differential without including the paper expense of depreciation.

Cash flow and profitability analysis for tax-paying clients involve simple addition, subtraction, and multiplication of core factors on a spread sheet. The task is easily performed by hand, or extremely adaptable to programmable calculators or personal computers.

The last cash flow analysis variation presented is in the cash flow spread sheet from the six-story Pittsburgh example of Chapter Seven (Table 8.11). This figure shows the cash flow analysis for a leasing strategy that anticipates a 50¢/ft^2 income to the owner during the first year of occupancy.

Table 8.11 is not substantially different from the financial value target

TABLE 8.11.   SIX-STORY PITTSBURGH EXAMPLE, DEVELOPER'S CASH FLOW ANALYSIS

Cash Flow Factors ($)	Yr 1	Yr 2	Yr 3
Additional cash for higher initial cost[a] ($23,500 × 20%)	(4,650)		
Additional interest on project loan[b] [($23,500 × 80%) × 20%]	(1,860)[d]	(3,720)	(3,720)
Additional income from difference between stop and actual energy costs of 50¢/ft^2 in year 2, 35¢/ft^2 in year 3[c]	0	10,200	16,958
Cash flow attributable to investment in energy-responsive building	(6,510)	6,480	13,238

[a]Initial cost differential is $23,250. 20% of this total is paid directly by the developer. The remainder is financed.

[b]80% of initial cost differential is financed on a 3-yr construction loan at 20%/yr; interest only due annually.

[c]Occupancy begins at 18th month. Second year occupancy assumed as 80% of last 6 months. Third year occupancy assumed as 95%. Income varies between year 2 and 3 because fuel escalation rate is assumed to be 30% in this case (intentionally set high to generate a conservative estimate of financial value). Total leasable area for the building is 51,000 ft^2.

[d]Construction loan interest at one half on partially constructed project.

Note: Parentheses indicate negative cash flow.

generated for this project and presented in Figure 8.3 of the preceding section. However, to make the analysis more complete, the initial developer equity and additional annual interest on the project loan are included in the cash flow spread sheet. Since the first-year cash outflow equals the second-year net cash inflow, and since the before-tax rate of return for the project as proposed is 59%, it is not necessary to extensively assess and document additional concerns such as tax differentials. The proposed solution is a sure winner and requires no additional calculations unless the client specifically asks for them. A return on equity of 99% and the assumption that the added income will favorably influence the resale value of the building to long-term investors is adequate financial analysis for this project. Knowing when not to add extraneous variables to this analysis method is as useful as knowing which additional factors should be included for specific clients.

The key variable left from all these preceding discussions of cash flow calculations is how the expected internal rate of return of the investment is calculated. Internal rate of return is properly figured on net cash flow and includes tax differentials where appropriate. In cases where the design team does not incorporate the tax impacts of an energy-responsive investment, as in the last cash flow example, IRR can be calculated on the core net cash flow figures and presented as a pretax IRR. To avoid confusion, the internal rate of return should always be specified as pre- or after-tax.

Formulas for Net Present Value and Internal Rate of Return

Net present value (NPV):

$$(P/F, i, n) = \frac{1}{(1 + i)^n} = (1 + i)^{-r}$$

where P/F = net present value
      i = interest rate or desired rate of return by client
      n = number of periods for which interest is calculated.

Net rate of return (IRR) is that rate that discounts the project's cash flow to a net present value of zero, satisfying the following mathematical relationship:

$$0 = \frac{CF_1}{1 + r} + \frac{CF_2}{(1 + r)^2} + \cdots + \frac{CF_n}{(1 + r)^n} - I = CF_n(P/F, r, n) - I$$

where CF = cash flow
    r = IRR
    n = number of periods
    I = initial cost of investment.

Calculating IRR, especially for projects with uneven cash flows, is an extremely tedious, mathematical exercise. The formula above can be used, but we highly recommend investing in a financial calculator or computer software that has IRR-computing capability. The user manuals for these items will clearly show how to enter the initial cost and annual cash flow amounts to solve for IRR. The inputs required will be the same as those already documented on the cash flow analysis spread sheets presented in this section.

ADDITIONAL REAL ESTATE INVESTMENT CONSIDERATIONS

To this point, this chapter has covered the basics of investment analysis for energy-responsive buildings. The intent of this material is to get the reader started rather than to show the countless variations possible with these simple methods and techniques. For most design firms and clients, presentation of the core factors—initial investment costs and the differential in significant operating costs—should be the primary focus. (Depreciation is included as a core factor for tax-paying clients.) However, awareness of other client considerations is important, and specific knowledge of the influence of these factors is valuable in certain situations. Real estate investors consider several other factors in their investment decision making. This chapter concludes by reviewing four additional factors that may be useful to specific real estate decision makers.

1. *Appreciation.* Chief among these is the appreciation potential of a project. Appreciation is the amount by which the project's value will be increased upon sale. Appreciation is based on many factors but fundamental is the net cash flow the project generates.

The appreciation rate for energy-efficient commercial buildings has not been established because of the lack of historical data. Valuation theory leads to the conclusion that the appreciation rate of energy-responsive buildings should be higher if their net cash flow is greater than that of their conventional counterparts.

Although real estate investors typically calculate appreciation in their internal rate of return estimates for projects, attempting to calculate the increased resale value of a project due to its energy cost savings is not recommended at the present time. However, the IRR should always be calculated without the appreciation factor. Clarifying this point will enable the client to make an adjusted comparison of the internal rate of return on energy-responsive projects and their conventional counterparts.

2. *Tax Credits.* Tax credits reduce investment costs. Familiarity with federal, state, and local tax credits can help reduce the initial project costs if

features and systems eligible for tax credits are included in the design solutions where appropriate. The amount eligible for tax credits should be presented to the client as a legal reduction in additional costs and entered directly beneath additional investment costs as a positive inflow on the cash flow analysis spread sheet.

3.   *Property Tax.* The effect of higher project costs for energy efficiency on property tax has not been documented. Twenty-six states prohibit a higher assessment because of energy-efficiency improvements. Local property tax officials can provide information on their assessment policy.

4.   *Insurance.*   Likewise, the impact of higher project costs on insurance expenses has not been documented. However, insurance is normally a small percentage of overall operating costs.

Investment analysis for energy-responsive buildings is like many other elements in the total design process. The wider the concerns within which it is immersed, the greater the likelihood of finding appropriate solutions that would be missed if one focused merely on energy-related issues. However, it is important to decide how many second-order investment factors are to be included in the analysis. To clarify the key issues, it is often better to eliminate small factors and state that they have been withheld from the analysis.

In conclusion, investment analysis is a valuable tool that can inform both building owners and designers of the value of energy-responsive design before solutions are conceived as well as assist in the evaluation of proposed solutions. In this book, the emphasis of economic analysis is shifted from final accountability and placed within the process to stimulate innovation and reinvention that may be missed by withholding cost-effectiveness assessments to the end of schematic design.

This chapter only presents the fundamentals and basics of the investment analysis technique suggested in this book. As the reader gains experience in these techniques, additional variations and investment analysis tasks will readily become apparent from this simple beginning.

chapter nine

BUILDING ENERGY ANALYSIS DURING EARLY DESIGN STAGES

Early schematic energy analysis need only be accurate enough to intelligently choose between design alternatives.

WILLIAM M. C. LAM

INTRODUCTION

Design is a synthetic activity. It seeks to create a complex whole that is greater than the sum of the individual parts. During the early phases of a design project, designers must intuitively balance many competing requirements, energy conservation being just one of these. A creative blending and balancing of all requirements must occur to produce an outstanding design.

Energy considerations differ from the other requirements in that few designers have an adequate intuitive understanding of when, where, why, and how energy is used in commercial buildings. The survey of 250 design professionals in Chapter Five clearly demonstrates this lack of intuitive insight.

In contrast to design, analysis starts with the whole and dissects it into individual parts. In the building profession, energy analysis is usually a reactive activity. After a building is defined, it is then analyzed for the optimization of subcomponents and/or the selection of mechanical and electrical equipment. There are many existing computer programs, algorithms, and engineering methods for analyzing energy consumption in buildings after the building concept is developed. These analysis methods can be used in later design phases to answer the questions of when, where, why, and how energy is used in a building.

Several pioneers in the field of energy-conscious building design have sought to use existing energy analysis techniques as aids to augment the energy intuition of the designer. The concept is simple. Generic buildings, design concepts, and components are analyzed before the building is designed. The purpose of this predesign analysis is to identify important energy-related parameters and their interaction.

These early attempts to conduct proactive analysis during conceptual design are not always successful or well received. Some of the implementation problems are obvious: What is a generic building? How should data be displayed? How precise must the assumptions be? Can the energy needs of a building, as yet undesigned, be predicted?

Other implementation problems are more subtle and reflect the fundamental differences between synthesis and analysis. Architectural designers tend to stress synthesis and rely on historical examples. Many dismiss the value of analysis as a learning tool before design. Analysts, on the other hand, are uncomfortable with the relatively unstructured synthesis process and the fact that the approach of the architectural designer is so open-ended.

The synthetic and analytic approaches should be merged into a more eclectic style. Designers must recognize that their "energy intuition" may not be valid for commercial buildings. Analysts must recognize that much of the data they can generate and interpret are superfluous or uninterpretable by the designers for the early "form giving" exercises that occur in conceptual design. What has emerged is not new analysis techniques but rather a way to use existing analysis methods to:

Identify the controlling and largest energy end uses (in both Btu and dollars).

Estimate approximate time of peak-load occurrence and the relative time phasing of loads, energy sources, and occupancy.

Develop simple graphic presentations that communicate to the designer during the conceptual design phase.

Educate the intuition of the designer over the course of several projects.

Energy analysis at the predesign level uses existing analysis techniques; however, the intent is to study relative relationships and sensitivities of intertwined energy needs in a given building type and climate rather than to compute actual energy consumption, define HVAC zones, or select equipment. Thus, this approach is fundamentally simpler than the reactive analysis described earlier.

This chapter is written for the design team members who perform the energy analysis tasks. It is assumed that the reader is familiar with energy analysis methods, ASHRAE or other calculation algorithms for determining loads, and has had experience with one or more of the many energy analysis programs such as TRACE, BLAST, E-CUBED, ACCESS, or DOE 2.1A.

The purpose of the chapter is fourfold. One objective is to show how analysis can be conducted before a building design exists and that this generic analysis can be used to augment the energy intuition of the designer during the earliest stages of a project. Second, the chapter describes the outputs from the predesign energy analysis that are known to be most useful to design team communication. Third, and central to the chapter, are the special problems of data collection and assumption making that exist because the analysis is conducted prior to the final building design. Fourth, the chapter presents summaries of five different building energy analysis tools (BLAST, DOE 2.1A, ECD, Energy Graphics, and NOMOG) for an office building example. These examples reinforce the point that the energy analysis products described in this chapter can be generated by a wide variety of methods. In addition, these examples will help the energy analyst in the selection of an appropriate tool for a particular project and design team capabilities.

DESIRED RESULTS

As mentioned above, predesign analysis is not a new form of analysis but a way of thinking about its role during the early stages of a design project. To perform this predesign analysis, analysts need to accept two key concepts. First, the analyst needs to shift emphasis and not seek *the* answer to a given, well-defined problem. Instead, the analysis should be directed toward identifying important parameters and their relationships. Specific answers are less important during predesign analysis than are relative values. In many cases, precise input data are unavailable and assumptions must be made. In these instances, the important step is not finding the correct input data but rather determining how much influence input data uncertainty has on the results. In the parlance of analysis, predesign analysis can be categorized as sensitivity studies rather than as analysis of a specific problem.

The second major concept that analysts need to accept is that not all the data they can generate are relevant to the design team. Many analysts fail to understand the broad issues the designer confronts in the early phases of a project. There are, of course, many useful analysis results that can be used during conceptual design, particularly if one of the prime objectives of predesign analysis is to educate the energy intuition of the designer. Frequently, however, too much data and analysis for a proposed building confuse the designer, resulting in a reversion to faulty intuition. In other cases, the apparent precision of the energy analysis relative to other subjective considerations will skew the design, resulting in a building that is energy efficient but ugly, nonfunctional, too costly to build, and inappropriate to the client's needs. Analysts should learn to condense and summarize results into a brief and easily comprehensible form that is compatible with other conceptual design information.

Most design teams report that after a few projects the team's collective intuition improves significantly and various items can be omitted. Some design teams have even reported that at a certain point the designers' energy intuition is developed to the point that energy can simply be treated along with other variables such as form, function, and cost. Until this point is reached, however, the following described items are a starting point for discussions between the energy analyst and the architectural designer.

Total Energy Use and Costs

Perhaps the single most important information one can get from studying a base building is the relative magnitude of energy need and cost for individual end use. These totals can be presented in tabular form as in Table 9.1 or in graphic form as shown in Figure 9.1. Table 9.1 is frequently useful in clarifying the differences between energy consumption and utility costs, and between consumption and demand. It is also useful to chart the total costs data as in Figure 9.1. The purpose of Table 9.1 and Figure 9.1 is not to dictate which energy problems the design team should address but to highlight the major energy end uses. Also, this type of information can help eliminate common mistakes such as adding passive solar features to a building that has such high internal loads that it needs year-round cooling.

Even in situations where the demand charges are currently low, analyzing the impact of peak-demand cost is recommended because these charges appear to be rising at a much faster rate than base energy cost. In many cases, energy conservation features that reduce both consumption and peak-demand costs can pay for themselves through reductions in mechanical equipment and duct sizes. By taking advantage of these size reductions, the design team can frequently save substantial first costs for the building. However, these kinds of features cannot be given proper attention unless both consumption and demand costs are considered.

Hourly Profiles for Typical or Peak Days

One common deficiency in the energy intuition of designers is a failure to recognize the importance of time phasing. Since many commercial buildings are occupied only during the day, design solutions that were originally developed for night occupancy residential structures (e.g., Trombe walls) are less appropriate in commercial buildings. Some type of

TABLE 9.1. BASE BUILDING ANNUAL ENERGY-USE ESTIMATES

HD-Use	Consumption								Demand			Total (Cons. + Dem.) ($/ft² yr)
	Elec. (kBtu/ft² yr)	Elec. ($/ft² yr)	Gas (kBtu/ft² yr)	Gas ($/ft² yr)	Total (kBtu/ft² yr)	Total ($/ft² yr)			Elec. (W/ft² yr)	Elec. ($/ft² yr)		
Equipment	0.649	0.0057	–	–	0.649	0.0057			1.195	0.0087		0.0144
Hot water	–	–	1.675	0.0058	1.675	0.0058			–	–		0.0058
Cooling	4.858	0.0427	–	–	4.858	0.0427			14.615	0.1064		0.1491
Lighting	18.967	0.1667	–	–	18.967	0.1667			28.571	0.2080		0.3747
Heating	0.613	0.0054	17.260	0.0595	17.873	0.0649			0.082	0.0006		0.0655
Total	25.087	0.2205	18.935	0.0653	44.022	0.2858			44.463	0.3237		0.6095

Notes: Cooling includes HVAC aux.
Lighting at 2.0 W/ft² connected load.
Equipment at 0.33 W/ft².

Rates: Gas—$3.45/MBtu = $.00345/kBtu.
Elec.—$0.03/kWh = $.00879/kBtu (cons.).
$7.28/kW = 0.728¢/W.

Light demand: (Assume one conference room in use at monthly peak)
[(800 × 1.0) + (9200 × 2.5)] ÷ 10,000 × 3.413 × 12 ÷ 1000 = 0.0975.

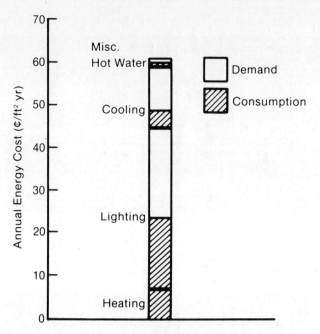

Figure 9.1.   Pittsburgh one-story base building, annual energy costs.

time-phasing information similar to Figure 9.2 can help focus the designer's attention on when energy loads occur relative to occupancy and energy source availability. These hour-by-hour charts can also be helpful to a designer in making orientation and fenestration decisions. For example, if the hourly profiles show that a building needs heat in the early morning hours of winter, it may be desirable for the design team to put more southeast-facing glass to make use of solar gain possibilities. Similarly, by examining typical fall and spring days, some preliminary indications and decisions can be made about the amount of shading needed and when the shading would be effective. Also, by examining outdoor air temperatures, an analyst can begin to develop some insight into the applicability of natural ventilation or economizer-cycle cooling. This has bearing on duct sizes and therefore on ceiling plenum spaces. Again, the purpose at this stage is not to define the mechanical system but to identify form-giving implications.

Hourly profile data are used in the opposite order of how they are developed. In Figure 9.2 the five variables (glazing solar, etc.) are summed to determine total gains/losses. Total gains/losses and deadband data are needed to determine heat extraction or addition. When using these data as a design aid, the heat extraction/addition chart is considered first, then the deadband data, then total gains/losses. In the examples of Chapter Seven, only the heat extraction and deadband data were needed to establish the major energy needs in the building and make a decision.

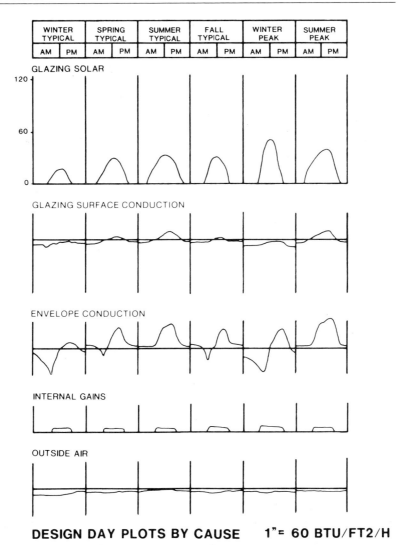

BTU/FT²H

TOTAL HEAT GAINS ( ) /LOSSES (−)

DESIGN DAY PLOTS BY CAUSE 1"= 60 BTU/FT2/H

Figure 9.2. Rainbow plots for a building perimeter zone.

100% Elimination Parametrics

One of the most important reasons for predesign analysis is sensitivity studies to identify the significant energy parameters and how they interact in commercial buildings. The concept illustrated in Figure 9.3 is simple. Total energy costs, including consumption and demand, are computed for the base case and then a single parameter at a time is eliminated. For example, to determine how sensitive total energy costs are to lighting

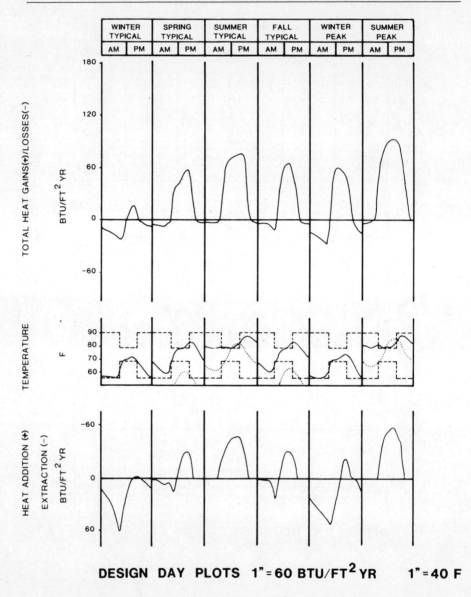

DESIGN DAY PLOTS 1"=60 BTU/FT²YR   1"=40 F

Figure 9.2. (*Continued*)

energy, a building energy analysis can be made with zero lighting energy. If total building energy costs change significantly, then lighting is an important parameter and deserves careful consideration during design.

The assumptions about which parameters to consider and how to eliminate them for the elimination parametric charts such as Figure 9.3 are shown in Table 9.2.

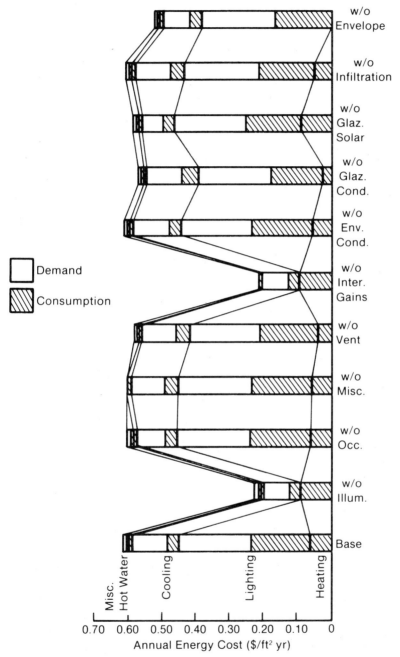

Figure 9.3. Elimination parametrics.

TABLE 9.2.   TYPICAL ELIMINATION PARAMETRIC VARIABLES

Parameter	Variable Changed
A. Illumination	Lighting load set at 0 W/ft^2
B. Occupants	Occupancy set at zero
C. Equipment	Equipment load set at 0 W/ft^2
D. Ventilation	Ventilation air needs set to 0 ft^3/min
E. Internal	A run with A, B, C, and D above
F. Glazing solar	Solar heat gain set at 0 Btuh/ft^2
G. Glazing conduction	Conduction loss/gain set at zero
H. Envelope conductance	Opaque surfaces R value set to 300
I. Infiltration	Infiltration set at 0 cfm
J. Envelope	A run with F, G, H, and I above

Some design teams prefer 10% or some other arbitrary percentages rather than 100% parametrics. Regardless of what sensitivity level is selected, the important point is that these parametrics do include coupling. Reducing energy input to the lights, for example, increases heating energy, decreases cooling energy, and impacts the peak demand.

Summary Matrix

As an alternative to the 100% elimination parametrics, some design teams have found that the energy summary matrix shown in Figure 9.4 is useful in visualizing where to concentrate attention and effort. Is the problem heating, cooling, or lighting? Or, given that the problem is cooling, what is the most significant contributing factor—windows, walls, roof, or infiltration? More discussion of these summary charts is given in the example applications of energy analysis techniques in this chapter.

There are some differences between the elimination parametrics and the summary matrix. The elimination parametrics require considerably more computer runs but are rather easy to interpret once the information is available. The summary matrix requires the analyst to interpret the total cost and consumption data to arrive at the same information. This interpretation requires the analyst to have considerable experience and intuition in order to establish the impact of the variables included in the summary matrix. The analyst may need to make elimination parametric runs to be able to learn how to use the summary matrix. In addition, even if the analyst can construct a summary matrix, the elimination parametric chart may be a better means to communicate the information to the design team. One of the major responsibilities of the design team analyst is to judge which presentation method is most appropriate for the team within the constraints of time, cost, and the need for effective communications.

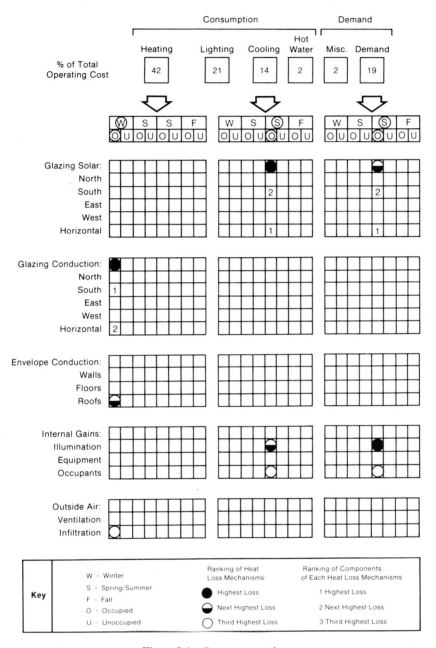

Figure 9.4. Summary matrix.

DATA COLLECTION

It is the assumptions made in the input that are significant.

William Fleming

In any analysis, the input assumptions are as important as the specific algorithms or calculation methodology. The "garbage in, garbage out" rule applies. A significant problem for any level of building energy analysis is the input assumptions related to occupancy schedules, diversity in lighting and internal equipment use, and microclimate. These same types of data collection problems exist for predesign analysis.

However, the purpose of predesign analysis is not to calculate the exact annual energy consumption. If specific input data are not available or are difficult to estimate, it may be more appropriate to treat these input data as parameters and determine how sensitive the final results are to uncertainties in these data. For example, in many large commercial buildings, internal loads are so great that major differences in climate have little effect on the annual energy consumption. In such cases there is no need to gather weather data meticulously or modify them for minor microclimate variations. By treating unavailable input data as parameters for predesign, the analyst can frequently reduce the effort spent collecting input data for later design phases.

The five major categories of input data that need to be obtained for predesign and other levels of energy analysis on a building are base building assumptions, and data on occupancy and use, climate, utility, and building construction cost. This section describes the special considerations of data collection as it relates to predesign analysis. It is assumed that the reader is familiar with energy analysis techniques and knows how to gather data for the analysis done in design development and later phases of the project. To reduce analysis time, the format of predesign analysis data should be compatible with these later efforts.

Base Building Assumptions

The most obvious problem with predesign analysis is that it precedes the actual design of the building. There are two approaches for generating input data and overcoming this problem: the "base building" and the "building block."

First, the design team working together can select the appropriate base-case building. There is no best base-case building. The appropriate base-case building is the one with which the design team is most comfortable. The idea is to select a building that is in some way characteristic of the building that the team wishes to design. Differences of opinion exist about whether this building should be the last building that the design team has developed, a comparable building (e.g., the last school that was designed for the school district prior to the current project), or a hypothetical typical building that has, for example, average glass areas, average aspect ratio, or average internal loads.

It should be recognized, however, that if a very energy-inefficient building is used, it may lead to erroneous problem identification. Also, subtle precedent is set in the selection of the base-case building. As discussed in earlier chapters, there are different types of energy-efficient buildings. The first case is the mechanically efficient, climate-rejecting building which would be analogous to a high-efficiency power boat. The other choice is the energy-efficient, climate-adapted building, analogous to a sailboat. In selecting the base-case building, the team will frequently prejudice the outcome toward one or the other case. Thus, it is important that the base-case building reflect this choice. If the intention is to design a climate-adapted building, then the base-case building should have climate-adapted features such as a larger surface-to-floor-area ratio or provisions for daylighting (i.e., windows). For the first few projects, it might even be desirable for the analyst to select more than one base-case building. This would be more for design team education than specific applicability to a given project.

Table 9.3 illustrates the kind of information needed to characterize a base building. These data represent the skylighted alternative design mentioned

TABLE 9.3. BASE BUILDING ASSUMPTIONS

$63 \times 158 \times 11$ ft.
1.5 ft ceiling cavity, 9.5 ft ceiling height
Glass area 50% of the 9.5 ft height
Skylight area 5% of the total roof area
Miscellaneous loads of 0.1 W/ft^2 in general space only
15 ft office perimeter
20×20 ft. conference room at building corners

Building area—10,000 ft^2, 1 story

General office—8,400 ft^2, open plan
   200 ft^2/person, occupied 9 h/day, 5 days/week
   Hung ceiling and carpeting
   68°F heating/78°F cooling, occupied; 55°F heating/90°F cooling, unoccupied

Conference area—4 rooms @ 400 ft^2 each; Total–1,600 ft^2.
   30 ft^2/person, occupied 5 h/day, 1 day/week
   Hung ceiling and carpeting
   Minimum of 1 wall exterior
   68°F heating/78°F cooling, office occupied hours; 55°F heating/90°F cooling, unoccupied office hours
   High-quality lighting system (2.5 W/ft^2)

Building characteristics—
   Concrete slab-on-grade and light steel
   Framing to minimize first cost

in Chapter Six, which is the building used to demonstrate the five energy analysis tools in this chapter.

Some designers feel that selecting a base-case building prejudices their form-making decisions. Thus, sometimes it is not desirable to select a base-case building. A second approach to developing building data is the building block approach suggested by coauthor Larry Bickle. Building blocks are as shown in their simplest form in Figure 9.5. They comprise five generic regions of the building (not equivalent to HVAC zones): north, east, south, and west perimeters plus the core. By analyzing each of these generic blocks, the designer can develop insight into form issues. If, for example,

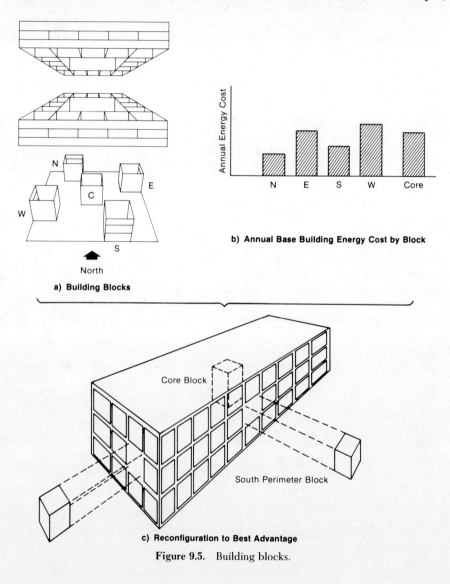

b) **Annual Base Building Energy Cost by Block**

a) **Building Blocks**

c) **Reconfiguration to Best Advantage**

Figure 9.5.   Building blocks.

north and south blocks use less energy than east, west, or core blocks (as shown in *b* in Fig. 9.5), then the form implication is that the building should be narrow and long with the long axis oriented east-west. Consideration could also be given to alternatives such as buffer zones on the east and west.

The analysis results described earlier must be generated five or more times. This aggravates the excess data problem and requires the analyst to work harder at summarizing results. For some analysis techniques, predominantly those that are computer-based, the additional calculations for the building blocks are relatively easy.

For the manual methods such as ASHRAE-TC4.7 and Energy Graphics, the burden of making five sets of calculations instead of one may become too time-consuming and a whole-building analysis may be a more appropriate use of time. In some cases, different occupancy categories, noncardinal building orientation, or other factors may prompt the use of more than five building blocks. Knowing where to start and stop analysis, to be most effective with finite resources, is a key responsibility of the design team analyst. However, the analyst should seriously consider whether or not the additional information is needed or desired early in the design process. Too much information may be as harmful as too little.

Whether the team decides to use a base-case building or a building block approach is not crucial. The important decision is selecting either climate-adapted or high-efficiency features for the base-case building or the building blocks.

Once again, it must be emphasized that useful analysis demands design team approval with the assumptions made by the analyst. Whether a base-case building is climate-adapted or climate-rejecting, it must reflect the building program, meet the state energy code, and represent an approach agreed upon by the design team.

Building Operation and Occupancy Schedule

The time at which a building is occupied and the manner in which its systems are operated are crucial variables in calculating energy consumption. Obtaining these types of data for predesign analysis is no different than obtaining them for other energy analysis. It is always vague, even after the building is in operation!

Wherever large uncertainties are encountered, it may be necessary to treat multiple occupancy schedules and diversity factors as parameters. The purpose of these parametric calculations is not to inundate the designer with data; rather, they are for the analyst to determine if occupancy schedule and diversity factors are significant variables. The occupancy schedule and building operation schedule selected for a test of five different energy tools are included in the base building data illustrated in Table 9.3. In the absence of other data, a reasonable starting point for estimating occupancy and operation patterns is available in Chapter Five of *Energy Conservation*

Design Manual of New Non-Residential Buildings, published by the State of California Energy Commission, Energy Conservation Division (available through the CEC Publications Unit, 1111 Howe Ave., Sacramento, CA 95825). When using data from this or other references, the analyst should determine if these data are for peak or average conditions. Diversity factors that have been developed for sizing equipment (e.g., ASHRAE) need to be carefully scrutinized because they usually reflect maximum/minimum conditions that are of short time duration during an entire year.

Climate Data

Predesign analysis presents no new difficulties or problems associated with obtaining climate data. There are the usual problems associated with finding data relevant to a specific site. Subjective judgement and extrapolation of weather data from nearby sites will probably be required.

Important for any level of energy analysis is average versus peak weather data. For energy consumption, average or typical values should be used. If peak demand or mechanical equipment sizes are the relevant issues, then reasonable peak values are likewise needed.

Since one of the recommended outputs from energy predesign analysis is the hour-by-hour charts, it is desirable to obtain some hourly data. Whether 8760 hourly values for an entire year are required or whether only 24 hourly values for three or four typical or peak days are required depends on the specific analysis methodology used.

Actual climate data and additional information on selecting climate data can be found in the following references:

1. NOAA National Climatic Center Federal Building
    Asheville, NC 28801
    (704) 258-2850

    Available Computer Tapes
    "Test Reference Year" (TRY)
    "Typical Meteorologist Year" (TMY)
    "SOLMET"
    "WBAN"
    "TDF-14" (50-year data base)
2. Engineering Weather Data Department of Air Force, Army, Navy.
    Available as AFM 88-29, TM 5-785 or NAVFAC P-Bg
3. *Insolation Data Manual*
    Solar Energy Research Institute
    1617 Cole Blvd.
    Golden, CO 80401
    Available from NTIS Stock # SERI/SP-755-789

4. *Local Climatological Data Annual Summary*
   NOAA National Climate Center
   Asheville, NC 28801
   (704) 258-2850

Utility Rate Data

Many building owners and designers are woefully ignorant of the influence and impact they have on supporting utilities. Few realize that for every dollar invested in a building, the supporting electric utility alone must eventually invest $0.35–$0.50. While the electric utility investment is by far the highest, the gas, water, and sewer utilities also have to make additional capital investments.

In the case of the electric utility, the capital invested in additional power plant capacity is recovered in two ways. First, there is a charge for the actual energy that is consumed—generally measured in kilowatt-hours. In addition there is usually a "demand charge" associated with stand-by equipment to meet peak demand. This demand charge is easy to justify if one considers that a building only reaches peak electrical demand a few hours per year. The equipment to meet this peak demand sits idle most of the time. This equipment must be paid for even though it may not be generating electricity to sell. Clearly it is best for the utility if the building's average demand is a large fraction of its peak demand. This ratio of average demand to peak demand is referred to as the "load factor" and is an important parameter to utility companies. A high load factor is also good for society because it minimizes the capital and embodied energy invested in mostly idle equipment.

Obtaining current rate schedules from the supporting utilities is almost always possible. The problem, as for any level of energy analysis, is to predict future rates. The utility rate structure used in our example was based upon an operating utility located in the Pittsburgh area. The 1982 costs were: oil at $1.25/gal, gas at $3.45/MBtu, and electricity at 3¢/kWh and $7.28/kW.

Someone from the design team should begin working with the supporting utilities at the earliest possible stages of a project. Frequently, utility companies can make available expected demand and consumption data. They may also be extremely helpful in defining the base-case building or building blocks. As a minimum, the data can serve as a valuable check during the early phase of a project.

Frequently, utility companies are anxious to support design of energy-responsive buildings. While these buildings may use slightly less energy, they have higher load factors which allow the utility to sell more energy for each dollar of capital invested.

Understanding energy issues on a scale broader than that of an individual building may lead designers to consider features that actually use more energy at the building site but that save net energy for the community and reduce utility costs. An example is off-peak storage of chilled or heated water. In this case, the loss associated with getting the energy in and out of storage and the stand-by losses during storage can result in more energy use. However, the overall effect is to reduce peak demands on the supporting utility. Because of the increased efficiency in the use of capital investment for the utility and for the community as a whole, the owner may reduce his utility costs through reduced demand charges. It is not uncommon to find situations where a 5% increase in local energy consumption with a storage system can result in a 20%–30% reduction in utility bills because of reduced demand charges.

Building Construction Cost Data

The final category of data for the predesign analysis is the estimated building construction cost data. Most design teams have their own technique for establishing construction costs on a project. Means Construction Cost Index data that have been city-indexed with an allowance for inflation were used in all of the examples presented in Chapters Six and Seven. One important deficiency in many early energy-conscious building designs is a failure to recognize the construction cost implications of simple changes in the building. For example, a climate-adapted building may have more wall area per square foot of usable floor area than a climate-rejecting building. What fraction of a building's cost is the exterior enclosure? What is the trade-off between increased exterior enclosure and decreased mechanical equipment costs? A design team must have at least a cursory understanding of which elements of a building most influence costs.

Building costs are also crucial in the cost-effectiveness analysis discussed in Chapter Eight. Having energy-operating cost data without construction cost data precludes the capability of generating cost-effectiveness information.

EXAMPLES OF PREDESIGN ENERGY ANALYSIS

This section illustrates how existing conventional energy analysis methods can be used to provide predesign and schematic design energy analysis data. The BLAST, DOE 2.1, Energy Graphics, NOMOG, and ECD programs and methods are applied to the 10,000-ft² office building in Pittsburgh that was used as an example in the Data Collection section of this chapter. None of these energy analysis tools was developed specifically for the methodologies described in this book.

This section shows that the recommended analysis approach is just a special case of more general energy analysis. As demonstrated, tools ranging from simple manual procedures to the most sophisticated computer

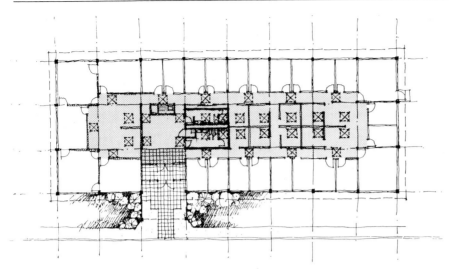

Figure 9.6. Pittsburgh one-story building with sky lights.

simulations, applied during the early stages of design, can meet the needs of building energy analysis. While the specific goals and viewpoints are different, the actual mechanics of execution are the same or simpler than the typical, after-the-fact, reactive energy analysis.

Five different organizations were asked to conduct a building energy analysis for the same example problem to demonstrate how different analysis tools could best be used. To keep the comparisons meaningful, each group was given the same base-case building and other data. The example building was the typical single-story office building in Pittsburgh as shown in Figure 9.6. The energy analysis tools, organizations, and individuals involved in this comparison are presented in Table 9.4.

These specific tools were chosen for presentation because they are in the public domain. In each case, the organization and specific individuals were deemed to be among the most knowledgeable in the use of the tool. Each

TABLE 9.4. ENERGY ANALYSIS TOOLS

Energy Analysis Tool	Organization	Authors
NOMOG	Burt Hill, Kosar, Rittelman Associates	A. Sain
Energy Graphics	Booz, Allen & Hamilton	K. Hart
		W. Whiddon
ECD	The Bickle Group	R. Busch
DOE 2.1A	Los Alamos Scientific Laboratory	B. Hunn
		J. Petersen
BLAST	Lawrence Berkeley Laboratory	R. Kammerud
		W. Carrol

participant was free to make reasonable accommodations and variations in the application of the tool to produce results similar to those shown earlier in this chapter. Each participant was also asked to document his work according to the following standard outline.

1. *Background.* A brief description of this particular analysis tool; its history, characteristics, applicability, and so on.

2. *Availability of Outputs.* A list of the recommended outputs which can technically be obtained from this particular analysis tool. Outputs should be classified as (*a*) standard reports, (*b*) derivable from standard reports, or (*c*) unavailable.

3. *Procedures.* A detailed description of the derivation procedure for outputs that are derived from standard reports. Note: It is assumed that procedures to obtain standard reports are described in publicly available user's manuals and will not be described further in this document.

4. *Input Requirements.* A complete list of input requirements in terms of the example building descriptions, and a list of any further information that is required or assumed.

5. *Additional Outputs.* A brief description of analysis tool outputs that are in addition to those recommended, and the author's opinion of the usefulness of these additional outputs in predesign.

In addition to the building data already discussed in this chapter, some of the tools required additional data to analyze the example building. Some of the major additional assumptions are listed in Table 9.5. Additional

**TABLE 9.5.   ADDITIONAL TOOL-SPECIFIC INPUTS
REQUIRED TO ANALYZE THE BUILDING**

Use of daylighting to reduce lighting quantity to 1.0 W/ft^2

Windows, U = 0.58, SC = 0.58, T = 0.36 (heat absorbing out, clear in)

Skylights, U = 0.65, SC = 0.82, T = 0.61 (clear out, clear in)

R-14 opaque walls, R-25 opaque roof, R-4 perimeter slab insulation

Central VAV system with perimeter baseboard

Absorption of surfaces—0.5 wall and 0.7 roof

0.25 ac/h infiltration in external zones

140,000 Btu/gal oil

450 Btuh/person total

Conference rooms have coincident occupancy

Floor adiabatic

Efficiencies 60% heating and DHW, COP-3.0 cooling

DHW @ 1 gal/person/day, 50°F in and 120°F out

assumptions made by each of the teams are documented in the results for each analysis tool.

Summaries of the five predesign energy analysis tools and the results for the example building are presented here.

NOMOG

NOMOG is a set of Energy Nomographs that have been developed to estimate the energy consumption of design options during schematic design. In contrast to analytical models that calculate the energy consumption at the end of a design process, the Energy Nomographs assist the designer in making decisions about energy during the design process.

The Energy Nomographs are simply a graphical calculation procedure using equations and methods found in the ASHRAE and IES Handbooks. Documentation available to the user includes a user's manual, analyst data manual, and reusable nomographs. The suggested procedure for calculating energy consumption using the nomographs is given by the following steps:

Determine the watts per square foot of lighting required, and calculate the total electrical consumption necessary for lighting.

Determine the domestic hot water (DHW) demand and the total annual load required for DHW consumption.

Determine the building balance point temperature (BBPT) for use in calculating heating and cooling loads. (The building balance point temperature is the outside air temperature at which the skin heat loss is equal to the internal heat gain.) See Figure 9.7 for the BBPT nomograph.

Determine the total air supplied by the fans. [The total cubic feet per minute (cfm) supplied by the fan will be used in calculating the fan electrical consumption and the amount of free cooling that can be obtained from the economizer cycle.]

Determine the electrical consumption of the fans.

Select the appropriate weather data from the input data manual. [The weather data are given in degree days (heating and cooling) and Btu days (solar) for various BBPTs and various locations in the United States.]

Determine the annual heating and cooling loads for the various components of the building (roof, walls, people, lights, etc.).

Determine the annual fuel consumption and cost for the six basic components of energy consumption of buildings: heating, cooling, lighting, miscellaneous, DHW, and fans.

Construct daily load profiles for a typical and/or design day in each season.

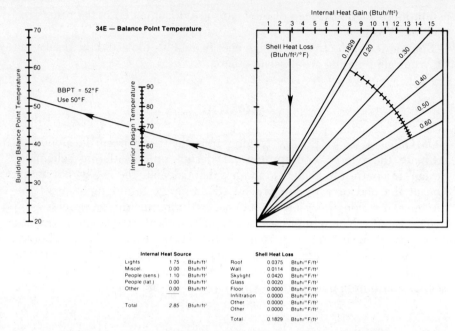

Figure 9.7. Sample of building balance point temperature nomograph.

The output of the NOMOG procedure consists of a complete set of nomographs containing the input data, the actual calculation (in graphic form), and the final answers. Four items, generated by the nomographs, are extremely useful in determining energy problems and their causes:

Summary of heating loads.
Summary of cooling loads.
Building totals.
Daily load profiles.

The summary of heating loads sheet displays the heating load by building component and season. It shows what components are the major contributing factors, in what seasons the load occurs, and what effects the internal and solar gains have on the heating load.

The summary of cooling loads sheet is similar to the heating summary. It also looks at all components contributing to the load by season. It differs from the heating load in that it takes into account the free cooling due to ventilation.

The building totals sheet is a summary of the four major components of energy consumption: heating, cooling, lighting, and domestic hot water (see Table 9.6). It shows the load, fuel consumption, and cost for each of these components in each zone. This complete summary is extremely useful in pointing out the major energy costs and the zone in which they occur.

Finally, the daily load profiles can be constructed for various typical and design days to show the time relationship of the various component loads. These profile can help the designer address the sharp peaks and the use of nonfossil fuel sources to reduce loads.

Figure 9.8 presents a composite output result for the Pittsburgh example building in the standardized format used in this book. The annual building load, annual energy consumption, and annual energy cost for consumption are depicted for each major component of energy consumption.

Energy Graphics

Energy Graphics is a graphic technique developed to help architects and engineers visualize energy requirements and thereby design more energy-efficient buildings. It also provides a simple means for prospective owners and users of a building to discuss energy use intelligently with architects and engineers.

Energy-efficient design includes two interrelated aspects: design of a building's physical characteristics to minimize heating, cooling, and lighting loads; and design of mechanical and electrical subsystems to handle energy loads efficiently. Energy Graphics focuses primarily on the first aspect: manipulation of design variables to limit heat gains and losses.

The Energy Graphics technique is visual, designed to illustrate how a building uses energy. It is intended to highlight energy issues that are often unnecessarily lost in complicated calculations. The technique can be done manually or by computer.

The first step in performing an Energy Graphics analysis is to collect information about the building program and the site climate. Since the analysis is done at the predesign stage, only very general conclusions about building energy performance may be available. Therefore, neither building program information nor site information need to be at a particularly fine level of detail.

The Pittsburgh example building has two distinct functional spaces—a general office area and conference rooms. For the sake of this analysis each is defined as an energy-use group.

Energy Graphics analysis routinely produces five plots for each energy-use group:

Internal heat gain.

Solar heat gain.

Envelope gain and loss.

Ventilation gain and loss.

Combined plot of energy performance for each energy-use group.

TABLE 9.6. SAMPLE OF THE BUILDING TOTALS SHEET

Areas	Gen'l. Office Zone 1		Conf. Rms. Zone 2		Zone 3		Zone 4		Zone 5		Building Total	
	8400	84%	1600	16%								
	MBtu/ft²	%	MBtu/ft²	%	MBtu/ft²	%	MBtu/ft²	%	MBtu/ft²	%	MBtu/ft²	%

Loads on the System

	MBtu/ft²	%	MBtu/ft²	%							MBtu/ft²	%
Heating	11.64	37	21.7	65							13.25	42
Cooling	9.66	31	9.5	28							9.63	31
Lighting	9.08	29	2.2	7							7.98	25
DHW	0.80	3	0.0	0							0.67	2
Total	31.18	100	33.4	100		100		100		100	31.53	100

Consumption of Fuel

	MBtu/ft²	%	MBtu/ft²	%							MBtu/ft²	%
Heating	19.40	56	36.2	86							22.09	62
Cooling	4.87 (1.65)	14	(3.15 + 0.49)	9							4.67	13
Lighting	9.08	26	2.2	5							7.98	22
DHW	1.30	4	0.0	0							1.09	3
Total	34.65	100	42.04	100		100		100		100	35.83	100

Cost

	$/ft²	%	$/ft²	%	$/ft²	%	$/ft²	%	$/ft²	%
Heating	0.470	49	0.318	82					0.194	55
Cooling	0.057	16	0.042	11					0.055	15
Lighting	0.110	32	0.025	7					0.096	27
DHW	0.012	3	0.000	0					0.010	3
Total	0.649	100	0.385	100		100		100	0.355	100

Consumption of Fuel

	MBtu/ft²	%	MBtu/ft²	%	MBtu/ft²	%	MBtu/ft²	%	MBtu/ft²	%
Heating	23.0	34	43.0	71					26.2	39
Cooling	15.0	23	11.0	18					14.4	22
Lighting	28.0	41	6.6	11					24.6	37
DHW	1.6	2	0.0	0					1.34	2
Total	67.6	100	60.6	100		100		100	66.54	100

BEPS = 112

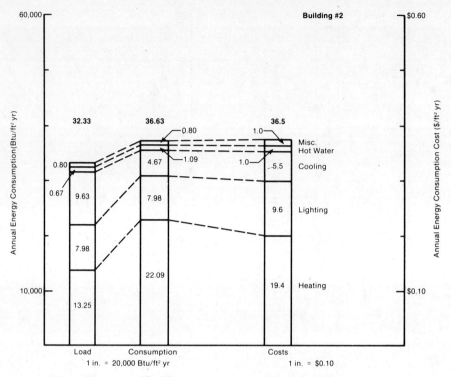

Figure 9.8. Annual building energy consumption and consumption costs.

When a building has more than one distinct energy-use group, a final plot of overall building performance—combining all energy-use groups—is also provided. The following is a brief discussion of each plot and any assumptions in addition to those listed necessary to produce it.

Heat gains from internal sources (people, lights, equipment) have already been specified as part of the definition for each energy-use group. The estimated internal heat gain in the general office energy-use group is measured in millions of Btu (MBtu) and plotted.

The amount of insolation available at the site has already been defined as part of the original information-gathering process. To estimate the solar heat gain within an energy-use group two important assumptions must be made:

Approximate area exposed to available insolation.

The proportion of incident solar heat transmitted from outside into each energy-use group.

In the sample SERI problem, the building configuration is specified so it is easy to compute the exposed area in each orientation. Had the dimensions not been specified for this analysis, we would have assumed a simple base-case configuration, such as a rectangular solid, and continued the analysis by modifying the assumed configuration to improve energy performance.

Solar heat transfer from the exterior to the interior of each energy-use group is a function of the construction of the building envelope. Using techniques described in the user's manual and transmission values given in the sample problem, an estimated percent transmission figure is computed for each wall and roof surface based on the weighted average of building materials assumed.

With this information, estimated solar gain is computed by simple multiplication. For example, on the roof (horizontal orientation) at noon in winter:

Available Solar Heat (72 Btuh/ft^2 from user's manual)
(times) Area (8400 ft^2 from building program)
(times) Transmission (4% from user's manual)
(equals) 24 MBtuh (rounded).

The estimated solar heat gain from the roof is added to all four walls to produce the total solar heat gain (52 MBtuh).

Envelope heat gain and loss are the result of conduction of heat through the exterior envelope of an energy-use group due to a difference in temperature inside and outside the space. The computation depends on three variables:

Temperature difference.
Exposed area.
Thermal conduction (transmission rate).

The method of computing temperature difference is described in the user's manual. This method basically calculates the difference between outside temperature and the allowable inside temperature as specified by the building program. Exposed area is simply the wall (or roof) area as computed for solar gains. Thermal conduction is based on a weighted average of building materials in each wall (or roof) but is computed slightly differently than solar transmission. Note that this thermal component is the first one described that offers the potential for heat loss from the space because of the fluctuation of exterior temperatures above and below the allowable interior temperature.

Another important characteristic of heat gain and loss to be considered in doing these calculations is that not all heat gain is necessarily bad. It is possible, in fact, to have some heat gain within allowable limits. While computing envelope gain and loss, it is necessary to keep track of the potential for a heat gain that is not excessive. The precise calculations for allowable heat gain are explained in the user's manual. Allowable heat gain is plotted on the same graph as envelope gain and loss.

Ventilation heat gain or loss is caused by the introduction of outside air at a different temperature from that being maintained in a space. Ventilation, as used here, means either uncontrolled introduction of air (infiltration) or controlled introduction (ventilation) usually by mechanical means. Calculations are based on two variables:

Ventilation rate.
Temperature difference.

Temperature differences, computed as part of envelope gain and loss, are used again here. Ventilation rates are part of input data. These two variables are combined (by multiplication) to compute overall gains and losses.

When the temperature within the space under study exceeds the outside temperature, some heat gain can be dumped outside using ventilation. The amount of heat gain that can be offset by the dumping is a function of the maximum ventilation rate and is called the allowable heat gain related to ventilation.

When all four thermal components have been computed and plotted, they are combined (by addition) into a plot of overall performance for each energy-use group. The composite plot for the general office area is shown in Figure 9.9. A quick look at this plot shows modest heat losses (requiring heating) in winter and more significant heat gains (requiring cooling) in spring, summer, and fall.

Figure 9.9 is based upon the assumption of only minimum ventilation rates. The sample problem for the Pittsburgh Building calls for use of an

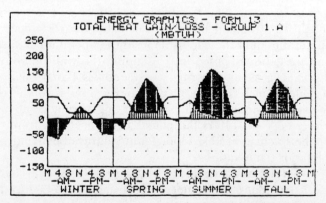

Figure 9.9. Composite of overall energy performance for general office area including internal gain, solar gain, envelope gain and loss, and ventilation gain and loss.

economizer cycle in the mechanical system. The Energy Graphics plot shows that a possibility for this cycle exists. However, because Energy Graphics is basically a load calculation, it is not possible to simulate the effects of an economizer cycle precisely. Instead, ventilation rates were modified according to the user's judgment. In this problem, ventilation rates were increased during occupancy in the spring and fall and during mornings only in the summer because of assumed high temperature and humidity on summer afternoons.

Figure 9.10 is a redrawn plot of ventilation gains and losses. It shows that increased ventilation augments heat losses in the spring and fall and increases allowable heat gain in all three seasons. The new ventilation plot is then combined with the previous three plots to obtain a new composite plot for the general office area. The revised ventilation schedule (economizer) removes excess gains in the spring and fall and reduces excess gains in the summer.

Although not shown in this summary, a similar series of steps was taken to develop a composite plot of energy performance for the conference rooms. The results show that modest excess heat gains occur in the conference rooms during spring, summer, and fall but only during periods of occupancy—one day a week.

Finally, the composite graph of the general office area is combined, by addition, with the composite graph of the conference rooms to produce a graph of overall building thermal performance (Fig. 9.11). This final graph is a summary of many base-case assumptions. According to the results, the proposed building is relatively energy-efficient. Winter heat losses are modest (less than 100,000 Btuh). Summer heat gains are somewhat more serious.

The sample problem was designed to end with an analysis of the base-case building. For a complete Energy Graphics analysis used in designing a

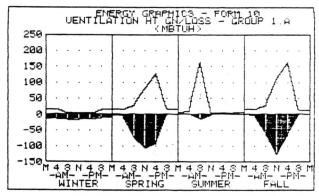

Figure 9.10. Revised ventilation gain and loss plot based on adjusted ventilation rates used to represent the effects of an economizer cycle.

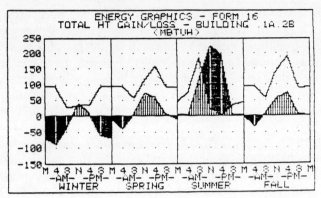

Figure 9.11. Composite energy performance of the entire proposed building including both the general office area and conference rooms.

proposed building, the designer would return to the original set of assumptions, alter them in ways that would improve energy performance, and then redo the calculations to see if these modified assumptions produced better results. This process is repeated until the designer is satisfied that a reasonable trade-off has been found among program, architectural, and energy considerations.

The final step in an Energy Graphics analysis is to prepare a simple estimate of energy costs based on heating and cooling loads. Typical daily loads are converted to annual dollar costs in five simple steps:

1. Average daily heating and cooling loads in each season are calculated from the area of heat loss and the area of excess heat gains shown on the graph of composite building performance.
2. Average daily loads are converted into seasonal loads by multiplication.
3. Seasonal loads are totaled to get annual loads.
4. Annual loads are adjusted by an average coefficient of performance (COP)—0.7 for heating equipment and 2.0 for cooling equipment—to arrive at energy consumption.
5. Consumption is multiplied by averaged utility costs to ge estimated annual heating and cooling costs.

Figure 9.12 presents the results for annual building load, annual energy consumption, and annual energy cost.

ECD

ECD is a mainframe loads program that calculates the hour-by-hour energy use in a building based upon the heating, cooling, lighting, and occupant loads. Calculations are performed for four seasons and are based upon an

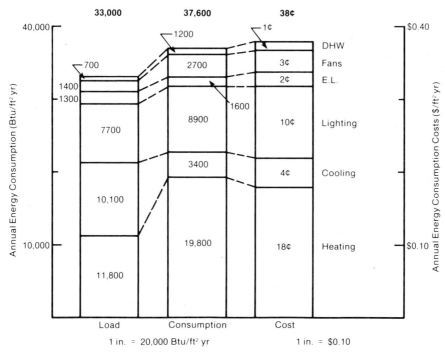

Figure 9.12. Annual building load, annual energy consumption, and annual energy cost (for consumption only) per square foot of building.

average day in each season. Each run assumes a single zone composed of a massless air node coupled to a lumped mass node containing all of the interior building mass. Individual zones or entire buildings are treated similarly with simultaneous heating and cooling loads not allowed; only the net load is calculated. ECD is an architectural design tool and does not calculate any internal or external latent loads.

ECD uses the graphical format and basic assumptions of Energy Graphics but extends the technique to include the concept of interior thermal mass and deadband thermostat. Thus, the design team is able to use timelag to shift energy loads. The ECD program is written in simplified FORTRAN and is interactive so the designer can sit down and ask "what if" questions to get a feel for the important parameters and how they interrelate.

The progam consists of three parts that are independent subprograms. First is MAKEFILE, an interactive routine that requests pertinent building and site data. Second is ECD, an energy analysis routine that calculates annual energy use based on typical days for the four seasons. Third is PLOT, a plotting routine that allows the user to graphically display any combination of 27 variables (e.g., auxiliary loads, shell transmission loads, inside air and mass temperatures, and internal loads) with up to three variables on each plot.

Typical use of the package would involve the following steps:

1. Use MAKEFILE to create a building data file.
2. Use ECD to do annual energy analysis.
3. Use PLOT to graphically show auxiliary load requirements and timing and identify major causes for loads.
4. Propose design concepts that reduce auxiliary loads.
5. Use ECD to change parameter(s) and redo annual energy analysis.
6. Repeat steps 3 through 5 as required.

ECD loads analysis is based upon steady-state U-values and sol-air temperatures for the shell load. The glass load is calculated considering the effects of overhang shading and solar altitude and azimuth angles. In addition, the Fresnel equations are used to determine the variation of glazing reflectance with incidence angle. Solar transmittance can also be modified through a shading coefficient for draperies or other interior shades.

The ECD subprogram creates a table of seasonal and yearly loads based upon the data file and weather selected. Outputs from ECD consist of the following:

Season with (a) winter, (b) spring, (c) summer, and (d) fall.
Total sensible heating load for the season or year.
Total sensible cooling load for the season or year.
Sensible lighting load.
Sensible appliance load.
Sensible occupant load.
Sensible ventilation and infiltration load.
Solar gains through all the glazed surfaces.
Total conductance load through building skin including glazing.
Total instantaneous sensible load.

Hourly results for a typical day in each season are stored in a plot file for later retrieval. Variables can be plotted on a graph to indicate hourly occurrences of loads and interactions among variables. Combinations of variables that provide insight into building energy use are as follows.

Indoor air temperature, indoor mass temperature, and outdoor dry bulb temperature. These indicate the stabilizing and delay effects of internal mass and also indicate the potential for using increased amounts of outdoor air for cooling or night flushing.

Total gain/loss to air, allowable heat gain, and allowable heat loss. These indicate the effects of deadband and mass on the heating and cooling loads.

Auxiliary load and glass solar gain. These show the loads that need to be met by HVAC equipment and the effect of solar gains on the timing and magnitude of the auxiliary loads.

Plotting the allowable gain and allowable loss for each hour creates an envelope in which no auxiliary energy is required. If a plot of the allowable envelope and the actual gain or loss for each hour is made, then the auxiliary energy requirements can be determined. The dashed line in Figures 9.13 and 9.14 represents the actual heat gain or loss to the indoor air for each hour. In Figure 9.13, there are times when the actual gain/loss is outside the allowable envelope. Because this occurs in the heat loss region of the plot, these deviations represent auxiliary heating requirements. The actual magnitude of the heating load is represented by the area outside the envelope. This dark area represents the total kBtuh load that must be met to maintain the internal environmental temperatures as prescribed in the building program. Similarly, in Figure 9.14, the deviations are in the heat gain region and represent cooling loads to be met by auxiliary equipment.

Once the auxiliary loads are identified, then the design team can minimize them by:

Reducing gains/losses (corresponds to a change in signal amplitude).

Shifting the timing of the loads (corresponds to a change in signal phase).

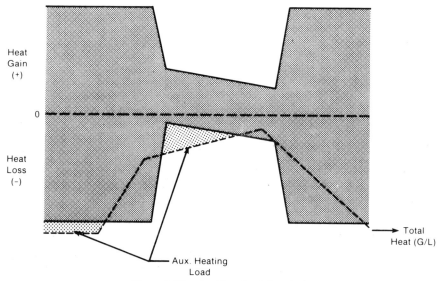

Figure 9.13. Auxiliary load (heating).

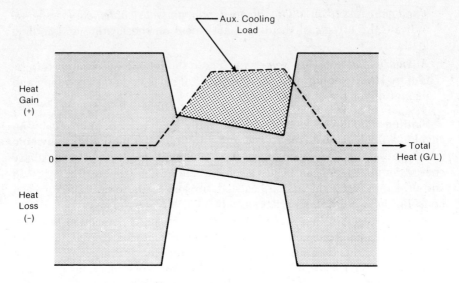

Figure 9.14. Auxiliary load (cooling).

Techniques used to reduce gains/losses may include additional insolation, a change in building form and external surface area, or the addition of shading devices for glazing. Shifting the load timing may involve a change in glazing orientation, use of internal mass for storage, or the addition of external mass for time delay. Since load reduction techniques act on the instantaneous heat gain/loss and have minimum interactions with other building components, it is relatively easy for the design team to determine the results of applying load-reducing techniques.

However, changes in load timing are not as easily understood. The addition of storage or delays does not just shift the peak by x hours. Load timing changes tend to widen the time range effects while reducing the magnitude of the load at any one hour. Thus, it is usually necessary to make some parametric runs to show the effects of load shifting. This will demonstrate mass effects and load shifting to the design team.

If the design team is to avoid the common mistakes in energy-responsive design, then they must have visual information that characterizes the energy use in the building. Because the architect has control over those features that directly influence the energy loads, he or she needs information that describes the magnitude, timing, and causes of those loads. Also needed is a graphic display of the relationship between loads, consumption, and cost.

ECD provides plots that characterize the magnitude, timing, and causes of the energy loads. Comparing plots of auxiliary load with causes such as ventilation, internal loads, and shell transmission allows the design team to determine possible concepts that would reduce the auxiliary loads. This helps the design team avoid the mistake of spending time and effort on

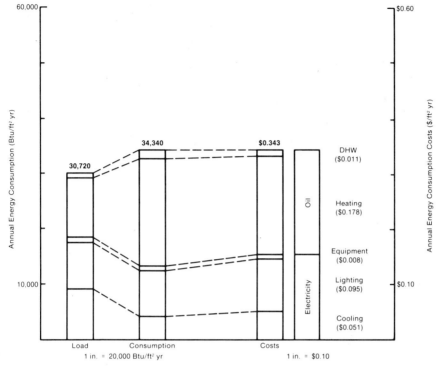

Figure 9.15.   Annual energy consumption costs.

parts of the energy problem that have minimal impact on end use and energy cost.

Figure 9.15 shows the relationship between load, consumption, and energy costs for the sample problem. Data for creating this graph are available from the ECD runs and plots.

DOE-2.1A

DOE-2.1A is a specialized version of DOE-2, a public-domain computer program for energy-use analysis of residential and commercial buildings. The program requires a minimum of 64K 60-bit words of storage on a CDC 6000 or 7000 series computer or a minimum of 500K bytes on an IBM 370 series computer. Modification packages are being developed by others to convert the code to other types of computers, including minicomputers. DOE-2 cannot be run on programmable calculators.

DOE-2 calculates the hour-by-hour energy end use of a building by determining the dynamic heating, cooling, and lighting loads and simulating the response of primary energy conversion and secondary heating, ventilating, and air-conditioning (HVAC) system equipment to these loads.

Response factors are used to calculate the energy flux through exterior walls, and weighting factors are used to determine the energy flux within individual building spaces. Annual consumption is the sum of the fuel used by the primary energy conversion equipment over the 8760 hours in a year.

DOE-2 can be used for both the design of energy-efficient new buildings and the analysis of existing buildings for energy-conserving modifications. It is intended for architects and engineers with a basic knowledge of the thermal performance of buildings. The program has four main sections: LOADS, SYSTEMS, PLANT, and ECONOMICS.

The LOADS program is based largely on the American Society of Heating, Refrigerating, and Air-Conditioning Engineers (ASHRAE) algorithms and uses the weighting-factor loads calculative method to account for the storage effects of the building elements. Hourly heating and cooling loads are calculated for each user-designated space, assuming a constant space temperature. An hourly weather tape provides the ambient conditions to which the building is subjected. LOADS does not take into account outside air brought into the building for ventilation purposes. The LOADS input for the annual energy end-use computer run includes information about the building location, dimensions of each thermal zone, type of construction (walls, floors, and roof), internal loads (people, lights, and equipment) with schedules, infiltration rates with schedules, and hot water use.

Some 23 HVAC systems are simulated in the SYSTEMS program. Features include modeling of control strategies, economizer cycles, exhaust air heat recovery, and operation of the supply and return fans. Ventilation air is simulated in the SYSTEMS program. The SYSTEMS input data include information about the system type, size, and the spaces served; ventilation air flow rates; control strategies; and fan characteristics.

The PLANT program simulates the operation of the primary energy supply and conversion equipment, including boilers, chillers, cooling towers, and electric generators. An active solar system simulator includes both preconnected and user-assembled solar heating and cooling systems. Energy storage and heat recovery equipment are also modeled in PLANT. Accurate simulation of the part-load performance of all plant equipment is a key feature of the PLANT program. The PLANT input data include information about the capacity, number, first cost, and maintenance of the primary equipment simulated.

The ECONOMICS program calculates the present value of the life-cycle cost of the building, including the cost of fuel, equipment, operation, and maintenance. It can be used to compare the cost of different building designs or to calculate savings-to-investment statistics for retrofits to an existing building. Input data for the ECONOMICS simulation were not developed because life-cycle cost comparisons were not a part of the Pittsburgh example building analysis.

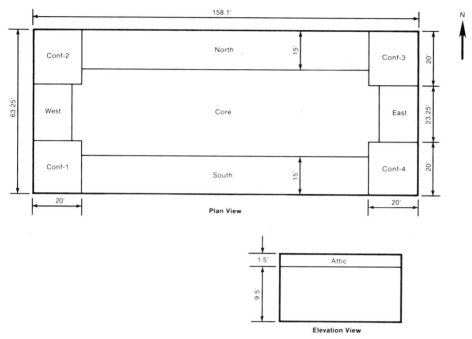

Figure 9.16. Zoning arrangement for SERI example building.

An important part of any building energy analysis is the way that a building is zoned. Figure 9.16 illustrates the zoning configuration selected for the Pittsburgh example building. Ten zones were modeled in all: five office zones, four conference zones, and an attic space. A simpler configuration could have been used, but it was assumed that the two main functional spaces, that is, the general office areas and the conference rooms, should be subdivided into smaller units reflecting the effect that the environment has on different orientations of a building envelope.

A total of five complete DOE-2 computer runs are required to develop the output supporting the predesign process:

An annual energy use run.
A system SUM run (see SYSTEMS chapter of DOE-2 Reference Manual).
An annual run without mechanical ventilation.
Two typical-day runs.

These runs are made for each zone of the building and are summed to obtain the total thermal loads. Table 9.7 summarizes the calculative procedure. The heating and cooling output is taken directly from the SYSTEMS summary report for each of the individual zone runs. A SUM run was made to determine the building thermal loads with the thermostatic air

TABLE 9.7.   ANNUAL THERMAL LOADS (Btu $\times$ 10⁶)

Thermal Load	Annual – Annual = Vent			SUM + Vent = Total		
		No Vent	Load		Load	Load
Heating	99.54 –	95.19	= 4.35	67.62 +	4.35	= 71.97
Cooling	125.98 –	124.93	= 1.05	136.40 +	1.05	=137.45
DHW	2720 Btuh $\times$ 2268 h		= 6.17	The number of operating hours is taken from the PLANT summary report.		

temperature strategy defined for each zone. However, a SUM run does not simulate mechanical ventilation loads, so another annual run without ventilation air was executed to determine the ventilation loads. Figure 9.17 summarizes the annual loads, consumption, and energy cost for the SERI building example in a single plot.

Two DOE-2 runs simulating typical-day input for the four seasons were completed to show the time phasing of the building loads. The time phasing for the Pittsburgh example building is shown in Figure 9.18. Most of the heating and cooling loads of the example building occur during the periods when the building is occupied. Thus, one need not perform a series of parametric runs to generate a specific typical day if the objective is to determine the time phasing of building loads.

An important observation in Figure 9.18 is the sharp trough shown for the winter heating load. This trough is the result of resetting the thermostat in

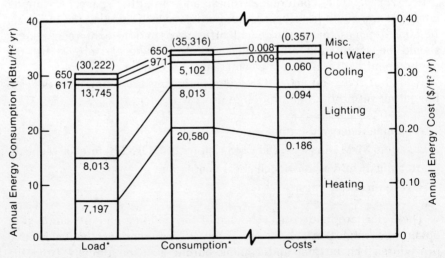

*Fans are included in cooling load, consumption and costs.

Figure 9.17.   Annual energy consumption costs.

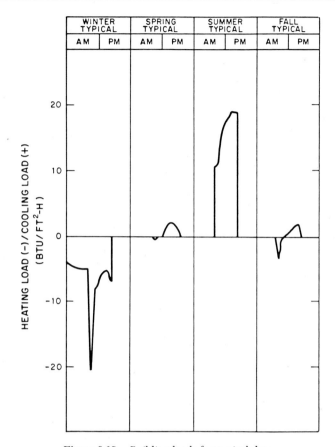

Figure 9.18. Building loads for typical days.

the individual zones of the Pittsburgh example building to 68°F from the 55°F night thermostat setting. Obviously, the mass of even a fairly light (spandrel glass) building plays a significant role in the magnitude and phasing of the building loads when a thermostat setback control strategy is used. Certainly, the mass of a building must be considered in any predesign analysis that wishes to account for the time phasing of building loads.

In conclusion, the DOE-2 computer program can be used as an extremely valuable tool in the energy analysis of a building. Only five complete computer runs are required to develop the information supporting the predesign process suggested in this book. Because each of these runs is built upon a common input data base, significant savings in the development of input data are realized. However, the time expended to use DOE-2 in the predesign analysis of a building (about 1 man-week) cannot be justified unless potential solutions to the design problem are also desired. Once a base building is defined for a predesign analysis performing multiple parametrics, using DOE-2 to identify potential design solutions is a simple matter. Herein lies the basic strength and cost-effectiveness of the DOE-2 computer program.

BLAST

The Building Loads Analysis and System Thermodynamics (BLAST) computer program was developed by the U.S. Army Construction Engineering Research Laboratory (CERL), in collaboration with Lawrence Berkeley Laboratory (LBL). The program requires a CDC 6000 or 7000 series computer, with a minimum of 170K (octal) single precision words of memory.

BLAST provides sequential hourly calculation of space loads (using the ASHRAE-based detailed heat balance method), HVAC system simulation, plant equipment simulation, building boundary utility cost, and life-cycle economics. The simulation period is variable and user-selected. The BLAST program consists of four major in-line subprograms; the major characteristics of each are as follows.

INPUT PROCESSOR. User communication with BLAST is through a structured English language syntax processor developed specifically to simplify input. The building is described in a hierarchical manner. First, the user specifies names for materials and defines them in terms of their thermophysical properties. Constructions are then defined as combinations of material names. Similarly, control strategies, interval load profiles, HVAC and plant equipment components, and other design parameters are given names and defined in terms of their operating characteristics. It is possible to make references to entries in an on-line library containing information about many common building materials, construction types, and control schedules, which can greatly facilitate user input. Next, the user defines the building geometry, surface construction types, and HVAC systems on a zone-by-zone basis, and includes internal loads and system control information by referencing previously defined schedules and other information. Appropriate interzone energy couplings are specified. The plant equipment that satisfies the HVAC system energy demands is specified in a similar manner. Finally, utility rates and other economic assumptions are specified.

BUILDING HEATING AND COOLING LOAD CALCULATIONS. Once the building is defined, BLAST first performs hourly computations of the space heating and cooling loads due to (a) the building environment, such as solar gains, heat transfer induced by temperature differences, and infiltration; and (b) internally generated thermal loads from occupants, electric and gas equipment or appliances, and lights. The loads are based on user-defined thermostat setpoints and equipment control schedules. In the computation of zone and building loads, BLAST 3.0 uses a thermal balance method developed by CERL. The method represents the state of the art for thermal load calculations. For each hour of the simulation, energy balance equations are set up for each internal surface of each zone of the building and for the air in each zone. These equations are intrinsically coupled and are solved simultaneously for all zones using iterative techniques. The individual equations include all dynamic thermal excitations for the surface or air node that they represent, and include:

Radiative excitations of the surfaces due to solar absorption (visible wavelengths) and to long wavelength radiative sources, such as occupants, equipment, lighting, baseboard heating, and other zone surfaces.

Conductive excitations through the construction that define the surfaces of the individual zones.

Convective excitations of the zone air resulting from infiltration and from thermal couplings to the surfaces defining the zone, air handling equipment, baseboard heating equipment, occupants, lighting, and other equipment.

The simultaneous solution of the energy balance equations produces the zone loads directly in terms of the baseboard energy input and the convective input from the air handler. The simulation is driven by hourly weather data either from files created by the weather data preprocessor or from design-day profiles created as part of the load simulation. In the latter case, the user specifies the extreme dry bulb and wet bulb temperatures, wind speed, and clearness for solar radiation. The program then internally generates the hourly data used in the analysis and performs the load calculation in the same manner that would be used if a weather tape was available. The result of the calculation is a temperature and a heating or cooling load for each zone, for each hour of the simulation. The loads calculation subprogram generates an output file containing the hourly load components which are read by the HVAC systems simulation subprogram.

AIR HANDLING (HVAC) SYSTEM SIMULATION ROUTINES.   The HVAC system simulation allows the user to select the air handling system type (e.g., constant volume, variable volume) and the specific thermal performance and operational characteristics for components in that system, such as terminal reheat units, fans, blowers, and hot and cold deck temperatures. This section of the program calculates the hourly secondary energy requirements that need to be supplied to the heating and cooling coils to meet the individual space loads under the constraints imposed by the design of the conventional systems, including outside ventilation air requirements, latent load control, distribution energy requirements, and component efficiencies.

CENTRAL PLANT SIMULATION AND ECONOMIC ANALYSIS ROUTINES.   The coil loads calculated in the HVAC system simulation program are the energy requirements imposed on the primary equipment in the central plant where the operation of boilers, chillers, cooling towers, and so on, are simulated. Given the energy conservation efficiencies of the plant components, and the operational control characteristics of the overall plant configuration (sequencing of multiple-unit boilers, chillers, etc.), the energy requirements that must be input to the plant to meet the demands of the HVAC system are calculated (i.e., building boundary fuel requirements). The fuel requirements (including peak-use rate information used to determine demand charges) are then used to calculate utility costs in subsequent life-cycle economic analyses.

In addition, the BLAST program includes two off-line processors:

An off-line weather data preprocessor that converts standard format weather tapes such as Typical Meteorological Year (TMY) and Test Reference Year (TRY) to BLAST-compatible files.

An off-line report generator postprocessor that outputs user selected quantities computed during the simulation.

PASSIVE ANALYSIS CAPABILITIES.   The current version of the program, BLAST 3.0, incorporates a number of features that permit energy analysis of the variety of passive solar systems. The presence of the mechanical systems and central plant simulation capabilities indicates the original thrust of the program to provide total energy analysis capabilities for nonresidential building types. This intent in no way limits the ability of the program to analyze residential-scale structures or unconventional structures of any type. On the contrary, the detailed heat-balance loads calculation approach that BLAST uses includes the capability to analyze more passive solar features than any other available building energy analysis tool. The passive analysis capabilities are thus a natural addition to the standard analysis capabilities of the program. They allow a thorough analysis of the energy consumption implications of a variety of passive design options, as well as standard building configurations, in either commercial or residential buildings. These capabilities are summarized in Table 9.8.

BLAST has a wide range of output reports available, only part of which were necessary to produce the "Standard Outputs" requested for this project. These reports are normally in printed form, but can be retained in the computer for subsequent processing. Essentially any physical variable

TABLE 9.8. BLAST 3.0 PASSIVE ANALYSIS CAPABILITIES

Direct Solar Gain
      User-defined window locations
      Proper radiation distribution on interior surfaces
      Transmission through external to internal zones

Solar Walls (Trombe/Morse Walls)
      User-defined glazing/absorber construction
      Unvented, vented, or fan-forced convection
      Convective heating or natural ventilation

Sunspaces
      Buffer
      Conductive and fan-forced convective coupling to occupied space

Natural Lighting
      Requires experimental data (solar usability)
      Dynamic control of conventional lights

Direct Ventilation Cooling
      Scheduled or thermostat control

Ground Coupling

Roof Ponds/Roof Evaporation (Planned Update to BLAST-3.0)

that is calculated as part of the simulation is available in some form of report. These variables range from monthly and annual total loads or energy use either zone-by-zone or for the entire building, to hourly values of the solar gains or components of the heat balance performed on the air in each zone, such as infiltration or internal loads. It is even possible to obtain hourly temperatures, heat fluxes, and convection coefficients on a surface-by-surface basis for the inside and outside of every surface in the building, although information at this level was not needed for this effort.

For the seasonal design-day analyses of the Pittsburgh example building, hourly reports were produced. The hourly outputs, in the form of "print image" (but unprinted) mass storage files were stored on the computer system. Subsequent to storage, they were processed off-line by standard graphics software to produce plots of total heat addition/extraction, components of this total, and zone temperatures. An example of one of these plots is shown in Figure 9.19. These plots are an extremely effective way of summarizing and conveying large amounts of information. For this

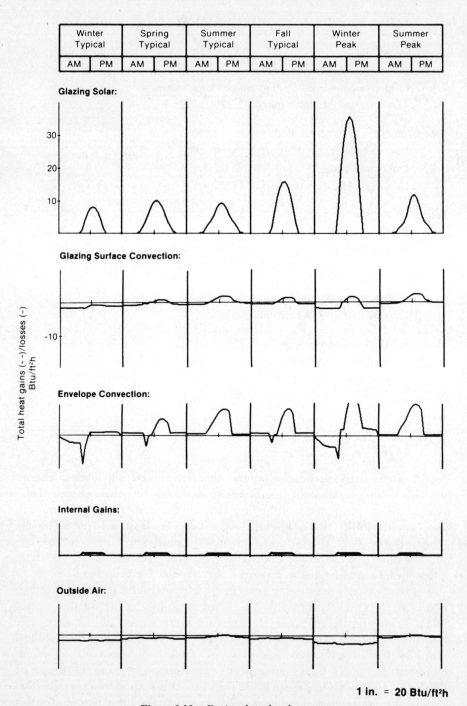

Figure 9.19. Design day plots by cause.

338

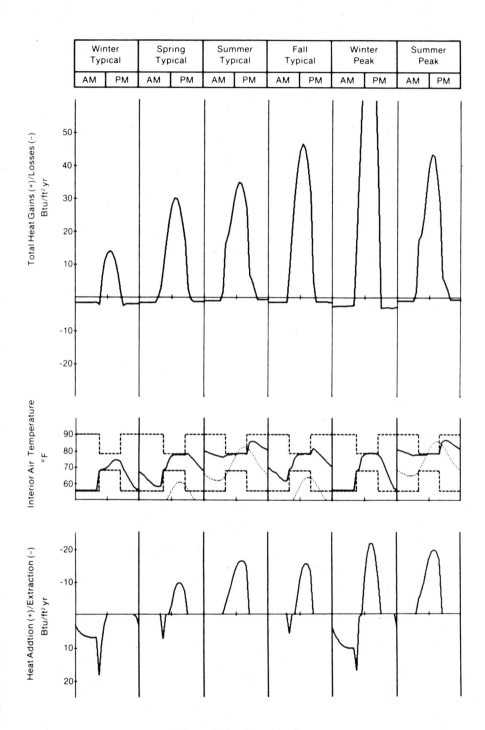

Figure 9.19. (*Continued*)

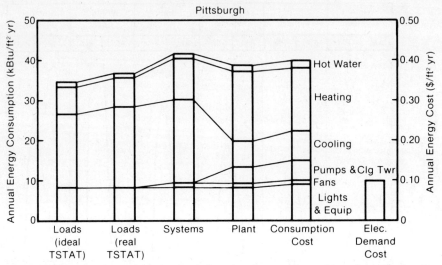

Figure 9.20.   Annual energy consumption bar chart/energy demand bar chart: Pittsburgh.

analysis of a nine-zone building there are 432 diurnal plots for the six design-day simulations, and yet the information is in a perfectly manageable form.

In addition to hourly results from the design simulations, other required simulation outputs are the bar charts of the annual loads, HVAC coil energy requirements, building boundary energy requirements, and utility consump-

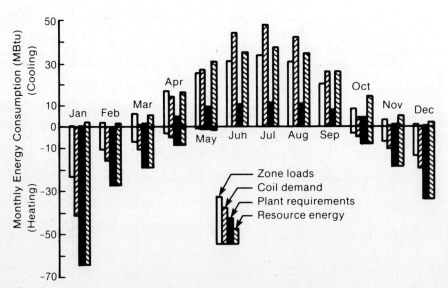

Figure 9.21.   Monthly energy requirements.

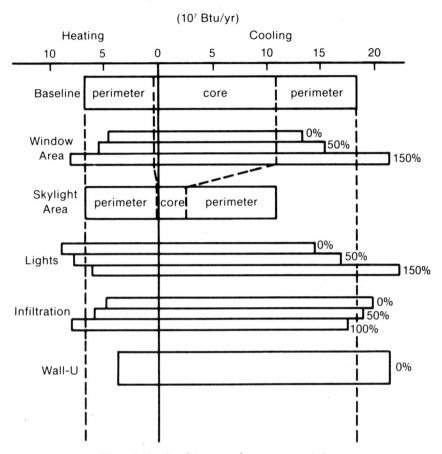

Figure 9.22. Load impacts of parameter variations.

tion costs (see Fig. 9.20). For each bar, the fraction of the total by end use (heating, cooling, hot water, fans, pumps and other auxiliaries, lights, and other electrical consumption) is indicated.

Several other outputs were produced that provide additional information and insights into the energy performance of the example building. The first is a bar chart of the monthly performance of the building, with the same loads-system-plant-cost breakdown of Figure 9.20. This chart is shown in Figure 9.21. The last is a bar chart showing the results of a number of additional BLAST analyses to explore the effects of architectural parameter changes to the basic building. The effects due to changes of vertical window area, skylight area, lighting power levels, infiltration/ventilation rates, and exterior wall thermal resistance were examined. These results, for heating/cooling loads only, are shown in Figure 9.22.

chapter ten

COMPONENT ENERGY ANALYSIS DURING EARLY DESIGN STAGES

INTRODUCTION

In Chapters Six and Seven, the case studies presented the concept of the recommended approach as it applies to the whole building. This chapter considers the concept of daylighting in more detail to illustrate how a particular subsystem was analyzed using the energy analysis methodology presented in Chapters Six and Seven.

The approach taken in this chapter illustrates how the analyst can fool the design tool. This is a relatively common practice that requires the analyst to assess the impact of a new and possibly innovative technology with the use of inputs already considered by the building energy analysis tool. That there are many tools with specific limitations, as well as an infinite variety of possible design and subsystem options, precludes describing all of the possibilities. One example of how this type of analysis is done, as shown in this chapter, will aid the reader in understanding how innovative subsystems and design concepts can be analyzed during the early stages of the design process.

DETERMINING NECESSARY INPUT VARIABLES

Analyzing the impact of any environmental subsystem that is not part of the normal analysis capabilities of a building energy analysis tool involves several preliminary steps. It is first necessary to determine the standard parameters that describe, or represent, the common environmental subsystem which performs the same function as the innovative subsystem. Once these parameters have been determined, the innovative environmental subsystem can be described, in identical terms, so that it can be input to the computer.

In the case of daylighting, the corresponding environmental subsystem is electric lighting. Electric lighting is often input to the building energy analysis tool as an average lighting load, in watts per square foot, for an individual zone or the entire building. If daylighting is to be included in the building energy analysis, the electric lighting load must be modified to represent the daylit building. For example, daylighting impacts the electric lighting, cooling, and heating loads of the building. To allow for the use of daylight in the building, the analyst must reduce the electric lighting load when appropriate. The energy analysis tool must also reduce or increase the cooling load and cooling COP to account for the impact of daylight on cooling. Similarly, the impact of the use of a daylighting system on the heating subsystem must be accounted for by the tool. At the same time the analyst must be sure that the solar gains and losses through the glazing are included in the analysis. Although most computer tools will keep track of this information automatically, many manual tools require the analyst to keep track of the impact of any environmental subsystems on the whole building.

A review of the thermal analysis tools discussed in Chapter Nine shows that the lighting load is represented as a Btu-hour or watts-per-square-foot load for distinct time periods representing occupied and unoccupied periods of a day. The lighting load for any one period is discrete from the lighting load of any other period. In addition, there may be the capability to distinguish between occupied and unoccupied days; that is, weekdays and weekends or holidays. Each time period of each design-day condition may have a different electric lighting load that must be represented as an input variable.

In order to determine the impact of daylighting on electric lighting, it is necessary to establish a new electric lighting load that represents the average lighting load for a given time period (an hour, day, month, season, year) when electric and natural light are being used simultaneously.

The impact of lighting on the cooling load is also represented by using an appropriate value as an equivalent electric lighting load to represent the combination of electric and natural light. Reducing or increasing the lighting load will result in a corresponding decrease or increase in the cooling load according to the change in equivalent electric lighting load. The peak cooling load is also determined using the same kind of analysis, although some thermal analysis tools are not designed to provide information about both the average and the peak cooling loads.

The impact of lighting on the heating load is represented by the same set of changes in the equivalent electric lighting load. Decreases in the lighting load usually increase the heating load. Depending upon the fuel used for heating, the impact of daylighting may have a substantial impact on the cost of heating. If the fuel is electricity, then the impact of daylighting can be substantial, because decreasing the electric lighting will probably increase the winter peak heating demand. However, the importance of the peak heating demand is utility-specific. If the utility has a peak ratchet clause that does not differentiate between winter and summer peaking, then the importance of the heating demand is reduced. Without the ratchet, or if there is a seasonal ratchet, then the heating peak demand for electric heating may be important.

Thus, in order to represent daylighting in a building thermal simulation tool, the input data must be modified for electric lighting. The modification should represent the source of daylight used; that is, sunlight, skylight, or reflected light. It should represent the electric lighting control strategy used in the building to integrate daylight usage with electric light, and it should match the time periods of building use to the availability of daylight to offset electric lighting loads.

The first step in this process is to analyze the daylighting in the proposed building in order to determine new values for the electric lighting input data.

INCLUDING DAYLIGHT IN
THE DENVER OFFICE BUILDING

The Denver Office Building is a project for a privately owned corporation requiring 60,000 gross ft^2 of office space for a construction budget of about $3.1 million.

The base building energy analysis is illustrated in Table 10.1 and Figure 10.1. A set of elimination parametrics is shown in Figure 10.2. All of this information is identical to that found in Chapter Seven.

From the base building and associated elimination parametric analysis, it can be seen that the building is internally load dominated and that electric lighting is the primary cause of the energy use in the building. In Alternative Design #1, the electric lighting load was substantially reduced by redesigning the lighting system to incorporate an energy-efficient lighting system such as a parabolic troffer system. This load reduction is represented as an input to the building energy analysis tool in terms of a change in the connected lighting load (W/ft^2). In most building energy analysis tools, electric lighting is represented as a single weighted lighting load value representative of the occupied and unoccupied portions of the day, as well as occupied and unoccupied days of the year (i.e., weekday and weekend day).

In Alternative Design #2, the building was elongated to incorporate daylighting and to optimize the overall daylight penetration into the

TABLE 10.1. DENVER BASE BUILDING, ANNUAL UTILITY COST ESTIMATES

| End-Use | Consumption | | | | | | Demand | | Total Cost |
	Elec. (kBtu/ft²)	Elec. ($/ft²)	Gas (kBtu/ft²)	Gas ($/ft²)	Total (kBtu/ft²)	Total ($/ft²)	Elec. (W/ft²)	Elec. ($/ft²)	(Cons. + Dem.) ($/ft²)
Equipment	2.554	0.0138	—	—	2.554	0.0138	3.953	0.0425	0.0563
Hot water	—	—	1.675	0.0047	1.675	0.0047	—	—	0.0047
Cooling	9.304	0.0501	—	—	9.304	0.0501	25.963	0.2791	0.3291
Lighting	44.047	0.2374	—	—	44.047	0.2374	53.098	0.5708	0.8082
Heating	0.039	0.0002	2.504	0.0070	2.543	0.0072	0.000	0.0000	0.0072
Total	55.944	0.3015	4.179	0.0117	60.123	0.3132	83.014	0.8924	1.2055

Notes: Equipment at 0.33 W/ft².
     Lighting at 5.6 W/ft² (offices), 3.2 W/ft² (core).

Rates: Gas—$2.80/MBtu = $0.0028/kBtu (consumption only).
     Electric—$0.0184/kWh (consumption) = $0.00539/kBtu,
     $10.75/kW (demand) = 1.075¢/W.

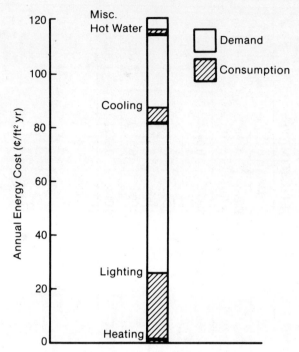

Figure 10.1.   Denver base building, utility cost.

building. In addition, some consideration needed to be given to the clear/ overcast daylight system performance and the impact of daylighting on peak cooling, average cooling, and heating loads.

The method used to analyze the daylighting potential in the Denver Office Building is the daylight factor (DF) method. The daylight factor method was developed during the 1930s and is used extensively in Europe, Asia, Africa, and Australia. It has also been used in the United States. The DF is defined as the ratio of exterior horizontal illuminance to the illuminance on the workplane in a space; this ratio is usually considered as a percent. A DF of 1.0 at a station point in the building would mean that 1.0% of the available exterior illuminance is reaching that station point.

The DF was developed primarily for overcast conditions where the ratio is reasonably constant throughout the day. Recent work by Bryan (1981) at MIT and Robbins (1983) at SERI has established techniques to calculate daylight factors for clear-sky conditions. Under clear-sky conditions, the DF is not a constant and varies with aperture orientation with respect to the location of the sun in the sky. Bryan has established ways to perform DF analysis for the clear sky without sun. Robbins has established ways to perform DF analysis with the sun included and exterior illuminance on a vertical surface in lieu of on a horizontal surface. To distinguish between a daylight factor based upon exterior illuminance on a vertical surface as

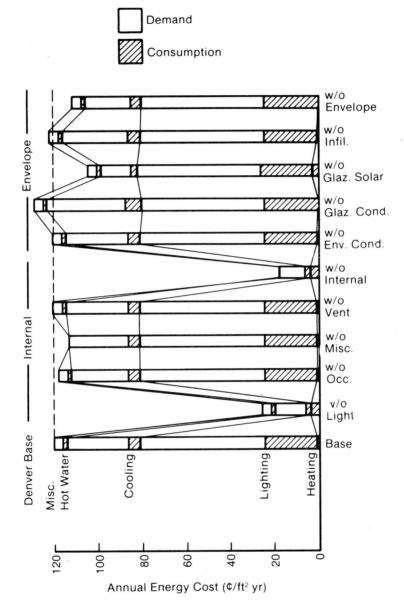

Figure 10.2. Denver base building, elimination parametrics.

347

opposed to the accepted definition of the term, the new method will be called a DFV; the traditional method will continue to be called a DF. The DFV method can be applied to clear and overcast conditions.

In building analysis the DF usually has three components: the sky component (SC), the external reflectance component (ERC), and the internal reflectance component (IRC). These components can be calculated, determined graphically, or evaluated through scale model investigation. The DF can be expressed in terms of these components as follows:

$$DF = (SC + ERC + IRC). \tag{1}$$

If mathematical or graphical analysis is being used to determine the DF, then the above equation is altered to allow for interior maintenance (as a maintenance factor, MF), glazing transmission (G), dust on glazing (D), and the framing around the glazing (G). These factors can be added to the equation:

$$DF = SC + ERC + (IRC)\ (G)\ (D)\ (F). \tag{2}$$

If scale model analysis is being used to determine the DF, then it is usually not possible to consider each of the components separately; and the DF is determined from a measured DF, DF_m, in combination with the reduction factors G, D, and F. That is,

$$DFV \quad or \quad DF = (DF_m)\ (G)\ (D)\ (F). \tag{3}$$

Currently, the DFV can only be determined from scale model analysis. The DF_m is determined from:

$$DF_m = \frac{E_{i,h}}{E_{e,v}}, \tag{4}$$

where $E_{i,h}$ is the measured illuminance on the horizontal work surface and $E_{e,v}$ is the global illuminance on the vertical surface at the plane of the aperture.

The physics used to describe daylight is based upon determining the light emitted from the sun that is considered to be an extended source rather than a point source as in electric lighting. Because the light rays from an extended source are considered to be parallel, light penetration into and reflected around a small-scale model is theoretically the same as it would be in the actual building. Thus, both the quantity and quality of the daylight in a scale model should be similar (theoretically they are exact) to the real, or full-scale, building.

For the Denver Office Building, a scale model at 0.5 in. = 1 ft is used to determine the daylight penetration into the building using a DFV. A different DF or DFV must be determined for clear and overcast conditions. Therefore, a scale model must be tested under both a clear and an overcast sky to establish these separate values.

Although the Commission Internationale de l'Eclairage (CIE) has established the theoretical definitions of a clear and an overcast sky, we must use more reasonable definitions of clear and overcast in order to test the scale models. In simple terms, the duration of sunshine can be used to establish the amount of clear and overcast sky in a day, month, or year. Hourly sunlight probability data are used to establish the probability of any hour being clear or overcast, as a percent of the hour. Typical data for Denver are shown in Tables 10.2 and 10.3.

Since a daylighting system is an instantaneous use of the incoming energy, it is more important to know how much sunshine is available during the operating schedule of the building than over the entire day from dawn to dusk. Sunshine probability data have been analyzed based upon 12 typical annual operating schedules for buildings; each annual schedule is called a standard work year. These data for Denver are shown, by month and on an annual basis, in Table 10.3 for the 12 typical standard work years.

Knowing the DF or DFV and the sunshine probability allows one to calculate the fraction of the standard work year, or any given hour, that the daylight can replace electric lighting in the building. Determining how much of a given time period daylight can replace electric light is also based upon the specific electric-lighting control system chosen for the building. Different control systems vary on the performance of the integrated lighting system with respect to the thermal performance of the building.

ELECTRIC LIGHTING CONTROL STRATEGIES

When enough daylight is present in a building or space, the electric lighting is not needed and may be turned off manually or with an automated on/off control. It is recommended that automated control systems be used wherever possible. An automated control system will be assumed in the Denver Office Building.

The purposes of any electric-lighting control system used in conjunction with daylighting are (a) to reduce the electric lighting load, and hence the energy use for electric lighting in the building, and (b) to maintain a relatively consistent level of light in the space by mixing quantities of daylight and electric light.

There are five different kinds of electric lighting control strategies that can be used in buildings. These fall into two groups: step switching and continuous dimming. Figure 10.3 illustrates the design illuminance for a building for an 0800–1800 h standard work year. In schematic analysis it will be assumed that the lighting load is a constant throughout the work day. Figure 10.4 illustrates the available daylight for the same time period. By overlaying Figure 10.3 and 10.4 it is possible to see how much of the time the daylight could replace or supplement the electric light; this is shown in Figure 10.5.

TABLE 10.2. SUNLIGHT AVAILABILITY FOR DENVER

Hour Solar	Jan.	Feb.	Mar.	Apr.	May	Jun.	Jul.	Aug.	Sept.	Oct.	Nov.	Dec.	Annual Fraction	Annual Hours
05:00–06:00	0.000	0.000	0.000	0.339	0.836	0.782	0.875	0.376	0.000	0.000	0.000	0.000	0.537	98.3
06:00–07:00	0.000	0.146	0.792	0.754	0.804	0.790	0.894	0.823	0.849	0.288	0.000	0.000	0.672	187.5
07:00–08:00	0.621	0.627	0.805	0.761	0.790	0.810	0.911	0.824	0.822	0.853	0.729	0.752	0.777	283.5
08:00–09:00	0.732	0.642	0.811	0.755	0.804	0.818	0.913	0.830	0.831	0.860	0.749	0.798	0.797	290.8
09:00–10:00	0.754	0.678	0.843	0.758	0.786	0.821	0.896	0.836	0.846	0.864	0.744	0.772	0.801	292.3
10:00–11:00	0.775	0.750	0.872	0.764	0.792	0.823	0.877	0.852	0.871	0.851	0.764	0.784	0.815	297.6
11:00–12:00	0.818	0.711	0.829	0.766	0.796	0.837	0.864	0.791	0.866	0.847	0.812	0.810	0.813	296.7
12:00–13:00	0.839	0.721	0.789	0.734	0.758	0.794	0.879	0.754	0.859	0.852	0.776	0.822	0.799	291.5
13:00–14:00	0.854	0.739	0.745	0.707	0.717	0.769	0.814	0.752	0.861	0.860	0.763	0.845	0.786	286.9
14:00–15:00	0.829	0.716	0.726	0.675	0.684	0.774	0.741	0.710	0.821	0.854	0.748	0.878	0.764	278.7
15:00–16:00	0.831	0.715	0.704	0.649	0.649	0.715	0.641	0.711	0.797	0.865	0.747	0.861	0.741	270.3
16:00–17:00	0.736	0.731	0.693	0.623	0.627	0.694	0.662	0.724	0.748	0.855	0.760	0.816	0.723	263.8
17:00–18:00	0.000	0.150	0.679	0.639	0.618	0.712	0.756	0.718	0.774	0.276	0.000	0.000	0.582	162.4
18:00–19:00	0.000	0.000	0.000	0.227	0.618	0.699	0.796	0.335	0.000	0.000	0.000	0.000	0.448	82.0
Monthly average	0.779	0.610	0.774	0.654	0.734	0.774	0.823	0.717	0.829	0.760	0.759	0.814		
Monthly fraction	0.779	0.618	0.735	0.654	0.669	0.677	0.720	0.713	0.746	0.760	0.721	0.814		
Monthly average hours of sunlight per day	7.8	7.3	9.3	9.2	10.3	10.8	11.5	10.0	9.9	9.1	7.6	8.1		

TABLE 10.3. SUNLIGHT AVAILABILITY BY STANDARD WORK YEAR FOR DENVER

Standard Work Year	Jan.	Feb.	Mar.	Apr.	May	June	July	Aug.	Sept.	Oct.	Nov.	Dec.	Annual (SA$_s$)
07:00–16:00	0.705	0.644	0.792	0.732	0.758	0.795	0.843	0.788	0.842	0.799	0.683	0.732	0.760
07:00–17:00	0.708	0.652	0.783	0.722	0.746	0.786	0.827	0.782	0.834	0.804	0.690	0.740	0.756
07:00–18:00	0.649	0.610	0.774	0.716	0.735	0.780	0.821	0.777	0.829	0.760	0.632	0.678	0.730
07:00–19:00	0.599	0.564	0.715	0.678	0.726	0.774	0.819	0.743	0.765	0.702	0.584	0.626	0.691
08:00–16:00	0.784	0.700	0.792	0.730	0.753	0.796	0.837	0.784	0.842	0.856	0.759	0.814	0.787
08:00–17:00	0.779	0.703	0.782	0.719	0.740	0.786	0.820	0.778	0.832	0.856	0.759	0.814	0.781
08:00–18:00	0.708	0.653	0.773	0.712	0.729	0.779	0.814	0.773	0.827	0.803	0.690	0.740	0.750
08:00–19:00	0.649	0.598	0.708	0.672	0.720	0.772	0.813	0.736	0.758	0.736	0.632	0.678	0.706
09:00–16:00	0.804	0.709	0.790	0.726	0.748	0.794	0.828	0.779	0.844	0.857	0.763	0.821	0.789
09:00–17:00	0.796	0.711	0.779	0.715	0.735	0.783	0.810	0.773	0.833	0.856	0.762	0.821	0.781
09:00–18:00	0.717	0.655	0.769	0.707	0.723	0.776	0.804	0.768	0.827	0.798	0.686	0.739	0.747
09:00–19:00	0.652	0.596	0.699	0.663	0.714	0.769	0.804	0.728	0.752	0.726	0.624	0.672	0.700

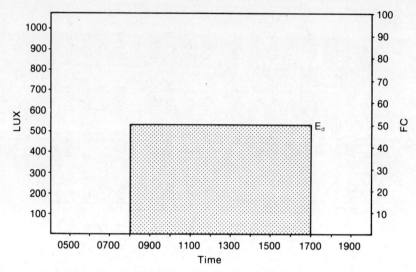

Figure 10.3.   Design illuminance for the 0800–1800 h standard work year.

If it is assumed that daylight can replace the electric light at the design illuminance level, then Figure 10.6 illustrates the portion of the day that the daylight is equal to or greater than the design illuminance. If an automatic electric-lighting control system were present in the room when this occurred, the electric lighting would be switched off during those times when daylight was sufficient to replace electric light. An automated control

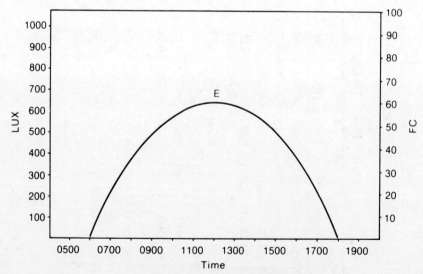

Figure 10.4.   Average interior daylight E_i.

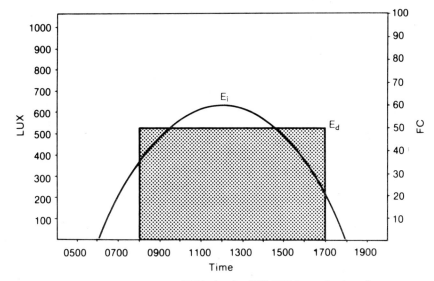

Figure 10.5. A comparison of E_iE_D for the 0800-1800 h standard work year.

system that turns all of the lamps in a luminaire on or off is called a two-step control system (one step = on, one step = off).

Since the design in a daylit building should optimize the period of time that daylighting can economically replace electric lighting, it is necessary to analyze a variety of control systems that attempt to maximize the area under the curve in Figure 10.5. The simple two-step system illustrated in Figure 10.7 is not totally effective at this process. Other step systems include three-

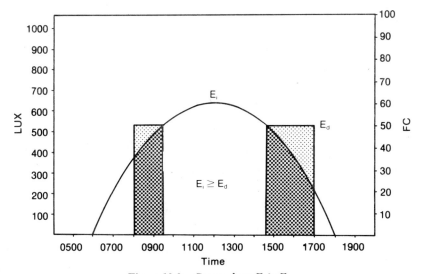

Figure 10.6. Cases where $E_i \geq E_D$.

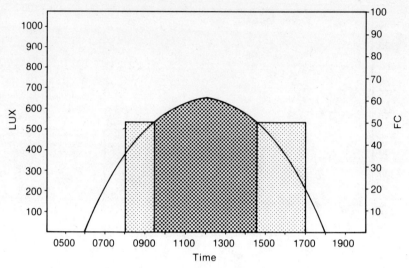

Figure 10.7. Two-step (on/off) control system.

step, four-step, and five-step control strategies. Each of these in turn increases the area under the curve that daylight can replace electric light in the building.

A three-step system requires a minimum of two lamps in a luminaire. The lighting control of such a system is illustrated in Figure 10.8. Notice that at 0800 h both lamps are in operation. As the daylight in the space increases, it reaches a point (at about 0830 h) where it is sufficient to replace one of the

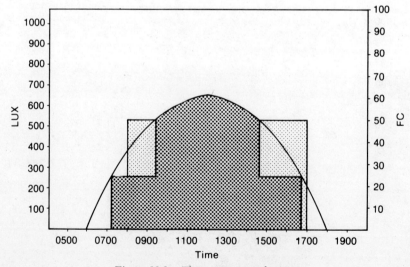

Figure 10.8. Three-step control system.

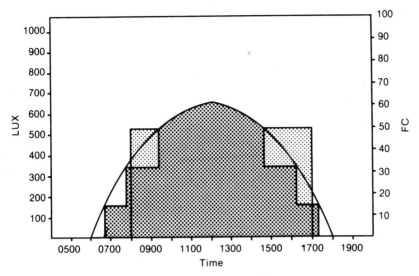

Figure 10.9.   Four-step control system.

lamps. When this occurs, one lamp is automatically turned off. Later in the day, the daylighting is sufficient to replace the second lamp and it is switched off. A comparison of Figure 10.7 with Figure 10.8 shows that the amount of area under the curve in Figure 10.8 has increased substantially. The three-step system is considerably more efficient than the two-step system. The three steps were: (*a*) all lamps on, step one; (*b*) one lamp on, step two; and (*c*) no lamps on, step three.

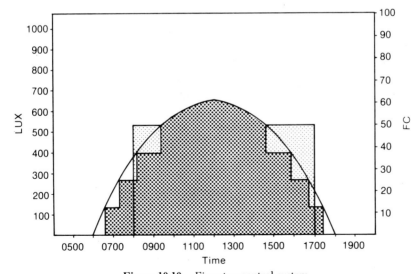

Figure 10.10.   Five-step control system.

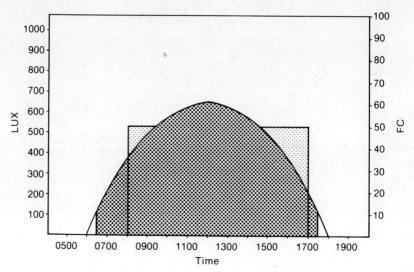

Figure 10.11.   Continuous dimming control system.

Four- and five-step switching systems operate in a similar manner. The four-step system requires a minimum of three lamps in the luminaire, and the five-step system requires a minimum of four lamps. The control strategies for the four- and five-step systems are illustrated in Figures 10.9 and 10.10, respectively.

The continuous dimming system is usually designed to continuously monitor the light level in the space and to adjust the current to the ballast of the lamps to equalize the daylight and electric light to maintain the design illuminance. An advantage of automatic dimming is that it can operate regardless of the number of lamps in the luminaire. A major disadvantage is that the current state of the technology allows them to operate only within about 15% of the input current; that is, there is a cut-off at that level. Figure 10.11 illustrates the continuous dimming system.

Each of these systems can be used simultaneously in different parts of a large space or different rooms or spaces in a building. The combination of daylighting system and electric lighting control can be used to determine the overall capability of the integrated lighting system to reduce lighting energy use and costs in commercial buildings.

ENERGY ANALYSIS OF THE DAYLIT DENVER OFFICE

Once the analysis of the daylighting system is completed, this information can be used as input to the building energy analysis tool. An equivalent electric lighting power budget is used to represent the daylighting and the associated electric lighting control strategy because this is typically the lighting input needed in most building thermal analysis tools. The first step is to determine the fraction of a given time period that one can daylight a space to a given design illuminance. This calculation is based upon the amount of time the daylight can achieve the design illuminance.

The design illuminance, E_d, represents the illuminance value used by the lighting designer to design the lighting systems of a room or space, including both daylight and electric light. Using hourly illuminance data, the contribution to interior illuminance from daylight, E_i, can be determined by rewriting the DF equation to solve for E_i:

$$E_i = E_e \times \frac{DF}{100}. \tag{5}$$

If average monthly E_i values are compared to E_d values, three distinct cases occur in which daylight can replace or supplement electric light:

1. $E_i \geq E_d$.
2. $E_i < E_d$ (part of the time).
3. $E_i < E_d$ (all of the time).

These three cases are illustrated in Figures 10.6, 10.12, and 10.13.

When E_i is greater than or equal to E_d, daylight can be used in lieu of electric light. The threshold exterior illuminance, E_t, necessary to establish that condition can be expressed as a function of DF:

$$E_t = \frac{E_d}{DF} \times 100. \tag{6}$$

When $E_i \geq E_d$, the electric lighting can be controlled by a simple two-step control system. It is possible to establish the frequency of occurrence of the exterior illuminance, E_t, as a function of the standard work year, orientation, and the fraction, F, of the standard work year for which E_t exceeds any specified value. Using a third order regression equation, the distribution curve of the fraction F can be expressed:

$$F = C_0 + C_1 E_t + C_2 E_t^2 + C_3 E_t^3. \tag{7}$$

Sample data are shown in Table 10.4.

When $E_i < E_d$ part of the time, then three-, four-, and five-step control systems as well as continuous dimming systems can be used to reduce the electric lighting usage in the building. It is assumed that when $E_i < E_d$, then $E_e < E_t$ and

$$\frac{E_i}{E_d} = \frac{E_e}{E_t}. \tag{8}$$

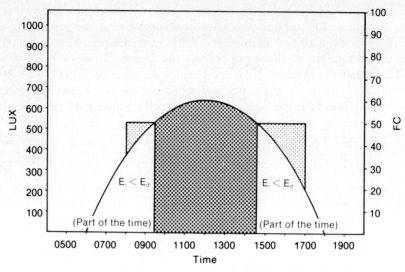

Figure 10.12. Cases where $E_i < E_D$ part of the time.

By multiplying this fraction by the frequency of occurrence of E_t and summing the result for each hourly occurrence over the year for the given switching strategy, the fraction F for each switching strategy can be determined.

When daylight is never sufficient to replace the electric light, then $E_t > E_{max}$, where E_{max} is defined as the largest single illuminance value occurring during the standard work year. In simple terms, the fraction F of

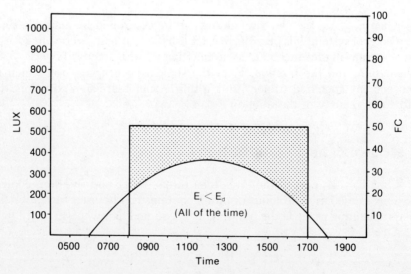

Figure 10.13. Cases where $E_i < E_D$ all of the time.

TABLE 10.4. REGRESSION COEFFICIENTS FOR PREDICTING ENERGY SAVINGS ATTRIBUTED TO DAYLIGHTING

Denver, CO (0800–1600)	Illuminance	Sky Condition	Orientation	C_0	C_1	C_2	C_3	Mean	G/D	Maximum
	Direct	Clear	Normal	1.081E+02	−1.326E−03	4.658E−08	−4.656E−13	80151		96311
	Global	Clear	North	9.935E+01	1.569E−03	−7.895E−07	2.265E−11	10856	2.186	18006
	Global	Clear	NE/NW	1.247E+02	−8.060E−03	1.849E−07	−1.441E−12	15569	3.135	53439
	Global	Clear	East/West	1.128E+02	−4.465E−03	8.300E−08	−5.922E−13	28150	5.668	73415
	Global	Clear	SE/SW	1.066E+02	−2.391E−03	4.189E−08	−3.871E−13	40142	8.083	75814
	Global	Clear	South	1.002E+02	3.603E−04	−4.539E−08	3.156E−13	45607	9.184	78843
	Diffuse	Clear	Vertical	1.004E+02	4.699E−03	−4.577E−06	3.218E−10	4966		8297
	Global	Overcast	Vertical	9.647E+01	1.438E−03	−7.890E−07	2.312E−11	10277		18218
	Global	Clear	Horizontal	9.850E+01	1.778E−04	−2.319E−08	1.187E−13	58736	5.914	100372
	Diffuse	Clear	Horizontal	1.004E+02	2.350E−03	−1.144E−06	4.022E−11	9932		16594
	Global	Overcast	Horizontal	9.647E+01	8.631E−04	−2.840E−07	4.994E−12	17128		30363

359

the standard work year that can be illuminated by daylight can be approximated by

$$F = \frac{E_{max}}{2E_t} \tag{9}$$

The portion of the standard work year that is clear and overcast can be determined from Robbins and Hunter (forthcoming). The total fraction F_T for a given switching strategy is expressed as

$$F_T = F_c \rho_c + F_o \rho_o, \tag{10}$$

where F_T = total fraction of the standard work year that daylight can replace electric light usage

F_c = fraction of the clear portion of the standard year that daylight can be used to affect electric light usage

ρ_c = percentage of the standard work year that is clear

F_c = fraction of the overcast portion of the standard work year that daylight can be used to offset electric light usage

ρ_o = percentage of the standard work year that is overcast ($= 1 - \rho_c$).

The value of F_T was used to derive simple expressions for the equivalent of the working year that the electric lighting system would be off when using various types of automated control systems. The energy savings can be determined by modifying the Illumination Engineering Society (IES) lighting power budget, P_r, equations to include F_T (Hunt 1977). The Unit Power Density (UPD) equations can be used to determine the energy usage in a daylit space over the year, and the design load, P_d, can be used to design the heating and cooling plant.

The lighting power budget of an individual room or space is determined by

$$P_r = A \times UPD \times RF \times SUF, \tag{11}$$

where P_r = power budget of a room or space

A = area

UPD = unit power density

RF = room factor

SUF = space utilization factor.

Values for UPD, RF, and SUF can be determined from the IES Handbook (Kaufman 1981).

The power budget equation can be rewritten for a room or space that is daylit for some fraction F_T of the year:

$$P_r = (A \times UPD \times RF \times SUF \times (1 - F_T)) + (A \times UPD_d \times F_T). \tag{12}$$

This calculation is made for each step.

Values determined for the entire building can be used to establish the average unit power density of the building, which in turn is used to design the heating and cooling system for the building.

REFERENCES

Bryan, H. J. and R. D. Clear. 1981 (July). "Calculating Daylight Illumination with a Programmable Hand Calculator." *Journal of IES*, Vol. 10, No. 4, pp. 219-227.

Hunt, D. R. G. 1977. *Predicting Energy Savings from Photo-Electric Control of Lighting*. BRE Current Paper, CP32/77. Building Research Establishment, Garston, Watford, England.

Kaufman, J. E., ed. 1981. *IES Lighting Handbook*. Application Volume. New York: Illuminating Engineering Society.

Robbins, C. and K. Hunter, 1983 (May). *Daylight Availability Data for Select U.S. Cities*. SERI/TR-254-1687. Golden, Colorado: Solar Energy Research Institute.

INDEX